Germaine Greer

The Female Eunuch

A PANTHER BOOK

GRANADA

London Toronto Sydney New York

Published by Granada Publishing Limited in 1981

ISBN 0 586 05406 5

First published in Great Britain by
MacGibbon & Kee Ltd 1970
Published by Paladin 1971: Fourteenth reprint 1979
Copyright © Germaine Greer 1970

Granada Publishing Limited
Frogmore, St Albans, Herts AL2 2NF
and
3 Upper James Street, London W1R 4BP
866 United Nations Plaza, New York, NY 10017, USA
117 York Street, Sydney, NSW 2000, Australia
100 Skyway Avenue, Rexdale, Ontario, M9W 3A6, South Africa
61 Beach Road, Auckland, New Zealand

Printed and bound in Great Britain by
Cox and Wyman Ltd, Reading
Phototypesetting by Georgia Origination, Liverpool
Set in Baskerville

Granada ®
Granada Publishing ®

Germaine Greer was born in 1939 in Melbourne. She took a BA honours from Melbourne University in 1959, an MA with 1st class honours from Sydney in 1963 and a PhD from Cambridge in 1968. She wrote for *Oz* magazine and for *Suck,* and appeared in Granada Television's *Nice Time* series, before taking the world by storm with *The Female Eunuch.* Her nationwide US publication tour was the subject of an hour-long television documentary. Since then she has travelled widely and has been seen frequently both as guest and as hostess on TV talk shows. She writes regularly for the *Sunday Times*, and until recently was a lecturer in English at the University of Warwick.

This book is dedicated to LILLIAN, *who lives with nobody but a colony of New York roaches, whose energy has never failed despite her anxieties and her asthma and her overweight, who is always interested in everybody, often angry, sometimes bitchy, but always involved. Lillian the abundant, the golden, the eloquent, the well and badly loved; Lillian the beautiful who thinks she is ugly, Lillian the indefatigable who thinks she is always tired.*

It is dedicated to CAROLINE, *who danced, but badly, painted but badly, jumped up from a dinner table in tears, crying that she wanted to be a person, went out and was one, despite her great beauty. Caroline who smarts at every attack, and doubts all praise, who has done great things with gentleness and humility, who assaulted the authorities with valorous love and cannot be defeated.*

It is for my fairy godmother, JOY *with the green eyes, whose husband decried her commonsense and belittled her mind, because she was more passionately intelligent, and more intelligently passionate than he, until she ran away from him and recovered herself, her insight and her sense of humour, and never cried again, except in compassion.*

It is for KASOUNDRA, *who makes magic out of skins and skeins and pens, who is never still, never unaware, riding her strange destiny in the wilderness of New York, loyal and bitter, as strong as a rope of steel and as soft as a sigh.*

For MARCIA, *whose mind contains everything and destroys nothing, understanding dreams and nightmares, who looks on tempests and is not shaken, who lives among the damned and is not afraid of them, a living soul among the dead.*

Acknowledgements

Acknowledgement is made to the following for their kind permission to reprint material from copyright sources:

Sigmund Freud Copyrights Ltd, the Institute of Psycho-Analysis and the Hogarth Press Ltd (*Three Essays on the Theory of Sexuality* and *Some Psychical Consequences of the Anatomical Distinction between the Sexes*); André Deutsch Ltd (*An American Dream* by Norman Mailer); Collins Publishers (*The Loving Heart* by Lucy Walker and *Go to the Widowmaker* by James Jones); Hurst and Blackett (*The Wings of Love* by Barbara Cartland); Peter Owen (*La Bâtarde* by Violette Leduc); Stanford University Press (*The Promise of Youth* by Barbara Stoddard Burks, Dortha Williams Jensen and Louis M. Terman); George Allen and Unwin Ltd (*The Art of Loving* by Erich Fromm); Heinemann Educational Books Ltd (*Problems of Adolescent Girls* by J. Hemmings); Longmans (*The Secret of Childhood* by Maria Montessori); Faber and Faber ('Metaphors' from *Colossus* by Sylvia Plath); W.H. Allen (*The World is Full of Married Men* by Jackie Collins); Sphere Books (*Eros and Civilisation* by Herbert Marcuse); and Arthur Barker Ltd (*Bloody Sunrise* by Micky Spillane).

Contents

INTRODUCTION TO THE
PANTHER EDITION

When *The Female Eunuch* was written in 1968, it seemed that the world was changing very fast. Events in Europe and America seemed to point to if not a revolution, then such fundamental changes that life would have been as totally transformed. Students had taken over their universities, workers had taken over their factories. Social justice was everybody's concern, even if everyone was just as fervently convinced of the utter unimportance of material things. Young revolutionaries had not then begun to feel the deep tiredness of spirit that follows the orgasm of overt political action. It had not even occurred to them that the traditional authorities ruled mostly by the force of inertia and would simply wait the crisis out, until everyone was exhausted and old enough to tremble at the approach of economic recession.

In 1968 I was teaching at a university where the students had occupied the Registry and had liberated illegal secret documents; in the hectic weeks that followed we all tried to redesign our education on principles of greater relevance and utility. The high point of my teaching life was a day-long seminar on Shelley's *Revolt of Islam*, which we conducted in the occupied students' union building. New thoughts were indeed like lightnings alive, and we had no doubt that Custom's hydra brood lay bound and cowering before our victorious progress. Four years later I left the university; in that short time the light of 1968 seemed to have gone out forever. The university had become a degree factory again.

I had waited a long time for 1968 and the surge of energy that it brought. Although *The Female Eunuch* was itself a product of that simmer, it is also the distillation of all my life.

11

At last it seemed possible to break out of mere eccentricity into genuine change. I hoped, and indeed believed, that the expression of my own disgust with the traditional feminine postures and procedures would be added to the spurs which were forcing women to rise up and smash the mold made for them, so that in a few years no one would believe that we were expected to waste our spiritual and mental powers upon such foolishness.

The world has changed a great deal since then. Nowadays no political party dreams of contesting an election without including in its platform some plank for women. Governments of the left, the right and the middle have all signed international protocols guaranteeing equal pay for equal work. They can afford to, for women have not yet sufficient power to hold them to the word so easily given. The female voter exists only to be wooed; she has not yet the solidarity to be able to manipulate a candidate by the threat of withholding votes. Economic boycott punishes the boycotters more than the boycotted; the ERA is not yet ratified, and now women have the added humiliation of extended time limits to explain away. We are not yet tough enough to tell them damn their Constitution and its amendments. Yet when they talk of reintroducing the draft, they insist that women shall be included. Let them include us and let them fear that, like our brothers in 1968, we shall turn our weapons against our commanding officers.

We have "won" in most countires the right to abortion, provided we have the money to pay for it and the low cunning to manipulate the law – but the right was not won but granted, because our child-bearing faculty is no longer our most valuable contribution, but in these days of population panic has come to be subversive in itself. We cannot say that our right to bear our children is being eroded, for we never actually enjoyed that right either. Most women who had abortions did not have them because they absolutely did not want under any circumstances to bear a child but because they could not afford a child, could not afford to starve the other children, to drop out of school, to leave work, to slide into disgrace and destitution.

In 1968 we thought we had the contraception problem all but licked; now we know better and we unwillingly return to the disgusting diaphragm, while our tax dollars pay for the dissemination of our rejected methods of birth control through the entire world. The family planners, or baby-stoppers as their clients more often call them, justify what they do by reference to our feminist principles.

The reason to be learned is the same as the lesson of 1968 when all is said and done. History was not ours to make but ours to serve. In some areas our media presence caused immediate capitulation: speech writers were careful not to include vulgar sexist expressions, while the proprietors of flesh magazines boasted of their treatment of their female executives as if theirs was not the role that female madams have always played in male-owned brothels. Journalists, teachers and students all addressed themselves to the new subject matter of feminism, and a whole academic industry of women's studies sprang up. The trade unions were not attending school – they countenanced all kinds of job evaluation schemes which institutionalized the differences in the classification of men's and women's work so that women's work would always be less well paid than men's. Since *The Female Eunuch* was written the difference in men's and women's earnings has grown, not shrunk.

In the last ten years life has become more difficult for almost everyone, wherever she lives in the world. If the recession bites more deeply, if the job market shrinks still further, if the Islamic revival gathers more momentum, women the world over will suffer, but they may have a clearer idea of why they are suffering, of the nature of the politico-economic system which can only value them as passive consumers and counterweights for harassed men. We have nothing to be thankful for and nobody to thank, for the most significant change is that wrought in ourselves by ourselves. The nominal political struggles have their enduring value as ways of getting to know ourselves and our situation. All over the world there are small groups of women who are the future in microcosm, working joyously, cooperatively, inventively and courageously to care for one another and make one another's lives easier and more rewarding in ways that cannot be aped by the masculine machines for domination.

The view of women's plight developed in *The Female Eunuch* is unavoidably a typically western view. Unfortunately it is no less relevant for that; the cultural domination of most of the world by consumer society and its megamedia has meant that for many women in Asia, Africa and South America, the lifestyle of the western middle-class is fast supplanting the traditional ways of life in which female collectivity was alive and real. Women who have grown up in village societies where women lived in segregated groups with their own cultural values and economic contributions are moving into urbanized nuclear households in which women are dependent upon men for their emotional, intellectual and social satisfaction. Ironically, many western feminists are seeking just the kind of alternative female society which these women are abandoning along with the restrictions and disabilities of systems of purdah.

We now understand that the isolation of women from other women is even more bewildering and crippling than the exclusion of individual women from public affairs. It is an added source of anxiety for western feminists that their arguments are used to discredit the female society of the harem which is vanishing before we have had any opportunity to learn from it. The paradigm of a female collectivity which welcomes men as lovers and sires of children, but regards the bond between mothers and daughters as more central to its emotional life is fading from women's consciousness before they have had the opportunity to assess its positive value. Nevertheless, the vitality of this tradition together with the crudeness of the new repressiveness in Islamic societies, for example, may be the volatile combination which sets off the next revolutionary feminist wave. We may be on the point of discovering that in the sense that they are isolated from their own sex western women are more irrevocably crippled than women living in traditional societies, as the revolutionary initiative passes into the hands of others.

The basic idea of *The Female Eunuch* has never been very well understood, perhaps because I was unable to explain it properly. Nevertheless the concept of the castration of women is the key to the book and, I still believe, the key to the situation. Women's sexuality has been repressed because it served no social or domestic function. Whole women would have been restless, aggressive, unpredictable, curious, lustful, imaginative and in league with their naughtiest children against men and their machines. They might have been artists, inventors, explorers, revolutionaries, but they would not have been housewives, and housewives were what was wanted. Because they did not want them to be miserable, women connived in the deadening of their daughters.

None of the women were completely successfully castrated; their wild selves would peep through their eyes sometimes and create havoc, but, by the same token, they could not recover their completeness either, for the wild woman was etiolated and demented by her suppression.

But her time is coming, and it will not be granted to her. She will seize it.

Pianelli, April 1980

SUMMARY

'The World has lost its soul, and I my sex' (TOLLER, *Hinkemann)*

This book is a part of the second feminist wave. The old suffragettes, who served their prison term and lived on through the years of gradual admission of women into professions which they declined to follow, into parliamentary freedoms which they declined to exercise, into academies which they used more and more as shops where they could take out degrees while waiting to get married, have seen their spirit revive in younger women with a new and vital cast. Mrs Hazel Hunkins-Hallinan, leader of the Six Point Group, welcomed the younger militants and even welcomed their sexual frankness. 'They're young,' she said to Irma Kurtz, 'and utterly unsophisticated politically, but they're full of beans. The membership of our group until recently has been far too old for my liking.'[1] After the ecstasy of direct action, the militant ladies of two generations ago settled down to work of consolidation in hosts of small organizations, while the main force of their energy filtered away in post-war retrenchments and the revival of frills, corsets and femininity after the permissive twenties, through the sexual sell of the fifties, ever dwindling, ever more respectable. Evangelism withered into eccentricity.

The new emphasis is different. Then genteel middle-class ladies clamoured for reform, now ungenteel middle-class women are calling for revolution. For many of them the call for revolution came before the call for the liberation of women. The New Left has been the forcing house for most movements, and for many of them liberation is dependent upon the coming of the classless society and the withering away of the state. The difference is radical, for the faith that the suffragettes had in the existing political systems and their deep desire to participate in them have perished. In the old days ladies were anxious to point out that they did not seek to disrupt society or to unseat God. Marriage, the family, private property and the state were threatened by their actions, but they were anxious to allay the fears of conservatives, and in doing so the suffragettes betrayed their own cause and prepared the way for the failure of emancipation. Five years ago it seemed clear that emancipation had failed: the number of women in Parliament had settled at a low level; the number of professional women had stabilized as a tiny minority; the pattern of female employment had emerged as underpaid, menial and supportive. The cage door had been opened but the canary had refused to fly out. The conclusion was that the cage door ought never to have been opened because canaries are made for captivity; the suggestion of an alternative had only confused and saddened them.

There are feminist organizations still in existence which follow the reforming tracks laid down by the suffragettes. Betty Friedan's National Organization for Women is represented in congressional committees, especially the ones considered to be of special relevance to women. Women politicians still represent female interests, but they are most often the interests of women as dependants, to be protected from easy divorce and all sorts of Casanova's charters. Mrs Hunkins-Hallinan's Six Point Group is a respected political entity. What is new about the situation is that such groups are enjoying new limelight. The media insist upon exposing women's liberation weekly, even daily. The change is that suddenly everyone is interested in the subject of women.

They may not be in favour of the movements that exist, but they are concerned about the issues. Among young women in universities the movement might be expected to find strong support. It is not surprising that exploited women workers might decide to hold the Government to ransom at last. It is surprising that women who seem to have nothing to complain about have begun to murmur. Speaking to quiet audiences of provincial women decently hatted and dressed, I have been surprised to find that the most radical ideas are gladly entertained, and the most telling criticisms and sharpest protests are uttered. Even the suffragettes could not claim the grass-roots support that the new feminism gains day by day.

We can only speculate about the causes of this new activity. Perhaps the sexual sell was oversell. Perhaps women have never really belived the account of themselves which they were forced to accept from psychologists, religious leaders, women's magazines and men. Perhaps the reforms which did happen eventually led them to the position from which they could at last see the whole perspective and begin to understand the rationale of their situation. Perhaps because they are not enmeshed in unwilling childbirth and heavy menial labour in the home, they have had time to think. Perhaps the plight of our society has become so desperate and so apparent that women can no longer be content to leave it to other people. The enemies of women have blamed such circumstances for female discontent.

We may safely assert that the knowledge that men can acquire of women, even as they have been and are, without reference to what they might be, is wretchedly imperfect and superficial and will always be so until women themselves have told all that they have to tell.

John Stuart Mill

Women must prize this discontent as the first stirring of the demand for life; they have begun to speak out and to speak to each other. The sight of women talking together has always made men uneasy; nowadays it means rank subversion. 'Right on!'

The organized liberationists are a well-publicized minority; the same faces appear every time a feminist issue is discussed. Inevitably they are presented as the leaders of a movement which is essentially leaderless. They are not much nearer to providing a revolutionary strategy than they ever were; demonstrating, compiling reading lists and sitting on committees are not themselves liberated behaviour, especially when they are still embedded in a context of housework and feminine wiles. As means of educating the people who must take action to liberate themselves, their effectiveness is limited. The concept of liberty implied by such liberation is vacuous; at worst it is defined by the condition of men, themselves unfree, and at best it is left undefined in a world of very limited possibilities. On the one hand, feminists can be found who serve the notion of equality 'social, legal, occupational, economic, political and moral', whose enemy is discrimination, whose means are competition and demand. On the other hand there are those who cherish an ideal of a better life, which will follow when a better life is assured for all by the correct political means. To women disgusted with conventional political methods, whether constitutional or totalitarian or revolutionary, neither alternative can make much appeal. The housewife who must wait for the success of world revolution for her liberty might be excused for losing hope, while conservative political methods can invent no way in which the economically necessary unit of the one-man family could be diversified. But there is another dimension in which she can find motive and cause for action, although she might not find a blue-print for Utopia. She could begin not by changing the world, but by re-assessing herself.

It is impossible to argue a case for female liberation if there is no certainty about the degree of inferiority or natural dependence which is unalterably female. That is why this book begins with the *Body*. We know what we are, but know not what we may be, or what we might have been. The dogmatism of science expresses the status quo as the ineluctable result of law: women must learn how to question the most basic assumptions about feminine normality in order to reopen the possibilities for development which have been successively locked off by conditioning. So, we begin at the beginning, with the sex of cells. Nothing much can be made of chromosomal difference until it is manifested in development, and development cannot take place in a vacuum: from the outset our observation of the female is consciously and unconsciously biassed by assumptions that we cannot help making and cannot always identify when they have been made. The new assumption behind the discussion of the body is that everything that we may observe *could be otherwise*. In order to demonstrate some of the aspects of conditioning a discussion follows the effects of behaviour upon the skeleton. From *Bones* we move to *Curves*, which is still essential to assumptions about the female sex, and then to *Hair*, for a long time considered a basic secondary sexual characteristic.

Female sexuality has always been a fascinating topic; this discussion of it attempts to show how female sexuality has been masked and deformed by most observers, and never more so than in our own time. The conformation of the female has already been described in terms of a particular type of conditioning, and now the specific character of that conditioning begins to emerge. What happens is that the female is considered as a sexual object for the use and appreciation of other sexual beings, men. Her sexuality is both denied and misrepresented by being identified as passivity. The vagina is obliterated from the imagery of femininity in the same way that the signs of indpendence and vigour in the rest of her body are suppressed. The characteristics that are praised and rewarded are those of the castrate – timidity, plumpness, languor, delicacy and preciosity. *Body* ends with a look at the way in which female reproduction is thought to influence the whole organism in the operations of the *Wicked Womb,* source of hysteria, menstrual depression, weakness, and unfitness for any sustained enterprise.

The compound of induced characteristics of soul and body is the myth of the Eternal Feminine, nowadays called the *Stereotype.* This is the dominant image of femininity which rules our culture and to which all women aspire. Assuming that the goddess of consumer culture is an artifact, we embark on an examination of how she comes to be made, the manufacture of the *Soul.* The chief element in this process is like the castration that we saw practised upon the body, the suppression and deflection of *Energy.* Following the same simple pattern, we begin at the beginning with *Baby,* showing how of the greater the less is made. The *Girl* struggles to reconcile her schooling along masculine lines with her feminine conditioning until *Puberty* resolves the ambiguity and anchors her safely in the feminine posture, if it works. When it doesn't she is given further conditioning as a corrective, especially by psychologists, whose assumptions and prescriptions are described as the *Psychological Sell.*

Because so many assumptions about the sex of mind cloud the issue of female mental ability, there follows a brief account of the failure of fifty years thorough and diversified testing to discover any pattern of differentiation in male and female intellectual powers, called *The Raw Material.* Because the tests have been irrelevant to the continuing conviction that women are illogical, subjective and generally silly, *Womanpower* takes a coherent expression of all such prejudice, Otto Weininger's *Sex and Character*, and turns all the defects which it defines into advantages, by rejecting Weininger's concepts of virtue and intelligence and espousing those of Whitehead and others. As a corrective to such a thoretical view of how valuable such female minds might be, *Work* provides a factual account of the patterns that the female contribution actually takes and how it is valued.

Draw near, woman, and here what I have to say. Turn your curiosity for once towards useful objects, and consider the advantages which nature gave you and society ravished away. Come and learn how you were born the companion of man and became his slave; how you grew to like the condition and think it natural; and finally how the long habituation of slavery so degraded you that you preferred its sapping but convenient vices to the more difficult virtues of freedom and repute. If the picture I shall paint leaves you in command of yourselves, if you can contemplate it without emotion, then go back to your futile pastimes; 'there is no remedy; the vices have become the custom.'

Choderlos de Laclos, 'On the Education of Women', 1783

The castration of women has been carried out in terms of a masculine-femine polarity, in which men have commandeered all the energy and streamlined it into an aggressive conquistatorial power, reducing all heterosexual contact to a sado-masochistic pattern. This has meant the distortion of our concepts of *Love*. Beginning with a celebration of an *Ideal*, *Love* proceeds to describe some of the chief perversions, *Altruism*, *Egotism*, and *Obsession*. These distortions masquerade under various mythic guises, of which two follow – *Romance*, an account of the fantasies on which the appetent and the disappointed woman is nourished, and *The Object of Male Fantasy,* which deals with the favourite ways in which women are presented in specifically male literature. The *Middle-Class Myth of Love and Marriage* records the rise of the most commonly accepted mutual fantasy of heterosexual love in our society, as a prelude to a discussion of the normal form of life as we understand it, the *Family*. The nuclear family of our time is severely criticized, and some vague alternatives are suggested, but the chief function of this part, as of the whole book, is mostly to suggest the possibility and the desirability of an alternative. The chief bogy of those who fear freedom is insecurity, and so *Love* ends with an animadversion on the illusoriness of *Security,* the ruling deity of the welfare state, never more insubstantial than it is in the age of total warfare, global pollution and population explosion.

Because love has been so perverted, it has in many cases come to involve a measure of hatred. In extreme cases it takes the form of *Loathing and Disgust* occasioned by sadism, fastidiousness and guilt, and inspires hideous crimes on the bodies of women, but more often it is limited to *Abuse* and ridicule, expressed by causal insult and facetiousness. Rather than dwell upon the injustices suffered by women in their individual domestic circumstances, these parts deal with more or less public occasions in which the complicated patterns of mutual exploitation do not supply any ambiguous context. There are many subjective accounts of suffering to be found in feminist literature, so *Misery* deals with the problem on a broader scale, showing how much objective evidence there is that women are not happy even when they do follow the blueprint set out by sentimental and marriage guidance counsellors and the system that they represent. Although there is no pattern of female assault on men to parallel their violence to women, there is plenty of evidence of the operation of *Resentment* in bitter, non-physical sexual conflict, usually enacted as a kind of game, a ritualized situation in which the real issues never emerge. This unconscious vindictiveness has its parallels in more organized and articulate female *Rebellion,* in that it seeks to characterize men as the enemy and either to compete with or confront or attack them. Insofar as such movements *demand* of men, or *force* men to grant their liberty, they perpetuate the estrangement of the sexes and their own dependency.

Revolution ought to entail the correction of some of the false perspectives which our assumptions about womanhood, sex, love and society have combined to create. Tentatively it gestures towards the re-deployment of energy, no longer to be used in repression, but in desire, movement and creation. Sex must be rescued from the traffic between powerful and powerless, masterful and mastered, sexual and neutral, to become a form of communication between potent, gentle, tender people, which cannot be accomplished by denial of heterosexual contact. The Ultra-feminine must refuse any longer to countenance the self-deception of the Omnipotent Administrator, not so much by assailing him as freeing herself from the desire to fulfil his expectations. It might be expected that men would resist female liberation because it threatens the foundations of phallic narcissism, but there are indications that men themselves are seeking a more satisfying role. If women liberate themselves, they will perforce liberate their oppressors: men might well feel that as sole custodians of sexual energy and universal protectors of women and children they have undertaken the impossible, especially now that their misdirected energies have produced the ultimate weapon. In admitting women to male-dominated areas of life, men have already shown a willingness to share responsibility, even if the invitation has not been taken up. Now that it might be construed that women are to help carry the can full of the mess that men have made, it need not be surprising that women have not leapt at the chance. If women could think that civilization would come to maturity only then they were involved in it wholly, they might feel more optimism in the possibilities of change and new development. The spiritual crisis we are at present traversing might be just another growing pain.

Revolution does little more than 'peep to what it would'. It hints that women ought not to enter into socially sanctioned relationships, like marriage, and that once unhappily in, they ought not to scruple to run away. It might even be thought to suggest that women should be deliberately promiscuous. It certainly maintains that they should be self-sufficient and consciously refrain from establishing exclusive dependencies and other kinds of neurotic symbioses. Much of what it points to is sheer irresponsibility, but when the stake is life and freedom, and the necessary condition is the recovery of a will to live, irresponsibility might be thought a small risk. It is almost a hundred years since Nora asked Helmer 'What do you consider is my most sacred duty?' and when he answered 'Your duty to your husband and children', she demurred.

I have another duty, just as sacred... My duty to myself... I believe that before everything else I'm a human being – just as much as you are ... or at any rate I shall try to become one. I know quite well that most people would agree with you, Torvald, and that you have a warrant for it in books; but I can't be satisfied any longer with what most people say, and with what's in books. I must think things out for myself and try to understand them.[7]

The relationships recognized by our society, and dignified with full privileges, are only those which are binding, symbiotic, economically determined. The most generous, tender, spontaneous relationship deliquesces into the approved mould when it avails itself of the approval buttresses, legality, security, permanence. Marriage cannot be a *job* as it has become. Status ought not to be measured for women in terms of attracting and snaring a man. The woman who realizes that she is bound by a million Lilliputian threads in an attitude of impotence and hatred masquerading as tranquillity and love has no option but to run away, if she is not to be corrupted and extinguished utterly. Liberty is terrifying but it is also exhilarating. Life is not easier or more pleasant for the Noras who have set off on their journey to awareness, but it is more interesting, nobler even. Such counsel will be called encouragement of irresponsibility, but the woman who accepts a way of life which she has not knowingly chosen, acting out a series of contingencies falsely presented as destiny, is truly irresponsible. To abdicate one's own moral understanding, to tolerate crimes against humanity, to leave everything to someone else, the father-ruler-king-computer, is the only irresponsibility. To deny that a mistake has been made when its results are chaos visible and tangible on all sides, *that* is irresponsibility. What oppression lays upon us is not responsibility but guilt.

The revolutionary woman must know her enemies, the doctors, psychiatrists, health visitors, priests, marriage counsellors, policemen, magistrates and genteel reformers, all the authoritarians and dogmatists who flock about her with warnings and advice. She must know her friends, her sisters, and seek in their lineaments her own. With them she can discover co-operation, sympathy and love. The end cannot justify the means: if she finds that her revolutionary way leads only to further discipline and continuing in-comprehension, with their corollaries of bitterness and diminution, no matter how glittering the objective which would justify it, she must understand that it is a wrong way and an illusory end. The struggle which is not joyous is the wrong struggle. The joy of the struggle is not hedonism and hilarity, but the sense of purpose, achievement and dignity which is the reflowering of etiolated energy. Only these can sustain her and keep the flow of energy coming. The problems are only equalled by the possibilities: every mistake made is redeemed when it is understood. The only ways in which she can feel such joy are radical ones: the more derided and maligned the action that she undertakes, the more radical.

The way is unknown, just as the sex of the uncastrated female is unknown. However far we can see it is not far enough to discern the contours of what is ultimately desirable. And so no ultimate strategy can be designed. To be free to start out, and to find companions for the journey is as far as we need to see from where we stand. The first exercise of the free woman is to devise her own mode of revolt, a mode which will reflect her own independence and originality. The more clearly the forms of oppression emerge in her understanding, the more clearly she can see the shape of future action. In the search for political awareness there is no substitute for confrontation. It would be too easy to present women with yet another form of self-abnegation, more opportunities for appetence and forlorn hope, but women have had enough bullying. They have been led by the nose and every other way until they have to acknowledge that, like everyone else, they are lost. A feminist elite might seek to lead uncomprehending women in another arbitrary direction, training them as a task force in a battle that might, that ought never to eventuate. If there is a pitched battle women will lose, because the best man never wins; the consequences of militancy do not disappear when the need for militancy is over. Freedom is fragile and must be protected. To sacrifice it, even as a temporary measure, is to betray it. It is not a question of telling women what to do next, or even what to want to do next. The hope in which this book was written is that women will discover that they have a will; once that happens they will be able to tell us how and what they want.

The fear of freedom is strong in us. We call it chaos or anarchy, and the words are threatening. We live in a true chaos of contradicting authorities, an age of conformism without community, of proximity without communication. We could only fear chaos if we imagined that it was unknown to us, but in fact we know it very well. It is unlikely that the techniques of liberation spontaneously adopted by women will be in such fierce conflict as exists between warring self-interests and conflicting dogmas, for they will not seek to eliminate all systems but their own. However, diverse it may be, they need not be utterly irreconcilable, because they will not be conquistatorial.

Hopefully, this book is subversive. Hopefully, it will draw fire from all the articulate sections of the community. The conventional moralist will find much that is reprehensible in the denial of the Holy Family, in the denigration of sacred motherhood, and the inference that women are not by nature monogamous. The political conservatives ought to object that by advocating the destruction of the patterns of consumption carried out by the chief spenders, the house-wives, the book invites depression and hardship. This is tantamount to admitting that the oppression of women is necessary to the maintenance of the economy, and simply ratifies the point. If the present economic structure can change only by collapsing, then it had better collapse as soon as possible. The nation that acknowledges that all labourers are worthy of their hire and then withholds payment from 19,500,000 workers cannot continue. Freudians will object that by setting aside the conventional account of the female psyche, and relying upon a concept of woman which cannot be found to exist, the book is mere metaphysics, forgetting the metaphysical basis of their own doctrine. The reformers will lament that the image of womanhood is cheapened by the advocacy of delinquency, so that women are being drawn further and further away from the real centres of power. In the computer kingdom the centres of political power have become centres of impotence, but even so, nothing in the book precludes the use of the political machine, although reliance on it may be contra-indicated. The most telling criticisms will come from my sisters of the left, the Maoists, the Trots, the I.S., the S.D.S., because of my fantasy that it might be possible to leap the steps of revolution and arrive somehow at liberty and communism without strategy or revolutionary discipline. But if women are the true proletariat, the truly oppressed majority, the revolution can only be drawn nearer by their withdrawal of support for the capitalist system. The weapon that I suggest is that most honoured of the proletariat, withdrawal of labour. Nevertheless it is clear that I do not find the factory the real heart of civilization or the re-entry of women into industry as the necessary condition of liberation. Unless the concepts of work and play and reward for work change absolutely, women must continue to provide cheap labour, and even more, free labour exacted of right by an employer possessed of a contract for life, made out in his favour.

This book represents only another contribution to a continuing dialogue between the wondering woman and the world. No questions have been answered but perhaps some have been asked in a more proper way than heretofore. If it is not ridiculed or reviled, it will have failed of its intention. If the most successful feminine parasites do not find it offensive, than it is innocuous. What they can tolerate is intolerable for a woman with any pride. The opponents of female suffrage lamented that woman's emancipation would mean the end of marriage, morality and the state; their extremism was more clear-sighted than the woolly benevolence of liberals and humanists, who thought that giving women a measure of freedom would not upset anything. When we reap the harvest which the unwitting suffragettes sowed we shall see that the anti-feminists were after all right.

Body

Gender

It is true that the sex of a person is attested by every cell in his body. What we do not know is exactly what that difference in the cells means in terms of their functioning. We cannot even argue from the observed difference in the cells to a significant difference in the tissues composed of those cells. To make any assumptions about superiority or inferiority on this basis is to assume what is very far from being proved. Perhaps when we have learnt how to read the D.N.A. we will be able to see what the information which is common to all members of the female sex really is, but even then it will be a long and tedious argument from biological data to behaviour.

It is an essential part of our conceptual apparatus that the sexes are a polarity, and a dichotomy in nature. Actually, that is quite false. The animal and vegetable worlds are not universally divided into two sexes, or even into two sexes with the possibility of freaks and indeterminate types; some lucky creatures are male and female by turns; some fungi and protozoa have more than two sexes and more than one way of coupling them. The degree of distinguishability between the sexes can vary from something so tiny as to be almost imperceptible to a degree of difference so great that scientists remained for a long time ignorant of the fact that species classified as distinct were in fact male and female of the same species. Nazi anthropologists maintained that the secondary sexual characteristics are more highly developed in more highly evolved species, pointing out that Negroid and Asiatic types frequently had less defined secondary characteristics than Aryans.[1]

In fact many simple forms of life are more strikingly differentiated sexually than humans are. What we do notice however is that the differentations between the human sexes are stressed and exaggerated, and before justifying the process we must ask *why*.

We can see the differentation which is essential to human sex if we magnify a body cell so much that we can see the chromosomes, say 2,000 times. Along with forty-five other chromosomes in the male body cell, there is one tiny one, called the Y-chromosome. It is not in fact a sex chromosome at all, and because of its isolation it has peculiar problems.

Since mutation within a chromosome can only be tested in different combinations when they can be freely distributed by crossing over, suppression of crossing over prevents mutations occurring within the Y-form being so tested. Since crossing over does not occur, the Y cannot undergo any structural interchange by means of interchange of parts. The Y-chromosome, therefore, during its evolution, would come to lose its effectiveness in the matter of sex determination and its place would be taken by the autosomes interacting with X.[2]

The autosomes are the chromosomes which are neither X nor Y, and of them there are twenty-three pairs in the body cells. Female sex is assured by the presence alongside them of a pair of chromosomes, which look exactly like them, but are in fact sex-determining, and are designated as XX. Instead of an XX pair added to his twenty-three pairs of autosomes the male has XY. The Y-chromosome has a negative function: when a Y-carrying sperm fertilizes an ovum, it simply reduces the amount of femaleness which would result in the formation of a female foetus. Along with his maleness, the foetus then inherits a number of weaknesses which are called sex-linked, because they result from genes found only in the Y-chromosome. Strange deformities like hypertrichosis, meaning excessive growths of hair mainly on the ears, horny patches on hands and feet, bark-like skin and a form of webbing of the toes are some which are less well-known than haemophilia, which is in fact the result of a mutant gene in the X-chromosome which the Y-chromosome cannot suppress, so that it is transmitted by females, but only effective in males. Colour-blindness follows the same pattern. About thirty other disorders are to be found in the males of the species and seldom in the females for the same reason. There is much evidence that the female is constitutionally stronger than the male; she lives longer, and in every age group more males than females die although the number of males conceived may be between ten and thirty per cent more. There is no explanation for the more frequent conception of males, for female-producing spermotozoa are produced in the same number as male-producing ones. It is tempting to speculate whether this might not be a natural compensation for the greater vulnerability of males.[3]

> While woman remains nearer the infantile type, man approaches more to the senile. The extreme varational tendency of man expresses itself in a larger percentage of genius, insanity and idiocy; woman remains more nearly normal.
>
> W.I. Thomas, 'Sex and Society', 1907, p. 51

Recently, criminologists have come up with another disconcerting observation about the Y chromosome. They found that there was a high proportion of males with the XYY chromosome, that is an extra Y, among those men in prison for crimes of violence, and it seemed to be linked to certain deficiencies in mental ability.[4]

The development of the sexual characteristics is not simply determined by the chromosomes: these constitute the primal difference, but the development of the different physical characteristics involves the whole endocrinal system and the interaction of various hormones. Women have been made especially aware of their hormones because of the use of synthetic hormones in the contraceptive pill; as usual when such notions are popularized, the function of the hormones has been too simply described. In fact, the full range of activity of hormones is very imperfectly understood. In tampering with the delicate and fluctuating balance of female hormones, physicians have had to admit that they have produced alterations in non-sexual and non-reproductive functions which they did not expect. It is difficult enough to understand the simple mathematics of genes and chromosomes: when it comes to the chemistry of hormones, the processes are much more difficult to trace. We know that the male hormone, testosterone, induces the growth of male sexual characteristics, and that it is linked somehow with the other male hormone, androgen, which stimulates the growth of muscle, bone and guts. The secretion of androgen is under the control of the pituitary interstitial cell hormone, as is the female hormone oestrogen which is very like it. Both sexes produce both; all we know is that if we give oestrogen to men their secondary sexual characteristics become less evident, and if we give androgen to women the same thing happens. For some functions oestrogen needs the help of the other female hormone, progesterone. All of our secretions have complementary and catalytic reactions: almost every investigation of these turns up new chemicals with new names. Despite the haphazard bombardment of women with large doses of hormones in order to prevent conception, the commonest attitude towards them among those who know is one of respect and wonder. The search still goes on for a pill which will inhibit only the function essential to conception, and women ought not to feel confident until it is found.

The sex of a child is established at conception because each spermatozoona contains one Y and one X chromosome, and

the mature ovum contains one X. The specialized chromosome causes the primary difference, but the development of
sexual features grows out of specialized chemical substances
in the chromosomes. Up to the seventh week the foetus
shows no sexually differentiated characteristics, and when
sexual development begins it follows a remarkably similar
pattern in both sexes. The clitoris and the head of the penis
look very alike at first, and the urethra develops as a furrow
in both sexes. In boys the scrotum forms out of the genital
swelling, in girls, the labia. If we examine the tissue in these
analogous sites we see that it is in fact different, although
women do have tissues similar to the male tissues in different
sites.[5]

Nature herself is not always unambiguous. Sometimes a
girl child may have so well-developed a clitoris that it is
assumed that she is a boy. Likewise, many male children
may be under-developed, or their genitals deformed or
hidden and it is assumed that they are girls. Sometimes they
accept their sex as described, and regard themselves as
defective members of the wrong sex, assuming the behaviour
and attitudes of the sex, despite special conflicts. In other
cases, some sort of genetic awareness creates a problem
which leads to investigation and the right sex of the child is
established.[6] Some, like little girls born without vaginas, are
wrongly considered neuter: others having the XXY
construction are considered women without ovaries. Some of
these difficulties can be resolved by cosmetic surgery, but too
often surgeons perform such operations for peculiar motives,
when scanning the body cell structure would reveal that no
congenital abnormality is present. Most homosexuality
results from the inability of the person to adapt to his given
sex role, and ought not to be treated as genetic and
pathological, but the prejudiced language of *abnormality*
offers the homosexual no way of expressing this rejection, so
he must consider himself a freak. The 'normal' sex roles that

we learn to play from our infancy are no more natural than the antics of a transvestite. In order to approximate those shapes and attitudes which are considered normal and desirable, both sexes deform themselves, justifying the process by referring to the primary, genetic difference between the sexes. But of forty-eight chromosomes only one is different: on this difference we base a complete separation of male and female, pretending as it were that all forty-eight were different. Frenchmen may well cry 'Vive la différence', for it is cultivated unceasingly in all aspects of life. It is easiest and most obvious to consider that deliberately induced deformity as it is manifested in the body and our concepts of it, for whatever else we are or may pretend to be, we are certainly our bodies.

Bones

Just how much sex is there in a skeleton? When archaeologists state categorically that half a femur comes from a twenty-year-old woman we are impressed with their certainty, not the less so because the statement, being a guess, is utterly unverifiable. Such a guess is as much based in the archaeologists' assumptions about women as anything else. What they mean is that the bone is typically female, that is, that it *ought* to belong to a woman. Because it is impossible to escape from the stereotyped notions of womanhood as they prevail in one's own society, curious errors in ascription have been made and continue to be made.

We tend to think of the skeleton as rigid; it seems to abide when all else withers away, so it ought to be a sort of nitty-gritty, unmarked by superficial conditioning. In fact it is itself subject to deformation by many influences. The first of these is muscular stress. Because men are more vigorous than women their bones have more clearly marked muscular grooves. If the muscles are constrained, by binding or wasting, or by continual external pressure which is not counterbalanced, the bones can be drawn out of alignment. Men's bodies are altered by the work that they do, and by the nutriment which sustains them in their growing period, and so are women's, but women add to these influences others which are dictated by fashion and sex-appeal. There have been great changes in the history of feminine allure in the approved posture of the shoulders, whether sloping or straight, drawn forward or back, and these have been bolstered by dress and corsetting, so that the delicate balance of bone on bone has been altered by the stress of muscles maintaining the artificial posture. The spine has been curved forward in the mannequin's lope, or backwards in the S-bend of art nouveau or the swayback of the fifties. Footwear reinforces these unnatural stresses; the high-heeled shoe alters all the torsion of the muscles of the thighs and pelvis and throws the spine into an angle which is still in some circles considered essential to allure. I am not so young that I cannot remember my grandmother begging my mother to corset me, because she found my teenage ungainliness unattractive, and was afraid that my back was not strong enough to maintain my height by itself. If I had been corsetted at thirteen, my rib-cage might have developed differently, and the downward pressure on my pelvis would have resulted in its widening. Nowadays, corsetting is frowned upon, but many women would not dream of casting away the girdle that offers *support* and *tummy control*. Even tights are tight, and can cause strange symptoms to the wearer. Typists' slouch and shop-girl lounge have their own effect upon the posture and therefore upon the skeleton.

Most people understand that the development of the limbs is affected by the exercise taken by the growing child. My mother discouraged us from emulating the famous girl swimmers of Australia by remarking on their massive shoulders and narrow hips, which she maintained came from their rigorous training. It is agreed that little girls should have a different physical education programme from little boys, but it is not admitted how much of the difference is counselled by the conviction that little girls should not look like little boys. The little girls look so pretty doing their eurhythmics, and the boys so manly when they chin them-selves.[1] The same assumptions extend into our suppositions about male and female skeletons: a small-handed skeleton *ought* to be female, small feet are feminine too, but the fact remains that either sex may exhibit the disproportion.

Medical students learn their anatomy from a male sample, except where they are explicitly dealing with the reproductive functions. They learn that *as a rule* the female skeleton is lighter and smaller, and the bone formation more childlike than the male. This last is an observation which is frequently made about the whole female body, that it is infantilized or *pedomorphic,* while the male body is aged, or *gerontomorphic.* This description, far from implying any defect in female development, implies an evolutionary advantage in greater elasticity and adaptability. We can assume nothing whatever about physical strength or mental ability from it.[2]

The difference between the childish type and the aged type must not be exaggerated: in fact there is a wide range of variation possible, without any hint of a functioning abnormality. Such categorization represents an effort to identify a tendency. In our search for distinctions to justify the inequalities in the male and female lot we have not only overstated the general difference but invented particular differences which do not exist, like the extra rib which is still widely believed to exist in women. It is assumed that the female pelvis, the seat of the most marked differentiation in the bone structure of the sexes, is quite different from the male. In fact the difference is one of comparative dimensions and angle of tilt: the basic design is common.[3] Well-bred sedentary women tend to have larger pelves than hard-working or poorly nourished women and in them the sexual difference is exaggerated by influences not connected with biological sex, but with the sociology of sex.[4] The prejudice that narrow pelves are inefficient in childbirth is unfounded; deformation in either direction will affect the efficiency of the mechanisms of the pelvis. Most people do not judge sex like archaeologists; when the actual sexual organs are hidden, the sex type is revealed by superficial characteristics, but even curves take their toll of the patient unseen bones, bearing them up, thrusting them out, wobbling and waggling them. Shall these bones live?

Curves

When the life of the party wants to express the idea of a pretty woman in mime, he undulates his two hands in the air and leers expressively. The notion of a curve is so closely connected to sexual semantics that some people cannot resist sniggering at road signs. The most popular image of the female despite the exigencies of the clothing trade is all boobs and buttocks, a hallucinating sequence of parabolae and bulges.

The female body is commonly believed to be enveloped in insulating fat, just so that she is more cuddly, Nature and Hugh Hefner being alike bawds in this traffic. It is true that women wear much fewer and lighter clothes than men do, but it is not so easy to determine whether the layer of fat results from the necessity to insulate such exposed portions or predates it. Men's habit of wrapping their nether quarters in long garments has resulted in a wastage of the tissues which can be seen in the chicken legs which they expose on any British resort beach.[1] Men have subcutaneous fat as well as women, but women build up larger deposit in specific sites. In fat people most of the fat is accumulated in the subcutaneous layer: what the pseudo-fact that women have subcutaneous fat really means is that women ought to be fatter than men. Historically we may see that all repressed,

---

The finest bosom in nature is not so fine as what imagination forms.

Gregory, 'A Father's Legacy to his Daughters', 1809, p. 64

---

indolent people have been fat, that eunuchs tend to fatten like bullocks, and so we need not be surprised to find that the male preference for cuddlesome women persists.[2]

The most highly prized curve of all is that of the bosom. The actual gland that forms the base of the breast is a convex structure extending from the second rib to the sixth beneath: the fat which gathers around it and forms the canyon of cleavage is not itself a sexual characteristic; in cases where the owner of huge breasts is not fat elsewhere the phenomenon is usually caused by endocrine derangement. The degree of attention which breasts receive, combined with the confusion about what the breast fetishists actually want, makes women unduly anxious about them. They can never be just right; they must always be too small, too big, the wrong shape, too flabby. The characteristics of the mammary stereotype are impossible to emulate because they are falsely simulated, but they must be faked somehow or another. Reality is either gross or scrawny.

A full bosom is actually a millstone around a woman's neck: it endears her to the men who want to make their mammet of her, but she is never allowed to think that their popping eyes actually see her. Her breasts are only to be admired for as long as they show no sighs of their function: once darkened, stretched or withered they are objects of revulsions. They are not parts of a person but lures slung around her neck, to be kneaded and twisted like magic putty, or mumbled and mouthed like lolly ices. The only way that women can opt out of such gross handling is to refuse to wear undergarments which perpetuate the fantasy of pneumatic boobs, so that men must come to terms with the varieties of the real thing. Recent emphasis on the nipple, which was absent from the breast of popular pornography, is in women's favour, for the nipple is expressive and responsive. The vegetable creep of women's liberation has freed some breasts from the domination of foam and wire. One way to continue progress in the same direction might be to remind men that they have sensitive nipples too.

The next curve in the joker's hourglass is the indentation of the waist. The waist is exaggerated in order to emphasize the outward curve of breast and buttock: it is hardly a natural phenomenon at all. In all those eras when it was *de rigueur* women have had to wear special apparatus to enforce it, and, in much the same way that a heap of brass rings really does elongate Bantu ladies' necks, the waist came to exist. Nineteenth-century belles even went to the extremity of having their lowest ribs removed so that they could lace their corsets tighter. One native tribe of New Guinea uses tight girdles for both men and women, and the flesh tends to swell above and below the ligature, so that men have hourglass curves too. If we may take the imposition of tight corsets on 'O' as any guide, we might assume that the tiny waist is chiefly valued as a point of frangibility for the female frame, so that it gratifies sadistic fantasies.[3]

Buttock fetishism is comparatively rare in our culture, although Kenneth Tynan did write a connoisseur article for a girlie mag on the subject not so long ago.[4] Sub-pornographic magazines still carry advertisements for girdles with built in cushions for inadequate arses, but generally the great quivering expanses of billowing thigh and buttock which titillated our grandfathers have fallen into obloquy.[5] Instead, the cheeky bottom in tight trousers, more boyish than otherwise, attracts the most overt attention. Girls are often self-conscious about their behinds, draping themselves in long capes and tunics, but it is more often because they are too abundant in that region than otherwise.

There is a kind of class distinction in sexual preferences. The darling of the working class is still curvy and chubby, but the fashionable middle class are paying their respects to slenderness, and even thinness. For women, there is one aspect which is common to both situations: demands are made upon them to contour their bodies in order to please the eyes of others. Women are so insecure that they constantly take measures to capitulate to this demand, whether it is rational or not. The thinnest women either diet because of an imagined grossness somewhere or fret because they are not curvaceous: the curviest worry about the bounciness of their curves, or diet to lose them. The curvy girl who ought to be thin and the thin girl who ought to be curvy are offered more or less dangerous medications to achieve their aims. In each case the woman is tailoring herself to appeal to a buyers' market; her most exigent buyer may be her husband, who goes on exacting her approximation to the accepted image as a condition of his continuing desire and pride in her.

Every human body has its optimum weight and contour, which only health and efficiency can establish. Whenever we treat women's bodies as aesthetic objects without function we deform them and their owners. Whether the curves imposed are the ebullient arabesques of the tit-queen or the attenuated coils of art-nouveau they are deformations of the dynamic, individual body, and limitations of the possibilities of being female.

Hair

The schoolboy who wrote to the Sunday papers asking why his headmaster was so agitated by the brown stuff that he had growing down his neck and on to his collar was being disingenuous. When men began to grow their hair in our generation they were not acting motivelessly, as they afterwards tried to maintain. Their hair was a sign that they did not accept the morality of the crop-haired generation of bureaucrats which sired them. By growing their hair they managed to up-end some strange presupposition about its sexual significance, for many young men sported full heads of tossing curls and long glossy tresses which their sisters tried vainly to emulate. The old supposition that women grew thicker and longer hair on their heads than men could did not die painlessly.[1] The long-haired men were called freaks and perverts, and the women resorted to immense cascades of store-bought hair to redress the balance. While they built up the hair on their heads and festooned their eyelashes they were resolutely stripping off every blade of hair in their armpits and on their arms and legs. When the summer brought the freaks out in the parks and gardens in singlets, they noticed that many of them had smooth arms and chests and scant beard; instead of understanding what this proved about the maleness of hairy chests, they took it to be further proof that these men were degenerates. Not so long ago Edmund Wilson could imply a deficiency in Hemingway's virility by accusing him of having crêpe hair on his chest.

The fact is that some men are hairy and some are not; some women are hairy and some are not. Different races have different patterns of hair distribution. That most virile of creatures, the 'buck' negro, has very little body hair at all.

Some dark-skinned Caucasian women have abundant growth of dark hair on their thighs, calves, arms and even cheeks; eradication of it is painful and time consuming; yet the more clothes women are allowed to take off, the more hair they must take off.

The rationale of depilation is crude. Sexuality is quite falsely thought to be an animal characteristic, despite the obvious fact that man is the most sexually active of the animals, and the only one who has sex independently of the instinctual reproductive drive. In the popular imagination hairinesss is like furriness, an index of bestiality, and as such an indication of aggressive sexuality. Men cultivate it, just as they are encouraged to develop competitive and aggressive instincts, women suppress it, just as they suppress all the aspects of their vigour and libido. If they do not feel sufficient revulsion for their body hair themselves, others will direct them to depilate themselves. In extreme cases, women shave or pluck their pubic area, so as to seem even more sexless and infantile. Mind you, if even Freud could consider that pubic hair was a screen supplied by some sort of physiological modesty, this shaving could also figure as a revolt. The efforts made to eradicate all smell from the female body are part of the same suppression of fancied animality. Nowadays it is not enough to neutralize perspiration and breath odours; women are warned in every women's magazine of the horror of vaginal odour, which is assumed to be utterly repellent. Men who do not want their women shaved and deodorized into complete tastelessness are powerless against women's own distaste for their bodies. Some men on the other hand take a pride in smelliness and hairiness, as part of their virile rejection of prettiness. There is a mean between the charm of a half-cured goatskin and the glabrous odourless body of the feminine toy, which is the body cared for and kept reasonably clean, the body desirable, whether it be male or female.

Sex

Women's sexual organs are shrouded in mystery.

It is assumed that most of them are internal and hidden, but even the ones that are external are relatively shady. When little girls begin to ask questions their mothers provide them, if they are lucky, with crude diagrams of the sexual apparatus, in which the organs of pleasure feature much less prominently than the intricacies of tubes and ovaries. I myself did not realize that the tissues of my vagina were quite normal until I saw a meticulously engraved dissection in an eighteenth-century anatomy textbook.[1] The little girl is not encouraged to explore her own genitals or to identify the tissues of which they are composed, or to understand the mechanism of lubrication and erection. The very idea is distasteful. Because of this strange modesty, which a young woman will find extends even into the doctor's surgery, where the doctor is loath to examine her, and loath to expatiate on what he finds, female orgasm has become more and more of a mystery, at the same time as it has been exalted as a duty. Its actual nature has become a matter for metaphysical speculation. All kinds of false ideas are still in circulation about women, although they were disproved years ago: many men refuse to relinquish the notion of female ejaculation, which although it has a long and prestigious history is utterly fanciful.

Part of the modesty about the female genitalia stems from actual distaste. The worst name anyone can be called is *cunt*. The best thing a cunt can be is small and unobtrusive: the anxiety about the bigness of the penis is only equalled by anxiety about the smallness of the cunt. No woman wants to find out that she has a twat like a horse-collar: she hopes she is not sloppy or smelly, and obligingly obliterates all signs of her menstruation in the cause of public decency. Women were not always so reticent: in ballad literature we can find lovely examples of women vaunting their genitals, like the lusty wench who admonished a timid tailor in round terms because he did not dare measure her fringed purse with his yard:

> You'l find the Purse so deep,
> You'l hardly come to the treasure.[2]

Another praised her shameful part in these terms:

> I have a gallant Pin-box,
>   the like you ne'er did see,
> It is where never was the Pox
>   something above my knee...
> O 'tis a gallant Pin-box
>   you never saw the peer;
> Then Ile not leave my Pin-box
>   for fifty pound a year.[3]

Early gynaecology was entirely in the hands of men, some of whom, like Samuel Collins, described the vagina so lovingly that any woman who read his words would have been greatly cheered. Of course such books were not meant to be seen by women at all. He speaks of the vagina as the Temple of Venus and the *mons veneris* as Venus's cushion, but he abandons euphemism to describe the wonders of the female erection:

...the Nymphs...being extended to compress the Penis and speak a delight in the act of Coition.... The use of the blood-vessels is to impart Vital Liquor into the substance of the Clitoris, and of the Nerves to impregnate it with a choyce Juyce inspired with animal Spirits (full of Elastick Particles making it Vigorous and Tense)....

The Glands of the Vagina... being heated in Coition, do throw off the rarified fermented serous Liquor, through many Meatus into the Cavity of the Vagina, and thereby rendereth its passage very moist and slippery, which is pleasant in Coition.... The Hypogastrick Arteries do sport themselves in numerous Ramulets about the sides and other parts of the Vagina, which are so many inlets of blood to make it warm and turgid in the Act of Coition.[4]

Collins's description is an active one: the vagina *speaks, throws,* is *tense* and *vigorous.* He and his contemporaries assumed that young women were even more eager for intercourse than young men. Some of the terms they used to describe the tissues of the female genitalia in action are very informative and exact, although unscientific. The vagina is said to be lined 'with tunicles like the petals of a full-blown rose', with 'Wrinckle on wrinckle' which 'do give delight in Copulations'. The vagina was classified as 'sensitive enough' which is an exact description. They were aware of the special role of the clitoris, in causing the 'sweetness of love' and the 'fury of venery'.

> **The Vagina is made so artificial (affabre is his word) that it can accommodate itself to any penis, so that it will give way to a long one, meet a short one, widen to a thick one, constringe to a small one: so that every man might well enough lie with any Woman, and every Woman with any Man.**
>
> **'The Anatomy of Human Bodies epitomised'**
> **1682, p. 156**

The notion that healthy and well-adjusted women would have orgasms originating in the vagina was a metaphysical interpolation in the empirical observations of these pioneers. Collins took the clitoris for granted, as a dear part of a beloved organ; he did not underemphasize the role of the vagina in creating pleasure, as we have seen. Unhappily we have accepted, along with the reinstatement of the clitoris after its proscription by the Freudians, a notion of the utter passivity and even irrelevance of the vagina. Love-making has become another male skill, of which women are the judges. The skills that the Wife of Bath used to make her husbands swink, the athletic sphincters of the Tahitian girls who can keep their men inside them all night, are alike unknown to us. All the vulgar linguistic emphasis is placed upon the *poking* element; *fucking, screwing, rooting, shagging* are all acts performed upon the passive female: the names for the penis are all *tool* names. The only genuine intersexual words we have for sex are the obsolete *swive,* and the ambiguous *ball.* Propagandists like Theodore Faithfull (and me) are trying to alter the emphasis of the current imagery. To a man who had difficulty getting an erection Faithfull wrote:

If you ignore any idea of erection and concentrate your attention on your girl-friend, ignore the clitoris and use your fingers to caress her internally and if you follow such activity by a close association of your sex organs you may soon find that she can draw your sex organ into her vagina without any need on your part for erection.[5]

This sounds like therapeutic lying, nevertheless serious attempts have been made to increase women's participation in copulation. A.H. Kegel, teaching women how to over-come the bladder weakness that often afflicts women, showed them how to exercise the pubococcygeal muscles and found inadvertently that this increased their sexual enjoyment.[6] What their mates thought of it is not on record. The in-continence resulted from the same suppression of activity that inhibited sexual pleasure; we might find that if we restored women's competence in managing their own mus-culature many of their pelvic disturbances would cease, and their sexual enjoyment might correspondingly grow. Of course we cannot do this until we find out how the pelvis ought to operate: as long as women cannot operate it, we cannot observe its action, and so the circle perpetuates itself. If the right chain reaction would happen, women might find that the clitoris was more directly involved in intercourse, and could be brought to a climax by a less pompous and deliberate way than digital massage. In any case, women will have to accept part of the responsibility for their own and their partners' enjoyment, and this involves a measure of control and conscious cooperation. Part of the battle will be won if they can change their attitude towards sex, and embrace and stimulate the penis instead of *taking* it. Enlightened women have long sung the praises of the female superior position, because they are not weighed down by the heavier male body, and can respond more spontaneously. It is after all a question of communication, and communication is not advanced by the *he talk, me listen* formula.

The banishment of the fantasy of the vaginal orgasm is ultimately a service, but the substitution of the clitoral spasm for genuine gratification may turn out to be a disaster for sexuality. Masters and Johnson's conclusions have produced some unlooked for side-effects, like the veritable clitoromania which infects Mette Eiljersen's book, *I accuse!* While speaking of women's orgasms as resulting from the 'right touches on the button' she condemns sexologists who

recommend...the stimulation of the clitoris as part of the prelude to intercourse, to that which most men consider to be the 'real thing'. What is in fact the 'real thing' for them is *completely devoid of sensation* for the woman.

This is the heart of the matter! Concealed for hundreds of years by humble, shy and subservient women.[7]

Not all the women in history have been humble and subservient to such an extent. It is nonsense to say that a woman feels nothing when a man is moving his penis in her vagina: the orgasm is qualitatively different when the vagina can undulate around the penis instead of vacancy. The differentiation between the simple inevitable pleasure of men and the tricky responses of women is not altogether valid. If ejaculation meant release for all men, given the constant manufacture of sperm and the resultant pressure to have intercourse men could copulate without transport or disappointment with anyone. The process described by the experts, in which the man dutifully does the rounds of the erogenous zones, spends an equal amount of time on each nipple, turns his attention to the clitoris (usually too directly), leads through the stages of digital or lingual stimulation and then politely lets himself into the vagina, perhaps waiting until the retraction of the clitoris tells him that he is welcome, is laborious and inhumanly computerized. The implication that there is a statistically ideal fuck which will always result in satisfaction if the right procedures are followed is depressing and misleading. There is no substitute for excitement: not all the massage in the world will ensure satisfaction, for it is a matter of psycho-sexual release. Real gratification is not enshrined in a tiny cluster of nerves but in the sexual involvement of the whole person. Women's continued high enjoyment of sex, which continues after orgasm, observed by men with wonder, is not based on the clitoris, which does not respond particularly well to continued stimulus, but in a general sensual response. If we localize female response in the clitoris we impose upon women the same limitation of sex which has stunted the male's response. The male sexual ideal or virility without languor or amorousness is profoundly desolating: when the release is expressed in mechanical terms it is sought mechanically. Sex becomes masturbation in the vagina.

Many women who greeted the conclusions of Masters and Johnson with cries of 'I told you so!' and 'I am normal!' will feel that this criticism is a betrayal. They have discovered sexual pleasure after being denied it but the fact that they have only ever experienced gratification from clitoral stimulation is evidence for my case, because it is the index of the desexualization of the whole body, the substitution of genitality for sexuality. The ideal marriage as measured by the electronic equipment in the Reproductive Biology Research Foundation laboratories is enfeebled – dull sex for dull people. The sexual personality is basically anti-authoritarian. If the system wishes to enforce complete suggestibility in its subjects, it will have to tame sex. Masters and Johnson supplied the blueprint for standard, low-agitation, cool-out monogamy. If women are to avoid this last reduction of their humanity, they must hold out not just for orgasm but for ecstasy.

The organization of sexuality reflects the basic features of the performance principle and its organization of society. Freud emphasizes the aspect of centralization. It is especially operative in the 'unification' of the various objects of the partial instincts into one libidinous object of the opposite sex, and in the establishment of genital supremacy. In both cases, the unifying process is repressive – that is to say, the partial instincts do not develop freely into a 'higher' stage of gratification which preserved their objectives, but are cut off and reduced to subservient functions. This process achieves the socially necessary desexualization of the body, leaving most of the rest free for use as the instrument of labour. The temporal reduction of the libido is thus supplemented by its spatial reduction.[8]

If women find that the clitoris has become the only site of their pleasure instead of acting as a kind of sexual overdrive in a more general response, they will find themselves dominated by the performance ethic, which would not itself be a regression, if the performance principle in our society included enterprise and creativity. But enterprise and creativity are connected with libido which does not survive the civilizing process. Women must struggle to keep alternative possibilities open, at the same time as they struggle to attain the kind of strength that can avail itself of them.

The permissive society has done much to neutralize sexual drives by containing them. Sex for many has become a sorry business, a mechanical release involving neither discovery nor triumph, stressing human isolation more dishearteningly than ever before. The orgies feared by the Puritans have not materialized on every street corner, although more girls permit more (joyless) liberties than they might have done before. Homosexuality in many forms, indeed any kind of sex which can escape the dead hand of the institution – group sex, criminal sex, child-violation, bondage and discipline – has flourished, while simple sexual energy seems to be steadily diffusing and dissipating. This is not because enlightenment is harmful, or because repression is a necessary goad to human impotence, but because sexual enlightenment happened under government subsidy, so that its discoveries were released in bad prose and clinical jargon upon the world. The permit to speak freely of sexuality has resulted only in the setting up of another shibboleth of sexual normality, gorged with dishonesty and kitsch. Women who understand their sexual expertise in the way that Jackie Collins writes of it are irretrievably lost to themselves and their lovers:

He took her to the bedroom and undressed her slowly, he made love to her beautifully. Nothing frantic, nothing rushed. He caressed her body as though there were nothing more important in the world. He took her to the edge of ecstasy and back again, keeping her hovering, sure of every move he made. Her breasts grew under his touch, swelling, becoming even larger and firmer. She floated on a suspended plane, a complete captive to his hands and body. He had amazing control, stopping at just the right moment. When it did happen it was only because he wanted it to, and they came in complete unison. She had never experienced *that* before, and she clung to him, words tumbling out of her mouth about how much she loved him. Afterwards they lay and smoked and talked. 'You're wonderful,' he said, 'You're a clever woman making me wait until after we were married!'[9]

Miss Collins's heroine is prudish, passive, calculating, selfish and dull, despite her miraculous expanding tits. When her husband grows tired of playing on this sexual instrument she can have no recourse but must continue to loll on her deflated airbed, wondering what went wrong. There is no mention of genitals: everything happens in a swoon or a swamp of undifferentiated sensation. He labours for her pleasure like a eunuch in the harem. Sex is harnessed in the service of counter-revolution.

Embraces are cominglings from the Head to the Feet, And not a pompous High Priest entering by a Secret Place.
                    Blake, 'Jerusalem', pl. 69, II. 39–40

What Jackie Collins is expressing is the commonest romantic ideal of the perfect fuck. It shows how deeply we believe in the concept of male mastery. Miss Collins's heroine was manipulating her mate's colonizing sexual urge, making him wait, as long as his importunacy lasts, until she is ready. In manipulating his violent impulses she exercised an illusory superiority, for she is tender, sentimental and modest, loving not for her own gratification, but in expression of esteem, trust and true love, until she could civilize him into marriage and the virtuoso sexual performance. The complicated psychic aspect of his love is undervalued; she is still alone, egotistical, without libido to desire him or bring him to new pleasure in her. Jackie

Collins and the sex-books show that we still make love to organs and not people: that so far from realizing that people are never more idiosyncratic, never more totally *there* than when they make love, we are never more incommunicative, never more alone.

The Wicked Womb

Sex is not the same as reproduction: the relation between the two is especially tenuous for human beings, who may copulate when they will, not only when they are driven thereto by heat or an instinctual urge. The difference must be at least partly caused by the fact that human beings have memory, will and understanding to experience the pleasure of sex and desire it for itself. Little girls only learn about the pleasure of sex as an implication of their discoveries about their reproductive function, as something merely incidental. Much more care is taken to inform them about the approaching trauma of menstruation and the awful possibility of childbirth if they should 'lose control' or 'give in' to sexual urges, than to see that they recognize and welcome these sexual urges in the first place. So the growing girl knows more about her womb than she does about her external genitalia, and not much of what she knows is good news.[1]

Her knowledge of the womb is academic: most women do not actually feel any of the activity of their ovaries or womb until they go wrong, as they nearly always do. Many women, one might say too many women, die of illnesses in organs that they have virtually ignored all their lives, the cervix, the vulvae, the vagina, and the womb. Some of the trouble is caused by late diagnosis of illnesses begun in a trivial treatable way, which stems from the obscurantism falsely dignified by the name 'modesty'. Since time immemorial the womb has been associated with trouble, and some of the reluctance shown by doctors to attend to anxieties that women feel about their tricky apparatus stems

58

from this atavistic fear. Frigidity for women is regarded as a
common condition, resulting from bad luck and bad
management; in men impotence is treated with the utmost
seriousness. Any trivial lesion on the penis is examined with
ostentatious care so that a man need not feel threatened by
castration anxieties, but the poor old womb must gush blood
or drop out before anybody takes its condition seriously. The
clitoris is ignored: a nurse once narrowly missed cutting
mine off when shaving me for an operation. Even the much
vaunted cervical smears are rarely given in our community.
I first managed to get one when I went to the V.D. clinic in
despair because my own doctor would not examine my
vagina or use pathology to discover the nature of an
irritation, which turned out to be exactly what I thought it
was. At the V.D. clinic cervical smears were given as a *matter
of course*: at the respectable G.P.'s they were not given at all.
The enormous hoo-ha about the strange impalpable results
of vasectomy upon the male psyche results from this
continuing phallocentricity: the devisers of the pill worried
so little about the female psyche that it was years before they
discovered that one woman in three who was on the pill was
chronically depressed. Exaggerated care for the male
apparatus, together with reluctance to involve oneself in
serious attention to the womb and its handmaids, is the fruit
of centuries of womb-fear, not to be eradicated by political
action or yelling at public meetings.[2] Women must first of all
inform themselves about their own bodies, take over the
study of gynaecology and obstetrics,[3] and, not least, conquer
their own prejudice in favour of men doctors.

The most recent form of fantasy about the womb is the
enormously prevalent notion of the pathology of *hysteria* in
Europe until the twentieth century. At first it was called the
mother, and was thought to be the wandering womb that rose
into the throat of a girl and choked her. The most sceptical
anatomists, while deploring the arts which quacks and

witches used to allay hysterics, believed that the womb was 'charged with blood and stale seed from whence arise foul and ill-conditioned damps', developing their own strange theory of pelvic congestion.[4] It was assumed that unmarried women and widows suffered most from hysteria, and that a good husband could fix it. The very seriously discussed but imaginary green-sickness, renamed 'chlorosis' by doctors anxious to obscure the folklorish origins of their ideas, came about in the same way.[5] The descriptions of the condition are vivid, and although some of them incorporate symptoms arising from other causes generally we can observe the same hypochondriacal syndromes that are put down to hysteria these days: epilepsy, asthma, breathlessness, flatulence, *sensus globi in abdomine se volventis,* lassitude, convulsions, painful menstruation. Some doctors really believed that *est femineo generi pars una uterus omnium morborum,* 'the womb is a part of every illness of the female sex.' Women were assumed to be by nature subject to the tyranny of the insatiate womb, and to suffer symptoms from which men only suffered if they indulged in excessive self-abuse.[6] Although the repression mechanism was described in various ways, the reaction to that mechanism was taken (as it usually is) to be a ground for continuing it. Women were too weak, too vulnerable to irrational influences to be allowed to

That the Mother (as they call it) gets into the throat of married women and Maids, is by thousands believed to be a truth; yea, that the string of the Mother is fast in the throat, and that the vein of the Mother is also seated there, which fancy is craftily managed by a certain Woman in this Town, who thereby deceives many innocent women, and marvellously enriches herself.

'In libellum Hippocrates de virginum morbis',
1688, p. 73

control their own lives. When one of my students collapsed in her final examination with cramps and bitter uncontrollable sobbing, the cause was officially recorded as *hysteria*: the aetiology of her case was particularly important but the word *hysteria* seemed to supply all the answers.

Although we do not believe in green-sickness any more, since maidens became an essential, if menial, part of the work force, we do believe that old maidens are apt to be consumed and wasted by frustration, Only recently have the other terrifying functions of the womb been publicized and accepted. Husbands are allowed to participate in the mysteries of birth, which need no longer be carried out in a coven of females. Women do not have to be purified or churched after child-bearing any more. Attempts are being made to reduce the impression that childbirth is a kind of punishment for women, and to reëducate them in breeding, while the more sinister companions of childbed – puerperal fever and sudden haemorrhage – have been brought under control. Although few men have still to watch in horror while their wives breed themselves through miscarriage and prolapse helplessly to death, we still have not come to terms with the sinister womb. The most pervasive and significant manifestation of that atavistic fear surviving is in the common attitude to menstruation.

Women who adhere to the Moslem, Hindu or Mosaic faiths must regard themselves as unclean in their time of menstruation and seclude themselves for a period. Medieval Catholicism made the stipulation that menstruating women were not to come into the church. Although enlightenment is creeping into this field at its usual pace, we still have a marked revulsion for menstruation, principally evinced by our efforts to keep it secret. The success of the tampon is partly due to the fact that it is hidden. The arrival of the menarche is more significant than any birthday, but in the Anglo-Saxon households it is ignored and carefully concealed from general awareness. For six months while I was waiting for my first menstruation I toted a paper bag with diapers and pins in my school satchel. When it finally came, I suffered agonies lest anyone should guess or *smell* it or anything. My diapers were made of harsh towelling, and I used to creep into the laundry and crouch over a bucket of foul clouts, hoping that my brother would not catch me at my revolting labours. It is not surprising that well-bred, dainty little girls find it difficult to adapt to menstruation, when our society does no more than explain it and leave them to get on with it. Among the aborigines who lived along the Pennefather river in Queensland the little girl used to be buried up to her waist in warm sand to aid the first contractions, and fed and cared for by her mother in a sacred place, to be led in triumph to the camp where she joined a feast to celebrate her entry into the company of marriageable maidens, it seems likely that menstruation was much less traumatic.[7] Women still buy sanitary towels with enormous discretion, and carry their handbags to the loo when they only need to carry a napkin. They still recoil at the idea of intercourse during menstruation, and feel that the blood they shed is of a special kind, although perhaps not so special as was thought when it was the liquid presented to the devil in witches' loving cups. If you think you are emancipated, you might consider the idea of tasting your menstrual blood – if it makes you sick, you've got a long way to go, baby.

Menstruation, we are told, is unique among the natural bodily processes in that it involves a loss of blood. It is assumed that nature is a triumph of design, and that none of her processes is wasteful or in need of reversal, especially when it only inconveniences women, and therefore it it thought extremely unlikely that there is any 'real' pain associated with menstruation. In fact no little girl who finds herself bleeding from an organ which she didn't know she had until it began to incommode her feels that nature is a triumph of design and that whatever is, is right. When she discovers that the pain attending this horror is in some way her *fault,* the result of improper adaptation to her female role, she really feels like the victim of a bad joke. Doctors admit that most women suffer 'discomfort' during menstruation, but disagree very much about what proportion of women suffer 'real' pain. Whether the contractions of the womb are painful in some absolute sense of could be rendered comfortable by some psychotherapy or other is immaterial. The fact is that no woman would menstruate if she did not have to. Why should women not resent an inconvenience which causes tension before, after and during; unpleasantness, odour, staining; which takes up anything from a seventh to a fifth of her adult life until the menopause; which makes her fertile thirteen times a year when she only expects to bear twice in a lifetime; when the cessation of menstruation may mean several years of endocrine derangement and the gradual atrophy of her sexual organs? The fact is that nature is not a triumph of design, and every battle against illness is an interference with her design, so that there is no rational ground for assuming that menstruation as we know it must be or ought to be irreversible.

The contradiction in the attitude that regards menstruation as divinely ordained and yet unmentionable leads to the intensification of the female revolt against it, which can be traced in all the common words for it, like the *curse,* and male disgust expressed in terms like *having the rags on.* We have only the choice of three kinds of expression: the vulgar resentful, the genteel ('I've got my period', 'I am indisposed'), and the scientific jargon of the *menses.* Girls are irrepressible though: in one Sydney girls' school napkins are affectionately referred to as *daisies;* Italian girls call their periods *il marchese* and German girls *der rote König.* One might envy the means adopted by *La Dame aux Camélias* to signify her condition to her gentlemen friends, but if it were adopted on a large scale it might look like a mark of proscription, a sort of leper's bell. There have been some moves to bring menstruation out into the open in an unprejudiced way, like Sylvia Plath's menstruation poem.[8] Perhaps we need a film to be made by an artist about the onset of menstruation, in which the implications emerge in some non-academic way, if we cannot manage a public celebration of a child's entry into womanhood by any other means.

Menstruation has been used a good deal in argument about women's fitness to undertake certain jobs: where women's comfort is concerned the effects are minimized –where the convenience of our masters is threatened they are magnified. Women are not more incapacitated by menstruation than men are by their drinking habits, their hypertension, their ulcers and their virility fears. It is not necessary to give menstruation holidays. It may be that women commit crimes during the pre-menstrual and menstrual period, but it is still true that women commit far fewer crimes than men. Women must be aware of this enlistment of menstruation in the anti-feminist argument, and counteract it by their own statements of the situation. Menstruation does not turn us into raving maniacs or complete invalids; it is just that we would rather do without it.

Soul

The Stereotype

In that mysterious dimension where the body meets the soul the stereotype is born and has her being. She is more body than soul, more soul than mind. To her belongs all that is beautiful, even the very word beauty itself. All that exists to beautify her.

> Taught from infancy that beauty is woman's sceptre, the mind shapes itself to the body, and roaming round its gilt cage, only seeks to adorn its prison.
>
> Mary Wollstonecraft,
> 'A Vindication of the Rights of Women', 1792, p. 90

The sun shines only to burnish her skin and gild her hair; the wind blows only to whip up the colour in her cheeks; the sea strives to bathe her; flowers die gladly so that her skin may luxuriate in their essence. She is the crown of creation, the masterpiece. The depths of the sea are ransacked for pearl and coral to deck her; the bowels of the earth are laid open that she might wear gold, sapphires, diamonds and rubies. Baby seals are battered with staves, unborn lambs ripped from their mothers' wombs, millions of moles, muskrats, squirrels, minks, ermines, foxes, beavers, chinchillas, ocelots, lynxes, and other small and lovely creatures die untimely deaths that she might have furs. Egrets, ostriches and peacocks, butterflies and beetles yield her their plumage. Men risk their lives hunting leopards for her coats, and crocodiles for her handbags and shoes. Millions of silkworms offer her their yellow labours; even the seamstresses roll seams and whip lace by hand, so that she might be clad in the best that money can buy.

The men of our civilization have stripped themselves of the fineries of earth so that they might work more freely to plunder the universe for treasures to deck my lady in. New raw materials, new processes, new machines are all brought into her service. My lady must therefore be the chief spender as well as the chief symbol of spending ability and monetary success. While her mate toils in his factory, she totters about the smartest streets and plushiest hotels with his fortune upon her back and bosom, fingers and wrists, continuing that essential expenditure in his house which is her frame and her setting, enjoying that silken idleness which is the necessary condition of maintaining her mate's prestige and her qualification to demonstrate it.[1] Once upon a time only the aristocratic lady could lay claim to the title of crown of creation: only her hands were white enough, her feet tiny enough, her waist narrow enough, her hair long and golden enough; but every well-to-do burgher's wife set herself up to ape my lady and to follow fashion, until my lady was forced to set herself out like a gilded doll overlaid with monstrous rubies and pearls like pigeons' eggs. Nowadays the Queen of England still considers it part of her royal female role to sport as much of the family jewellery as she can manage at any one time on all public occasions, although the male monarchs have escaped such showcase duty, which devolves exclusively upon their wives.

At the same time as woman was becoming the showcase for wealth and caste, while men were slipping into relative anonymity and 'handsome is as handsome does', she was emerging as the central emblem of western art. For the Greeks the male and female body had beauty of a human, not necessarily a sexual kind; indeed they may have marginally favoured the young male form as the most powerful and perfectly proportioned. Likewise the Romans showed no bias towards the depiction of femininity in their predominantly monumental art. In the Renaissance the female form began to predominate, not only as the mother in the predominant emblem of *madonna col bambino,* but as an aesthetic study in herself. At first naked female forms took their chances in crowd scenes or diptychs of Adam and Eve, but gradually Venus claims ascendancy, Mary Magdalene ceases to be wizened and emaciated, and becomes nubile and ecstatic, portraits of anonymous young women, chosen only for their prettiness, begin to appear, are gradually disrobed, and renamed Flora or Primavera. Painters begin to paint their own wives and mistresses and royal consorts as voluptuous beauties, divesting them of their clothes if desirable, but not of their jewellery. Susanna keeps her bracelets on in the bath, and Hélène Fourment keeps ahold of her fur as well!

What happened to woman in painting happened to her in poetry as well. Her beauty was celebrated in terms of the riches which clustered around her: her hair was gold wires, her brow ivory, her lips ruby, her teeth gates of pearl, her breasts alabaster veined with lapis lazuli, her eyes as black as jet.[2] The fragility of her loveliness was emphasized by the inevitable comparisons with the rose, and she was urged to employ her beauty in love-making before it withered on the stem.[3] She was for consumption; other sorts of imagery spoke of her in terms of cherries and cream, lips as sweet as honey and skin white as milk, breasts like cream uncrudded, hard as apples.[4] Some celebrations yearned over her finery as well, her lawn more transparent than morning mist, her lace as delicate as gossamer, the baubles that she toyed with and the favours that she gave.[5] Even now we find the thriller hero describing his classy dames' elegant suits, cheeky hats, well-chosen accessories and footwear; the imagery no longer dwells on jewels and flowers but the consumer emphasis is the same. The mousy secretary blossoms into the feminine stereotype when she reddens her lips, lets down her hair, and puts on something frilly.

Nowadays women are not expected, unless they are Paola di Liegi or Jackie Onassis, and then only on gala occasions, to appear with a king's ransom deployed upon their bodies, but they are required to look expensive, fashionable, well-groomed, and not to be seen in the same dress twice. If the duty of the few many have become less onerous, it has also become the duty of the many. The stereotype marshals an army of servants. She is supplied with cosmetics, underwear, foundation garments, stockings, wigs, postiches and hairdressing as well as her outer garments, her jewels and furs. The effect is to be built up layer by layer, and it is expensive. Splendour has given way to fit, line and cut. The spirit of competition must be kept up, as more and more women struggle towards the top drawer, so that the fashion industry can rely upon an expanding market. Poorer women fake it, ape it, pick up on the fashions a season too late, use crude effects, mistaking the line, the sheen, the gloss of the high-class article for a garish simulacrum. The business is so complex that it must be handled by an expert. The paragons of the stereotype must be dressed, coifed and painted by the experts and the style-setters, although they may be encouraged to give heart to the housewives studying their lives in pulp magazines by claiming a lifelong fidelity to their own hair and soap and water. The boast is more usually discouraging than otherwise, unfortunately.

As long as she is young and personable, every woman may cherish the dream that she may leap up the social ladder and dim the sheen of luxury by sheer natural loveliness; the few examples of such a feat are kept before the eye of the public. Fired with hope, optimism and ambition, young women study the latest forms of the stereotype, set out in *Vogue*, *Nova*, *Queen* and other glossies, where the mannequins stare from among the advertisements for fabulous real estate, furs and jewels. Nowadays the uniformity of the year's fashions is severely affected by the emergence of the pert female designers in Britain who direct their appeal to the working girl, emphasizing variety, comfort, and simple, striking effects. There is no longer a single face of the year: even Twiggy has had to withdraw into marketing and rationed personal appearances, while the Shrimp works mostly in New York. Nevertheless the stereotype is still supreme. She has simply allowed herself a little more variation.

The stereotype is the Eternal Feminine. She is the Sexual Object sought by all men, and by all women. She is of neither sex, for she has herself no sex at all. Her value is solely attested by the demand she excites in others. All she must contribute is her existence. She need achieve nothing, for she is the reward of achievement. She need never give positive evidence of her moral character because virtue is assumed from her loveliness, and her passivity. If any man who has no right to her be found with her she will not be punished, for she is morally neuter. The matter is solely one of male rivalry. Innocently she may drive men to madness and war. The more trouble she can cause, the more her stocks go up, for possession of her means more the more demand she excites. Nobody wants a girl whose beauty is

The myth of the strong black woman is the other side of the coin of the myth of the beautiful dumb blonde. The white man turned the white woman into a weak-minded, weak-bodied, delicate freak, a sex pot, and placed her on a pedestal; he turned the black woman into a strong self-reliant Amazon and deposited her in his kitchen. . . . The white man turned himself into the Omnipotent Administrator and established himself in the Front Office.

Eldridge Cleaver, The Allegory of the Black Eunuchs, 'Soul on Ice', 1968, p. 162

imperceptible to all but him; and so men welcome the stereotype because it directs their taste into the most commonly recognized areas of value, although they may protest because some aspects of it do not tally with their fetishes. There is scope in the stereotype's variety for most fetishes. The leg man may follow mini-skirts, the tit man can encourage see-through blouses and plunging necklines, although the man who likes fat women may feel constrained to enjoy them in secret. There are stringent limits to the variations on the stereotype, for nothing must interfere with her function as sex object. She may wear leather, as long as she cannot actually handle a motorbike: she may wear rubber, but it ought not to indicate that she is an expert diver or water-skier. If she wears athletic clothes the purpose is to underline her unathleticism. She may sit astride a horse, looking soft and curvy, but she must not crouch over its neck with her rump in the air.

> **She was created to be the toy of man, his rattle, and it must jingle in his ears whenever, dismissing reason, he chooses to be amused.**
>
> **Mary Wollstonecraft,**
> **'A Vindication of the Rights of Women', 1792, p. 66**

Because she is the emblem of spending ability and the chief spender, she is also the most effective seller of this world's goods. Every survey ever held has shown that the image of an attractive woman is the most effective advertising gimmick. She may sit astride the mudguard of a new car, or step into it ablaze with jewels; she may lie at a man's feet stroking his new socks; she may hold the petrol pump in a challenging pose, or dance through woodland glades in slow motion in all the glory of a new shampoo; whatever she does her image sells. The gynolatry of our civilization is written large upon its face, upon hoardings, cinema screens, television, newspapers, magazines, tins, packets, cartons, bottles, all consecrated to the reigning deity, the female fetish. Her dominion must not be thought to entail the rule of women, for she is not a woman. Her glossy lips and matt complexion, her unfocused eyes and flawless fingers, her extraordinary hair all floating and shining, curling and gleaming, reveal the inhuman triumph of cosmetics, lighting, focussing and printing, cropping and composition. She sleeps unruffled, her lips red and juicy and closed, her eyes as crisp and black as if new painted, and her false lashes immaculately curled. Even when she washes her face with a new and creamier toilet soap her expression is as tranquil and vacant as her paint as flawless as ever. If ever she should appear tousled and troubled, her features are miraculously smoothed to their proper veneer by a new washing powder or a bouillon cube. For she is a doll: weeping, pouting or smiling, running or reclining, she is a doll. She is an idol, formed of the concatenation of lines and masses, signifying the lineaments of satisfied impotence.

Her essential quality is castratedness. She absolutely must be young, her body hairless, her flesh buoyant, and *she must not have a sexual organ*. No musculature must distort the smoothness of the lines of her body, although she may be painfully slender or warmly cuddly. Her expression must betray no hint of humour, curiosity or intelligence, although it may signify hauteur to an extent that is actually absurd, or smouldering lust, very feebly signified by drooping eyes and a sullen mouth (for the stereotype's lust equals irrational submission) or, most commonly, vivacity and idiot happiness. Seeing that the world despoils itself for this creature's benefit, she must be happy; the entire structure would topple if she were not. So the image of woman appears plastered on every surface imaginable, smiling interminably. An apple pie evokes a glance of tender beatitude, a washing machine causes hilarity, a cheap box of chocolates brings forth meltingly joyous gratitude, a Coke is the cause of a rictus of unutterable brilliance, even a new stick-on bandage is saluted by a smirk of satisfaction. A real woman licks her lips and opens her mouth and flashes her teeth when photographers appear: *she* must arrive at the première of her husband's film in a paroxysm of delight, or his success might be murmured about.

> Discretion is the better part of Valerie
> though all of her is nice
> lips as warm as strawberries
> eyes as cold as ice
> the very best of everything
> only will suffice
> not for her potatoes
> and puddings made of rice
>
> **Roger McGough, 'Discretion'**

The occupational hazard of being a Playboy Bunny is the aching facial muscles brought on by the obligatory smiles.

So what is the beef? Maybe I couldn't make it. Maybe I don't have a pretty smile, good teeth, nice tits, long legs, a cheeky arse, a sexy voice. Maybe I don't know how to handle men and increase my market value, so that the rewards due to the feminine will accrue to me. Then again, maybe I'm sick of the masquerade. I'm sick of pretending eternal youth. I'm sick of belying my own intelligence, my own will, my own sex. I'm sick of peering at the world through false eyelashes, so everything I see is mixed with a shadow of bought hairs; I'm sick of weighting my head with a dead mane, unable to move my neck freely, terrified of rain, of wind, of dancing too vigorously in case I sweat into my lacquered curls. I'm sick of the Powder Room. I'm sick of pretending that some fatuous male's self-importance pro-

nouncements are the objects of my undivided attention, I'm
sick of going to films and plays when someone else wants to,
and sick of having no opinions of my own about either. I'm
sick of being a transvestite. I refuse to be a female
impersonator. I am a woman, not a castrate.

April Ashley was born male. All the information supplied
by genes, chromosomes, internal and external sexual organs
added up to the same thing. April was a man. But he longed
to be a woman. He longed for the stereotype, not to
embrace, but to be.

To what end is the laying out of the embroidered Hair,
embared Breasts; vermilion Cheeks, alluring looks,
Fashion gates, and artfull Countenances, effeminate
intangling and insnaring Gestures, their Curls and Purls
of proclaiming Petulancies, boulstered and laid out with
such example and authority in these our days, as with
Allowance and beseeming Conveniency?

Doth the world wax barren through decrease of Generations, and become, like the Earth, less fruitfull heretofore?
Doth the Blood lose his Heat or do the Sunbeams become
waterish and less fervent, than formerly they have been,
that men should be thus inflamed and persuaded on to
lust?

Alex. Niccholes, 'A Discourse of Marriage and Wiving',
1615, pp. 143–52

He wanted soft fabrics, jewels, furs, make-up, the love and
protection of men. So he was impotent. He couldn't fancy
women at all, although he did not particularly welcome
homosexual addresses. He did not think of himself as a
pervert, or even as a transvestite, but as a woman cruelly
transmogrified into manhood. He tried to die, became a
female impersonator, but eventually found a doctor in
Casablanca who came up with a more acceptable alternative.
He was to be castrated, and his penis used as the lining of a

surgically constructed cleft, which would be a vagina. He would be infertile, but that has never affected the attribution of femininity. April returned to England, resplendent. Massive hormone treatment had eradicated his beard, and formed tiny breasts: he had grown his hair and bought feminine clothes during the time he had worked as an impersonator. He became a model, and began to illustrate the feminine stereotype as he was perfectly qualified to do, for he was elegant, voluptuous, beautifully groomed, and in love with his own image. On an ill-fated day he married the heir to a peerage, the Hon. Arthur Corbett, acting out the highest achievement of the feminine dream, and went to live with him in a villa in Marbella. The marriage was never consummated. April's incompetence as a woman is what we must expect from a castrate, but it is not so very different after all from the impotence of feminine women, who submit to sex without desire, with only the infantile pleasure of cuddling and affection, which is their favourite reward. As long as the feminine stereotype remains the definition of the female sex, April Ashley is a woman, regardless of the legal decision ensuing from her divorce.[6] She is as much a casualty of the polarity of the sexes as we all are. Disgraced, unsexed April Ashley is our sister and our symbol.

Energy

Energy is the power that drives every human being. It is not lost by exertion but maintained by it, for it is a faculty of the psyche. It is driven to perverted manifestations by curbs and checks. Like the motive force that drives the car along the highway, when it meets with an obstacle it turns to destructive force and shakes its source to pieces. It is not too hard to point out to the averagely perceptive human being that women have plenty of the destructive kind of energy, but far fewer people can see that women's destructiveness is creativity turned in upon itself by constant frustration. Nervous diseases, painful menstruation, unwanted pregnancies, accidents of all kinds, are all evidence of women's energy destroying them. It extends beyond them wreaking havoc with the personalities and achievements of others, especially their husbands and their children. That is not to say that women must hate all their relatives, but that if

> The pure animal spirits which make both mind and body shoot out, and unfold the tender blossoms of hope, are turned sour and vented in vain wishes, or pert repinings, that contract the faculties and spoil the temper; else they mount to the brain, and sharpening the understanding before it gains proportional strength, produce, that pitiful cunning which disgracefully characterizes the female mind and I fear will characterize it whilst women remain the slaves of power.
>
> Mary Wollstonecraft,
> 'A Vindication of the Rights of Women', 1792, p. 378

children are presented to women as a duty and marriage as an inescapable yoke, then the more energy they have the more they will fret and chafe, tearing themselves and their dependants to pieces.

When children are falsely presented to women as their only significant contribution, the proper expression of their creativity and their lives' work, the children and their mothers suffer for it.

Although many people will see the justice of this description of the perversion of female energy, they will not so easily see that the solution does not lie in offering adult women other alternatives besides home and children and all that. The adult

> ...we are only happy so long as our life expands in ever widening circles from the upward gush of our early impulses...
>
> Herbert Read,
> 'Annals of Innocence and Experience', 1940, p. 55

woman has already established a pattern of perversity in the expression of her desires and motives which ought to fit her for the distorted version of motherhood: it will not disappear if she is allowed alternatives. Any substituted aim is likely to be followed in a 'feminine' way, that is, servilely, dishonestly, inefficiently, inconsistently. In most cases women are not offered a genuine alternative to repressive duties and reponsibilities: most would happily give up unskilled labour in a factory or the tedium of office work for the more 'natural' tedium of a modern household, because their energies are so thwarted by the usual kinds of female work that they imagine even housework would be a preferable alternative. Women who are offered education are offered a genuine alternative, insofar as they are offered genuine education, a rare commodity in these days of universal induction. And yet, when they were offered education at first the result was not the creation of an instant race of super-women. This is one contemporary's account of the first female undergraduates, and university teachers will recognize a familiar phenomenon:

At lectures women students are models of attention and industry; perhaps they even apply themselves too much to carrying home in black and white what they heard. They generally occupy the front seats because they enter their names early and then because they arrive early, well before the beginning of the lectures. Only this fact is noticeable, that often they merely give a superficial glance at the preparations that the professor passes around; sometimes they even pass them on to their neighbours without even looking at them; a longer examination would hinder their taking notes.[1]

What this rather prejudiced observer noticed is real enough: the girls were diligent, even too diligent, but their efforts were expended on mistaken goals. They were anxious to please, to pick up everything that they were told, but the preparations handed around by the lecturer were the real subject of the lecture, and in that they were not interested at all. Their energy is all expended on conforming with disciplinary and other requirements, not in gratifying their own curiosity about the subject that they are studying, and so most of it is misdirected into meaningless assiduity. This phenomenon is still very common among female students, who are forming a large proportion of the arts intake at universities, and dominating the teaching profession as a result. The process is clearly one of diminishing returns: the servile induce servility to teach the servile, in a realm where the unknown ought to be continually assailed with all the human faculties; education cannot be, and has never been a matter of obedience. It is not surprising then than women seldom make the scientific advances, but rather serve men as laboratory assistants, working under direction: it is merely a continuation of the same phenomenon that we observed in their undergraduate days. By the time they have come to apply for entrance to a university the pattern of their useless deflection of energy is already set. In the very great majority of cases they have not retained enough drive to desire to qualify themselves any further; the minority who go to university do so too often as a response to guidance and pressure from their mistresses at school, still not knowing what the real point is, still not interested in developing their own potential, at most hoping for a good degree and a qualification to join the Cinderella profession of teaching. The degree of satisfaction gained by women following this pattern is very slight; we were not surprised to find that many of them think of even their professional life either as a stop-gap or an indirect qualification for marraige.

All the blanket objections to women in professions may be understood as ways of stating this basic situation. They appear to be the judgments of prejudice, and, insofar as they adduce no other cause than sex, we must admit that they are. However, unless feminists admit that the phenomena described by critics of women's performance in industry, offices, schoolrooms, trade unions and in the arts and sciences are real, they must fail to identify the problem, and therefore to solve it. It is true that opportunities have been made available to women far beyond their desires to use them. It is also true that the women who avail themselves of opportunities too often do so in a feminine, filial, servile fashion. It must be understood that it will not suffice to encourage women to use an initiative that they have not got, just as it is useless to revile them for not having it. We must endeavour to understand how it is that women's energy is systematically deflected from birth to puberty, so that when they come to maturity they have only fitful resource and creativity.

In speaking of energy, I have had to use terms like resource, application, initiative, ambition, desire, motive, terms which have a masculine ring, because they convey marginal meanings which are incompatible with femininity. It is often falsely assumed, even by feminists, that sexuality is the enemy of the female who really wants to develop these aspects of her personality, and this is perhaps the most misleading aspect of movements like the National Organization of Women. It was not the insistence upon her sex that weakened the American woman student's desire to make something of her education, but the insistence upon a *passive sexual role*. In fact the chief instrument in the deflection and perversion of female energy is the denial of female sexuality for the substitution of femininity or sexlessness. For, no matter which theory of the energy of personality we accept, it is inseparable from sexuality. McDougall called it élan vital, Jung and Reich called it libido, Janet called it tension, Head called it vigilance, Flügel called it orectic energy.[2] All the terms amount to the same thing. One of the errors in the traditional theory is that it presupposes a sort of capitalist system of energy, as a kind of

---

The degree and essential nature of any human being's sexuality extends into the highest pinnacle of his spirit.

Nietzsche

---

substance which must be wisely invested and not spent all at once.[3] In fact, as we ought to know from the concept of energy we have derived from physics, energy cannot be lost but only converted or deflected. Freud saw that repression employs energy which might otherwise be expressed in creative action: what happens to the female is that her energy is deflected by the denial of her sexuality into a continuous and eventually irreversible system of repression. The women students expended as much energy taking notes and being early and attentive to lectures as their male counterparts did in exploring the subject: in the laboratory they expended it by dropping things and asking silly questions, fussing and fumbling. Male energy is contoured and deformed too, but in a different way, so that it becomes aggression and competitiveness. The female's fate is to become deformed and debilitated by the destructive action of energy upon the self, because she is deprived of scope and contacts with external reality upon which to exercise herself.

> **Energy is the only life and is from the body . . . . Energy is eternal Delight.**
>
> **Blake**

The acts of sex are themselves forms of inquiry, as the old euphemism 'carnal knowledge' makes clear: it is exactly the element of quest in her sexuality which the female is taught to deny. She is not only taught to deny it in her sexual contacts, but (for in some subliminal way the connection is understood) in all her contacts, from infancy onward, so that when she becomes aware of her sex the pattern has sufficient force of inertia to prevail over new forms of desire and curiosity. This is the condition which is meant by the term *female eunuch.* In traditional psychological theory, which is after all only another way of describing and rationalizing the status quo, the de-sexualization of women is illustrated in the Freudian theory of the female sex as lacking a sexual organ. Freud may not have intended his formulations to have been taken as statements of natural laws, but merely as coherent descriptions of contingent facts in a new, and valuably revealing terminology; nevertheless he did say:

Indeed, if we were able to give a more definite connotation to the concept of 'masculine' and 'feminine', it would also be possible to maintain that libido is invariably and necessarily of a masculine nature, whether it occurs in men or women, and irrespectively of whether its object is a man or a woman.[4]

If we are to insist on the contingency of feminine characteristics as the product of conditioning, we will have to argue that the masculine-feminine polarity is actual enough, but not necessary. We will have to reject the polarity of definite terms, which are always artificial, and strive for the freedom to move within indefinite terms. On these grounds we can, indeed we must reject femininity as meaning *without libido,* and therefore incomplete, subhuman, a cultural reduction of human possibilities, and rely upon the indefinite term female, which retains the possibility of female libido. In order to understand how a female is castrated and becomes feminine we must consider the pressures to which she is subjected from the cradle.

Baby

When a baby is born it has remarkable powers; it can stand upright, move its head about, its toes are prehensile, and its hands can grasp quite strongly. Within hours these powers fail, and the child must laboriously relearn skills it originally had. Nowadays we do not swaddle children so that they are transformed to rigid cigar-shapes which Mother can dispose of as she pleases, but we still treat a baby as a cross between a doll and an invalid. The initial struggles to move are quickly controlled by the nurse who applies the iron clutch on the back of the neck and the bottom which holds baby motionless. He may not be swaddled but he is put to bed and wrapped up tight. This process is somehow known not to be awfully good for him, for premature and weak babies are not subjected to it. It is in fact the cheapest and easiest way of insuring against heat loss: we might profitably wonder how the humidi-cribs and over-head infra-red heaters which are used in special cases have influenced the formation of the

> Throughout the whole animal kingdom every young creature requires almost continual exercise, and the infancy of children, conformable to this intimation, should be passed in harmless gambols, that exercise the feet and hands, without requiring every minute direction from the head, or the constant attention of a nurse. . . . The child is not left a moment to its own direction, particularly a girl, and thus rendered dependent —dependence is called natural.
>
> Mary Wollstonecraft,
> 'A Vindication of the Rights of Women' 1792, pp. 83–4

child's psyche, and then how the child reacts to the eventual
swaddling which will take place as soon as he is strong
enough.

> My mother groaned, my father wept;
> Into the dangerous world I leapt,
> Helpless, naked, piping loud,
> Like a fiend hid in a cloud.

> Struggling in my father's hands,
> Striving against my swaddling bands,
> Bound and weary I thought best
> To sulk upon my mother's breast.[1]

Energy does seem diabolical to us, because our whole
culture is bent on harnessing it for ulterior ends: the child
must be civilized; what this means is really that he must be
obliterated. From the beginning he is discouraged from
crowing and exercising his lungs at any time or in any place
where it might inconvenience the conduct of adult
intercourse. The new baby has enormous curiosity, and an
equal faculty for absorbing information, but he spends all of
it on specially constructed environments, featuring muted
sounds, insipid colours, and the massive, dominating figure
of Mother. The intense absorption of the baby in one human
being, whose familiarity gradually becomes indispensable to
him, is a necessary factor in the development of the character
which is considered normal in our society. The prejudice
against the substitution of any other person or number of
persons for the omnipotent mother is very strong indeed.
Even if the researches of Dr Jaroslav Koch in Prague, who
has kept babies in a special free environment with the result
that they can climb ladders at eight months, were to prove
beyond doubt that the childs acquisition of all faculties is
retarded ten-fold or a hundred-fold by the role he must play
as Mother's product, her toy and her achievement, his
conclusions would be ignored by a culture which insists upon

mother-domination as a prerequisite for character formation.[2] The child's attention must be weaned away from exterior reality on to an introverted relationship of mutual exploitation which will form the pattern of his future compulsions. Every marriage reënacts the Oedipal situation: children growing without any idea of the symbiosis of mother and child might be promiscuous or not, but they would not display the kind of obsessive behaviour in their relationships which suggest security and permanence.

The babies did not go towards the things which it was supposed would have pleased them, like for example, toys; neither were they interested in fairy stories. Above all they sought to render themselves independent of adults in all the actions which they could manage on their own; manifesting clearly the desire not to be helped, except in cases of absolute necessity. And they were seen to be tranquil, absorbed and concentrating on their work, acquiring a surprising calm and serenity.

Maria Montessori,
'Il Bambino in Famiglia', 1956, p. 36

'I have no name:
I am but two days old.'
What shall I call thee?
'I happy am,
Joy is my name.'[3]

The newborn baby is not conscious of any distinction between himself and everything he sees. He is first conscious of his ego when some wish of his is not gratified, and by frustration and confusion he finds the difference between himself and his mother.[4] Thus the first act of the ego is to reject reality, to adopt an inimical and anxious attitude to it. This sense of separateness and limitation inside the self is carefully fostered in our culture, to become the basis of our egotistic morality, which acts not from understanding and feeling the repercussions of action upon the community because of the continuity between the self and the rest, but by laws and restrictions self-imposed in a narcissistic way. The child's internal monitor must be set up, his conscience, better named his anxiety and his guilt. This process may fail or take a wrong turning very early on. Autism and other forms of disturbance make their appearance in children very early, and they are made the basis for rejection and segregation of the children away from the batches who are accepting their conditioning without difficulty. The high incidence of these troubles in gifted children would seem to indicate a correlation between the strength of the child's energy and the effect of the curbing upon it: for that such children can show any signs of ability at all is itself remarkable. It used to be the case that disturbed children were drilled and disciplined into order, and merely kept in special institutions where their failure to adapt was treated as a congenital pathological condition. It took a very gifted and courageous woman to penetrate these asylums, and begin reversing the processes of conditioning so that these children could start again on a less disastrous course.

Montessori's methods were so obviously successful that they have been made the basis of most infant schooling in England and Europe, but the significance of her insights as criticisms on the bringing up that children are subjected to outside school and in the crucial years before school has not been understood. As a result primary schooling is so far ahead of other forms of education in this country that new crises occur in the relationship between school and home, and between the junior school and the senior schools. In opening up the classroom so that her retarded children could run it, Montessori created a situation which was necessarily unique. There are intrepid schoolmistresses in England who move about undisciplined classrooms, listening to the

children when they stand up to communicate to the group
the results of their own inquiry, but most schoolmistresses
are too nervous to invite fruitful disorder, most classrooms
are too crowded to tolerate such methods, and most schools
have not the money for books and the other resources of such
study. Even at university level I have found it impossible so
far to run a research laboratory which would be a similarly
spontaneous cooperative effort. Montessori tells moving
stories of how the children expressed their corporate respect
for a royal visitor, of how one child, having been told of an
earthquake in Southern Italy, wrote upon a board, 'I am
sorry I am so small', so that she thought he had failed to
accept what he had heard, until he added the extra clause
which explained that he would have liked to help, and so
wrote his first ever compound sentence. Her children
progressed beyond the usual achievements of their own age
groups, but I guess that if follow-up studies had been made
of their problems of adjusting in a world which cannot use
spontaneity and cooperation the picture might have been
more depressing. Montessori's basic assumption is simple,
but radical:

A single fact lies at the source of all deviations, viz., that the child
has been prevented from fulfilling the original pattern of his
development at the formative age, when his potential energies
should evolve through a process of incarnation...thus welding the
acting personality into unity. If this unity is not achieved, through
the substitution of the adult for the child or through a want of
motives of activity in his environment, two things happen: psychic
energy and movement must develop separately, and a 'divided
man' results. Since in nature nothing creates itself and nothing
destroys itself, and this is especially true in the case of energies,
these energies since they have to work outside the scope designated
for them by nature become deviated... They have become
deviated about all because they have lost their object and work in
emptiness, vagueness and chaos. The mind that should have built
itself up through experiences of movement, *flees* into fantasy.[5]

The flight into fantasy is sanctioned in our culture, because it is part of the limitation of self-development which we call civilization. Although some aspects of it, like fetishism and masturbatory practices, are deplored, in general it is seen as a necessary and even pleasant concomitant of repression. Whole theories of art have been built up on the assumption that the proper function of art was to provide a harmless fantasy expression of tendencies which would otherwise have been destructive or anti-social.

So far we have not adduced anything about the repression of psychic energy in children which would apply to girls more than to boys, for both are treated in the same way up to a certain age. Discrimination does begin fairly early, however, despite the staunch refusal of British educators to distinguish between boys and girls in their primary schooling. Some baby girls are still dressed in pink rather than blue, are put into frilly, fragile dresses and punished for tearing and soiling them. Some have their hair curled up and bows put in it, and are told that they are pretty and Daddy's girl and so on. Even for the little girls who have rompers and no fuss with hair and Curly-pet and other infantile cosmetics, a system of rewards and encouragements begins to operate fairly early on. No one wants to bring up a child who doesn't know what sex he is, and in default of any other notion of female sexuality the styles of femininity are inculcated almost imperceptibly from the beginning. The baby soon discovers how to be coy and winsome, how to twist Daddy around her little finger.[6] When little boys discover the advantages of coyness they are eventually shocked out of them when their baby curls are shorn, but the little girl is praised and encouraged to exploit her cuteness. She is not directly taught how to do it, she simply learns by experience. It is an odd reflection that while we hear voices raised in protest against the destruction of innocence occasioned by showing sex films in the junior school, no voice is heard exclaiming at the awfulness of being flirted with by a three-year-old.

For little boys, a time eventually comes, soon or late, when the umbilical cord is finally broken, and the relationship with Mother becomes more distant. Where that does not happen, as it does not in strong matriarchies like the Jewish family, the result is what Philip Roth lamented in *Portnoy's Complaint*:

Ma, ma, what was it you wanted to turn me into anyway, a walking zombie like Ronald Nimkin? Where did you get the idea that the most wonderful thing I could be in life was *obedient*? *A little gentleman*? Of all the aspirations for a creature of lusts and desires! 'Alex,' you say, as we leave the Weequahic Diner – and don't get me wrong, I eat it up: praise is praise, and I take it however it comes – 'Alex,' you say to me all dressed up in my clip-on tie and my two-tone 'loafer' jacket, 'the way you cut your meat! the way you ate that baked potato without spilling! I could kiss you, I never *saw* such a little gentleman with his napkin in his little lap like that.' *Fruitcake*, Mother. Little *fruitcake* is what you saw – and exactly what the training programme was designed to produce. Of course! Of course! The mystery really is not that I'm not dead like Ronald Nimkin, but that I'm not like all the nice young men I see strolling hand in hand in Bloomingdale's on Saturday mornings.[7]

What happens to the Jewish boy who never manages to escape the tyranny of his mother is exactly what happens to every girl whose upbringing is 'normal'. She is a female faggot. Like the male faggots she lives her life in a pet about guest lists and sauce béarnaise, except when she is exercising by divine maternal right the same process that destroyed her lusts and desires upon the lusts and desires of her children.

Little boys can get out of their mother's way, eventually want to and are encouraged to. Little girls are not. It is agreed that 'girls take more bringing up' than boys: what that really means is that girls must be more relentlessly

supervised and repressed if the desired result is to ensue.[8] A
girl is early introduced to her menial role, as her mother
teaches her household skills (*mirabile dictu!*) and her recoil
from external reality is reinforced by the punishments she
gets for wandering off on her own. While little boys are
forming groups and gangs to explore or terrorize the
district,[9] she is isolated at home, listening to tales of evil-
minded strangers. Her comparative incarceration is justified
in the name of protection, although the home is the most
dangerous place there is. She is taught to fear and distrust
the world at large, for reasons which are never clearly stated.
As a form of forearming this forewarning is notoriously
unsuccessful. Sexual deviates are not so lacking in resource
that they cannot attack little girls as they go upon those
errands and journeys that are sanctioned by Mother. When
a little girl who missed her bus rang for her mother from the
bus-stop one evening, so spending the sixpence that would
have been her fare for the next one, her mother told her to
walk home because she didn't have the car. The child went
on her way weeping and terrified, and was accosted by a
smiling stranger who abducted, raped and strangled her.
The commonest result of the dark warning system is that
when little girls do meet an exhibitionist or do happen to talk
to a stranger who does something odd to them, they are too
frightened and guilty, as well as too worried about the effect
on their parents, even to tell them. It is a contributing factor
in the pattern of child violation that little girls think of
themselves as victims, and cannot even summon the energy
to scream or run away. Because they are prevented from
understanding the threat, they can have no adequate
defence. The bitterest irony is that the child violators are
themselves products of the same clumsy conditioning.

While little boys are learning about groups and
organizations, as well as the nature of the world outside their
homes, little girls are at home, keeping quiet, playing with

dolls and dreaming, or helping Mother. At school they use their energy to suppress themselves, to be good and keep quiet, and remember what they are hearing and doing. At home they perform meaningless physical rituals, with no mental activity attached to them. So the sensual and intellectual are even more widely separated in them than they are in their brothers. If the sensual retains its hold, they prefer to work with their hands, cooking, sewing, knitting, following a pattern designed by someone else. The designers, the master-cooks and the tailors are men. If women become 'intellectuals' they are disenfranchised of their bodies, repressed, intense, inefficient, still as servile as ever. Some geniuses have broken right through the chain reaction and have seen it for what it was, but most creative women bear the stamp of futility and confusion even in their best work. Virginia Woolf saw some of the way, but it cost her too much; George Eliot was one of the few who burst right through her strait-jacket. The difference may have been one of the energy of the psyche, or of intelligence, or simply that Eliot was plain and Virginia was graceful and lovely. Whatever the case, the foundations of the conflict were laid in their infancy.

Girl

I would not be doing justice to girls if I were to imply that they accepted all their enculturation without a struggle. The heaviness of maternal pressure in little girls to be neat and sneaking is very often met with the same degree of resistance. The growing girl may refuse to keep her room neat, may insist on mucking about with boyish affairs, even to the extent of joining a male group and fighting to maintain her place in it by being twice as tough as any of the boys. She may lose all her hankies and hair-ribbons, rip her knickers climbing trees, and swear and swagger with the best

> A girl whose spirits have not been damped by inactivity, or innocence tainted by false shame, will always be a romp. . .
>
> Mary Wollstonecraft,
> 'A Vindication of the Rights of Women', 1792, p. 87

of them. This is patronizingly referred to as going through a difficult phase, but we may find evidence of the duration of this kind of resistance over years and years, until puberty delivers the final crushing blow. The *tomboy* as this energetic rebel is pejoratively called may be of any age from five to fifteen; she may not be a tomboy all the time, either because she enjoys the coddling that neat, pretty little girls get, or because she has come to realize that it is advantageous to operate in the favoured way, or because she is simply denied opportunity or incentive to discover how vigorous she could be. Generally it is the little girls who are given presents of pretty things and spoilt and flattered who capitulate to the doll-makers earliest. The pattern of reward is kept up: at first it might be sweets and dolls' clothes, then dresses and shoes, and even the occasional perm and eyelash dyeing, and then pretty clothes for being seen at weekends in, outings, movies and all that.

However, even the little girl who gives in to the pressures applied by her mother and the rest of the feminizers is subjected to conflicting influences. At school her pretensions to jewellery and cosmetics are severely frowned on. She is required to do some form of physical exercise for a fixed period every week, despite Mother's notes pleading all kinds of delicacy and indisposition. She is given responsibilities, made to join in team efforts, all activities which, if her feminization is proceeding at good pace, she finds very unattractive. She would rather gossip and giggle with her confidantes in a corner of the playground than play soft-ball, even if soft-ball is a feminized form of a masculine sport. She does not like to get sweaty and dirty. Although her teachers praise her manners and her neatness, they lament her increasing dullness, and she may even feel the contempt of the more 'masculine', that is, active, girls in her class. She may be reviled as a cissy, a sook, a teacher's pet, a namby-pamby, a sneak.

But if Mummy's darling has trouble at school, the successful and active members of the school community run into trouble at home. Out of school, there is not the scope for team activity and adventure that school provides. Housework seems intolerable, and domestic conflicts can become a source of serious anxiety, so that many a teacher has discovered that a good pupil comes back from the summer holidays changed beyond recognition, principally by the abrasion of her training at home. As she grows older she finds her activities more serverly curbed; innocent exertions are ruled out because she is 'too big for that sort of thing now'. Sometimes she feels that she is being catapulted into a sort of shameful womanhood, and resists desperately, to the point of regressing into infantile and destructive behaviour. She may become unaccountably sullen or clumsy, long before the approach of puberty makes such changes explicable. Many of the changes thought to be intrinsically connected with puberty are actually connected with the last struggles of the little girl to retain her energy. The primary school has educated her as a person, making no distinction between boy and girl. We may expect the conflict to arise when she moves up to the junior school to find that, as a capitulation to womanly objections about the imposition of the masculine model of education on to girls, she has the unenviable options of studying dressmaking, domestic

---

Girls sometimes wish they were boys – You can see what man does – His work is wonderful – What is greater than man's work? Man – Who made the man? – Made by mother's training – Abraham Lincoln's mother – Great responsibility to train future President – Cannot tell what any child may become – No greater work than child training – The wife may think the husband's work greater than hers – Her work monotonous and tiresome – So is business – Woman's work not less than a man's – What Ruskin says about the wife – Man's success dependent upon woman – His health depends on his wife's cooking –The fate of a nation may depend upon a wholesome meal – If both man and woman were in business life would lose much brightness – Woman makes social life –Moral life –Keeps man thinking – Values of home education – Daniel Webster's table manners – Woman embroiders man's life – Embroider is to beautify – The embroidery of cleanliness – Of a smile – Of gentle words.

Summary of Mary Wood-Allen,
'What a Young Girl Ought to Know', 1928 (cited verbatim)

science and so forth. The bitter irony of having been inducted into a masculine-contoured form of education is counterpointed by the inclusion of these fatuous subjects in her regimen. Sitting in her absurd version of masculine uniform making sponge fingers with inky hands, she must really feel like the punching-bag of civilization.

The pre-pubescent girl, however sluggish and confused she may seem to the disenchanted observer, is a passionate creature. The conflicts that she is daily and hourly suffering absorb much of her energy, but she still has enough left to thrill to stories of adventure and achievement and to identify with heroes, male and female alike. Her sexuality is fundamental to these responses, just as it is to her actual genital practices. In the primary school, one may find this excited interest in an innocent and open form, sometimes quite sensual. I remember being warmly kissed once on a visit to a school in Manchester by a horde of little girls and boys, who flung their arms around my neck and snuggled into my fur, pressing questions and gifts indiscriminately. The classes of eleven and twelve-year olds that I taught in Australia could generate extraordinary intensity which had its expression in lots of odd ways, sometimes in crushes and rapt idealism, and sometimes in peculiar and deflected experiments within the playground community. Sometimes they could perform wonders of orchestrated cooperation in presenting their little plays and projects, or devising ways to recognize a birthday or thwart the school administration. More often they flagged or fell to quarrelling. Most often the authorities intervened because the classes had got too noisy, or because school routine was in danger of disruption. Gradually the scope for embracing, experiencing and expression was being limited as the pattern of submission, rejection and all the rest that is meant by adaptation was imposed.

It was remarkable that in view of the conflict and the

relentless enculturation to which they were subjected, these girls retained so much of their childhood energy and love. Some of its expression was specifically sexual, as the psychologists are prepared to admit, although they insist that the pre-adolescent girl's sexuality is masculine, clitoral and so forth.[1] So they grossly misinterpret the typical adolescent passion for horses as a reflection of the immature girl's penis envy. The horse between a girl's legs is supposed to be a gigantic penis. What hooey! What the younger rider feels is not that the horse is a projection of her own physical ego, but that it is an *other* which is responding to her control. What she feels is a potent love calling forth a response. The control required by riding is so strong and subtle that it hardly melts into the kind of diffuse eroticism that theorists like Dr Pearson would have us believe in. For many girls who are beginning to get the picture about the female role, horse-riding is the only opportunity they will ever have to use their strong thighs to embrace, to excite and to control. George Eliot knew what she was doing when she described Dorothea Brook's passion for wild gallops over the moors in *Middlemarch*. It is part and parcel of her desire to perform some great heroism, to be free and noble.

Those little girls who wrote passionate love-letters to each other and to me in the schools where I taught had no conscious understanding of their own passionate and amorphous feelings. Because of the taboos on their expression of these intense feelings, they become miserably agitated, sometimes hysterical, sometimes desperate and ridiculous. The feeling was expressed in a distorted fashion, like suppressed laughter, and so it was easily scorned and reviled. The reaction of most teachers to 'that sort of thing' is terribly destructive. I have even witnessed the public reading of a child's love poem, accompanied with sneers and deprecating gestures, as a punishment, while the little authoress stood impassive, feeling the iron enter her soul, waiting for the blessed time when she could escape to the lavatory and enjoy the obscenity of tears. However liberal a teacher may be she early discovers that the rigid embargo imposed upon physical contact between teacher and pupil must be observed, because the last flame of sexual energy is only destructive and can only be corrupted, given the wider context and the socializing function of the school. It is an aching nerve in the education situation and will remain so, must remain so, unless our whole sexual orientation is radically changed. To defy it piecemeal can only produce ever greater suffering.

The girl who directs her passion towards her peer is in a better situation than the girl who loves her teacher. It is usual to explain such deep and lasting attachments as the seduction of one girl by another who is especially aggressive, and sexually mature, or as transferred longing for the mother whose closeness is being withdrawn as sexual maturity and oedipal rivalry become pressing prognoses, or simply as the desire to confide sexual curiosity and share forbidden knowledge.[2] It is dangerous to admit that inseparable girls are often fascinated by each other, deeply altruistic and cooperative, and often genuinely spiritual, as well as utterly sexual if not literally genital. If we dignify these relationships by the name *love,* without patronizing diminutions, we imply a set of anti-social corollaries which cannot be allowed. Learning to dissemble these feelings, among the strongest and the most elevated that she will ever feel, is a squalid but inevitable business. However innocently one girl caresses the body of another, she cannot escape the necessity of furtiveness which she intuits right from the birth of her love. Gradually she learns to consider her own feelings in the light of the common appraisal of them and to ridicule and disown them. Such loss is enormous, and brings her much further on the way to the feminine pattern of shallow response combined with deep reserve. From the frank sharing of another's being she turns to the teasing and titillation of dating, which all the world condones. I can remember a scene with my mother when she discovered a letter written by me to my lover at school, a girl who introduced me to Beethoven by playing his sonatas to me in a dingy annexe where we retreated at every spare moment, who held my hand while we sang harmonies of Palestrina and Pachelbel in the crack school choir, and pretended I was George Sand and she was Chopin, and vice-versa, a girl who was obliterated by puberty and would end up singing in the chorus of *Damn' Yankees*. Mother was screaming that I was unnatural: to stem her flow, I repeated what I had read in the Sunday Supplements, that it was an adolescent homosexual phase, and I was through it anyway. I expiated that pusillanimous, lying betrayal of myself and my love for weeks. After such knowledge, what forgiveness?

Puberty

Puberty is when the still struggling woman-child receives her *coup de grâce*. The definition of puberty is difficult; much of the conflict which surrounds it is only arbitrarily connected to the necessary physiological changes. As usual physiology is made the excuse for destiny; contingency is described as necessity. If there have been studies made of the progress through the trauma of puberty by Trobriand Islanders or some such other people who are free from the neuroses which beset not only our society but most others that we know of, their results are not common knowledge. As it is, all that we are constantly aware of is that puberty is hell. It is hell for boys as well as girls, but for boys it is a matter of adjusting to physical changes which signify the presence of sex and genitality, as well as to the frustration of genital urges and the guilt and confusion occasioned by nocturnal pollutions and randy fantasies. For the girl it is a different matter: she has to arrive at the feminine posture of passivity and sexlessness. No sooner does her pubic hair appear than she has to learn how to obliterate it. Menstruation must be borne and belied. She has been so protected from accepting her body as sexual that her menstruation strikes her as a hideous violation of her physical integrity, however well she has been prepared for it. This is the time when she will reap the fruits of the whirlwind. All her conflicts come home to roost. If she cannot strike an equilibrium between her desires and her conditioning this is when she breaks down, runs away, goes wrong, begins to fail in school, to adopt forms of behaviour which are not only anti-social but self-destructive.

All observers of female psychology, from Freud and

Deutsch to Horney and Terman, agree that the girl's intellectual and other abilities suffer a marked diminution during and after puberty.[1] The slight advantage that she enjoys over the boys in school is lost. Dr Chapman thinks that 'women are to be congratulated on being able to traverse this stage of life retaining any semblance of emotional stability' but what he means by it is yet another discrimination against women.[2] It is a male chauvinist position to suppose that any creature that bleeds from the site of its torn-off sexual organ ought by rights to be a maniac. If we listen to what pubescent girls themselves are saying, we may find ample cause for conflict, without citing the secret ministry of biology.

I have a worry which is too embarrassing for me to seek the advice of my mother. I sometimes feel very lonely and simply long for a boyfriend. I yearn for an experience which I have never known. I know I am very young to be talking about this sort of thing as I am only thirteen but I can't help it and it reduces me to despair when I think I have so long to wait. Please don't advise me to forget this desire because I can't however much I try. My mind runs on it most of the time. Please help me.[3]

What help can there be? The writer of this plea must be convinced that she wants something else. She is already too well aware that such desire she describes is not supposed to exist. When she is fifteen she will have become convinced that it doesn't. On the other hand, this child's problem is tailored for solution:

I am the plain Jane in our family and just long for beauty. When I go to the pictures and see the beautiful girls it makes me nearly cry to think I'm so unattractive. Can you give me any beauty hints?[4]

This girl's uneasiness and shame are the result of the steady erosion of her personality. She is poised on the brink of a lifetime of camouflage and idiotic ritual, full of forebodings and failure which may be momentarily allayed while she is young and courted only to return with redoubled ferocity when that brief time is over. During the period of puberty the outward manifestations of conflict which may have existed from infancy become more conspicuous – irritability, nightmares, bed-wetting, giggling, lying, shyness, weeping, nailbiting, compulsive counting rituals, picking at sores, brooding, clumsiness, embarrassment, secretiveness.

There is no parallel in the young female groups, limited usually to the school situation, for the intense polymorphous genital activity which characterizes male puberty. The growing girl is encouraged to use her feminine charm, to be coy and alluring, while ignoring the real theatre in which such blandishments operate. Her strong desires become dissipated in passive fantasies, while their connection with sexuality is effectively underplayed or obscured. Kinsey's statistics that ninety per cent of males masturbated while sixty-two per cent of women have done so at least once, give a very imperfect idea of the actual difference in the auto-erotic activity of boys and girls.[5] In this critical period a girl is expected to begin her dealings with men, dealings based upon her attractiveness as a sexual object, dealings which can only be hampered by any consideration of her own sexual urge. In these palmy days of the permissive society this situation has given rise to some perversions which are extremely depressing. It is not uncommon for a girl seeking 'popularity' or approbation from boys to allow boys to take extraordinary liberties with her, while neither seeking nor deriving anything for herself. The phenomenon of girls agreeing to massage boys to orgasm, or even to let them have intercourse with them in rushed and sometimes squalid or public conditions is an unlooked for but not uncommon result of the inert force of inculcated passivity in the permissive society. Any Saturday afternoon in a provincial

English town one may see groups of girls clad in the uniform of their accepted image standing about the streets feigning to ignore the groups of boys who express clear scorn for them. Their susceptibility combined with insipidity and dishonesty offers them no ground for genuine intercourse with their male contemporaries. Ironically, the conditioning for femininity which ought to increase the market value of the sex object can and does become the worst devaluation.

When a girl fails to manipulate her sexual situation, as she often does, she turns her guidance for the answer cannot come from herself. James Hemming studied the correspondence sent to a weekly periodical magazine, noticing that twice as many letters came from girls as from boys, and most of them, unlike the boys', were concerned with problems of personal adjustment. He gives a number of reasons:

What accounts for the sex difference is not clear. It may be that boys find it easier to adjust to a society which is still predominantly controlled by men in spite of the growing emancipation of women. It may be that problems exist for the girl which the boy escapes because parents are more anxious about their adolescent daughters than about their adolescent sons. It may be that she is more disturbed by the existing confusion of values than are boys. It may be that the girl's greater facility in expressing herself in words makes her more willing to write about personal problems. Or it may be that what Dr James Suttie called 'our tabu on tenderness' makes boys shy about sharing their problems in case this should make them appear 'soft'. Whatever the reason, all research into problems of adolescence produces more problems of adjustment from girls than boys.[6]

All the causes that Hemming mentions are products of the root cause: the necessity for the adolescent girl to adopt the role of the eunuch. Her seeking guidance is one essential symptom of her abandonment of her autonomy. She has always been subjected to more control and supervision than her brother, and now she is required to adopt the proper feminine passivity and continue her own repression by herself. It is a delicate operation, and, given the stresses that have sprung from it since her infancy, it is not surprising that puberty appears as the breaking point.

In analysing women with neurotic troubles or character disturbances, one frequently finds two conditions: (1) although in all cases the determining conflicts have arisen in early childhood, the first personality changes have taken place in adolescence... (2) the onset of these changes coincides with menstruation.[7]

Karen Horney follows this observation by listing the main types of disintegration to be found in these neurotic characters – sexual guilt and anxiety, the fear that they do not measure up to the feminine ideal, deep defensiveness, and suspicion and antagonism. In considering her own observations, Horney finds that she must deny some of her own earlier Freudian opinions, and risk heterodoxy. The traditional argument was that what puberty aggravated was the individual's inability to accept her natural, proper sexual role, femininity miscalled womanhood. What Horney found was that femininity itself produced these aberrations, although she hardly dared say so in so many words. She closed her paper with a tentative admonition that it is better 'to educate children in courage and endurance instead of filling them with fears'.[8] Even so grudging a conclusion takes the weight of guilt for inability to adapt to the feminine role from the shoulders of those who suffer most by it.

But what is the use of courage and endurance when the whole point of a woman's existence is to be exploited by Mr Right? A girl finding that she is only valued in the dating situation for qualities which her school training sought to devalue must make a damaging decision either way. The adoption of the attributes of the sexual decoy is painful and halting. Waiting for the telephone to ring, learning not to seem too eager, pretending that she doesn't care, the girl applies a self-discipline which can become radical. On very rare occasions she may find herself in a situation where these curbs are not absolutely necessary. Those theorists who deny female sexuality ought to have seen as many pop concerts as I have, when thousands of girls between the ages of twelve and sixteen respond savagely to the stimulus of music and male exhibitionism. It is a commonplace in the music industry that the stars stuff their crutches, and that the girls wet the seat covers. The savagery and hysteria of the phenomenon is in direct relation to its rarity. The distortion is the same that the outlawed Bacchantes practised when they tore Pentheus to pieces.

> There's a little girl called Laetitia
> and she writes the most amazing letters
> to the cardboard cutout heroes
> of pubescent fantasy
> inviting rape by proxy
> a carnal correspondent
> she's the undisputed teenage queen
> of pop pornography.
>
> **Roger McGough, 'S.W.A.L.K.'**

The strength and concentration of the sexual desires and energies of young women has not always been denied as stoutly as it was by the Freudians. Women might learn something from the form of fantasy gratification used by seventeenth-century maidens.

Young wenches have a wanton sport which they call moulding of *cockle-bread*; viz. they get upon a Tableboard, and then gather up their knees and their coates with their hands as high as they can and then they wabble to and fro with the buttocks, as if they were kneading dough with their arses, and say the words, viz.

> My dame is sick and gone to bed,
> And I'll go mould my cockle bread
> Up with my heels and down with my head,
> And this is the way to mould cockle bread.

I did imagine [Aubrey comments] nothing to have been in this but mere Wantonesse of youth – *rigidas prurigine vulvae.* Juven. Sat. 6 (129).[9]

We no longer subscribe to the notion of the heated lust of the marriageable virgin, except in its etiolated form in the Lolita syndrome; we do not believe in the greensickness, but we do accept that puberty is a kind of natural disease of inorganic origin, which is a supposition no less arbitrary. What we ought to see in the agonies of puberty is the result of the conditioning that maims the female personality in creating the feminine.

To be sure he's a 'Man', the male must see to it that the female be clearly a 'Woman', the opposite of a 'Man', that is, the female must act like a faggot.

Valerie Solanas, SCUM Manifesto, p. 50

The Psychological Sell

Women are contoured by their conditioning to abandon autonomy and seek guidance. It ought to be *a priori* evidence of the synthetic nature of our concept of womanhood that it is so often expounded. The number of women who resort to the paternal guidance of the psychoanalyst is indicative of the same fact. The existence of continual strain in the feminine situation cannot be concealed so it must be explained; in explaining it, traditional psychology, like the Captain in Strindberg's *The Father*, assumed as arbitrarily as he did that women have been subjected to conditioning which is improper to their biological function, which is the breeding of children and supportive work in the home.[1] The woman who seeks academic guidance from psychologists might indeed find that some of the more galling conflicts are lessened as a result although this is a dubious conclusion. What she actually discovers is that the conditions against which she chafes are sanctioned by a massive structure of data and theory which she can only adapt to for there is no hope of shifting it. It takes another psychiatrist to explain to her the function of observer bias, and the essential conservatism of psychology.[2] As far as the woman is concerned, psychiatry is an extraordinary confidence trick: the unsuspecting creature seeks aid because she feels unhappy, anxious and confused, and psychology persuades her to seek the cause in *herself*. the person is easier to change than the status quo which represents a higher value in the psychologists' optimistic philosophy. If all else fails largactil, shock treatment, hypnosis and other forms of 'therapy' will buttress the claim of society. Psychologists cannot fix the world so they fix women. Actually they don't even manage that: one Eysenck study (1952) reported that of patients treated by psychoanalysis, 44 per cent improved; of those who were treated by other methods (drugs, shock, etc.) 64 per cent improved; and of those who received no treatment at all 72 per cent improved. The subsequent reports of Barron and Leary, Bergin, Cartwright and Vogel and Truax bear out these negative results.[3]

So much for the authority of psychoanalysis and the theory of personality. For the woman who accepts psychoanalytic descriptions of herself and of her problems there are specific perils far greater than the effects of personality prejudices on the other half of the community.

Freud is the father of psychoanalysis. It had no mother. He is not its only begetter, and subsequent structures of theory have challenged as well as reinforced his system. Probably the best way to treat it is as a sort of metaphysic but usually it is revered as a science. Freud himself lamented his inability to understand women, and became progressively humbler in his pronouncements about them. The best approach to Freud's assumptions about women is probably the one adopted by Dr Ian Suttie, that of psychoanalysing Freud himself.[4] The corner-stone of the Freudian theory of womanhood is the masculine conviction that a woman is a castrated man. It is assumed that she considers herself to be thus deprived and that much of her motivation stems either from the attempt to pretend that this is not so, typical of the immature female who indulges in clitoral sexuality, or from the attempt to compensate herself for this lack by having children. Basically the argument is a tautology which cannot proceed beyond its own terms, so that it is neither demonstrable nor refutable. Ernest Jones, himself a devout Freudian, began to suspect that something was wrong with the basic hypothesis because he took the trouble to observe the sexuality of female children:

There is an unhealthy suspicion growing that men analysts have been led to adopt an unduly phallocentgric view of the problems in question, the importance of the female organs being correspondingly underestimated.[5]

Unfortunately, the suspicion must have remained unhealthy, for it never flourished into a new theory. Psychoanalysts went on believing in the genital trauma despite evidence. Faith is not after all dependent upon evidence. The Freudian scheme sets out that the development of little girls parallels that of little boys with the complication that the girl discovers that she has lost her penis. Her infantile sexuality is essentially masculine, with important qualifications:

As we all know [*sic*] it is not until puberty that the sharp distinction is established between the masculine and feminine characters. From that time on, this contrast has a more decisive influence than any other on the shaping of human life. It is true that the masculine and feminine dispositions are already easily recognizable in childhood. The development of the inhibitions of sexuality (shame, disgust, pity, etc.) takes place in little girls earlier and in the fact of less resistance than boys; the tendency to sexual repression seems in general to be greater, and where the component instincts of sexuality appear, they prefer the passive form. The auto-erotic activity of the erotogenic zones is, however, the same in both sexes, and owing to its uniformity there is no possibility of a distinction between the two sexes such as arises after puberty. So far as the auto-erotic and masturbatory manifestations of sexuality are concerned we might lay it down that the sexuality of the little girl is of a wholly masculine character.[6]

This must be nonsense. The concepts of sameness and difference are without meaning. The description of personality regulating itself in a mysterious way towards repression is likewise not informative. What comes out strongly is only that Freud believed that all libido was male libido. We learn something about his linguistics, but nothing about the reality to which they refer.

The dualism of masculine–feminine is merely the transportation into genital terms of the dualism of activity and passivity; and activity and passivity represent unstable fusion of Eros and Death at war with each other. Thus Freud identifies masculinity with aggressiveness and femininity with masochism.[7]

If we are to achieve a stable relationship between the forces of creation and destruction, we will have to abandon the polarity. We cannot survive in the environment of male sadism and female masochism, a universe of aggressors and victims. Freud himself admitted this, but he did not link this insight with his own assumptions about the essential character of women.

Men have gained control over the forces of nature to such an extent that with their help they would have no difficulty in exterminating one another down to the last man. They know this, and hence comes a large part of their current unrest, their unhappiness and their mood of anxiety. And now it is to be expected that the other of the two 'Heavenly Powers', eternal Eros, will make an effort to assert himself with his equally immortal adversary.[8]

Freud wrote this long before Hiroshima and the concept of the megadeath. He did not suggest that one way Eros could recruit his forces would be by re-endowing women with their sexuality, their fealty to Eros. Instead, he and his followers elaborated the concept of female masochism as divinely ordained by biology.

The woman who resists her sexual role and ignores the message of her vaginal bleeding, that she should be bearing children, remains fixated in an infantile, aggressive state of penis envy. She may be sexually active but her response is still masculine, attached to her clitoris, and not originating in the receptive orifice, the vagina. The mature woman's masochism stems from her desire to submit to the aggression of the appetent male, and it is only controlled by her protective narcissism which causes her to impose moral, aesthetic and physical conditions. During the necessary interval between maturity and mating she expresses her sexuality in passive fantasies; only when impregnated is she completed, for the child signifies her lost genital and her achievement, the fantasies fade, the masochism-narcissism is replaced by energy in the protection and socialization of the child. It is quite a neat description of an existing mechanism, and it has proved seductive even to female theorists, who did not dare to counterpose their subjective experience against what seemed to be objective fact. Besides, it had a moral weight. The woman who knew that all her orgasms originated in the clitoris was shamed by the imputation of immaturity and penis envy. The woman who pursued active goals was by definition ill-adapted to her real role, and probably infantile.

The essentially sound activity and the social and intellectual energy developed by the young girl who renounces her fantasies often blight her emotional life and prevent her from achieving complete femininity and later motherhood. That women frequently remain entangled in infantile forms of emotional life while their minds and activities are extremely well developed is an interesting fact that still requires explanation. It appears that the development from fantasy life into fully mature femininity is a psychologic achievement that can be inhibited by intellectualization.[9]

Helene Deutsch's priorities are obvious. If intellect impedes feminization, intellect must go. Her psychoanalytic theory could not supply her with an answer to her interesting academic problem, because the answer lies in the social context in which active, intelligent women exist. To suggest that neither the wife-to-be nor the spinster schoolteacher ought to be inventing compensatory activities because they are not involved in child-bearing would upset the whole applecart. Both examples, the feminine and the pseudo-masculine, represent castrations. Even Deutsch came to reconsider her basic theory of feminine masochism, and argued feebly that it 'cannot be related to factors inherent in the anatomical-physiological characteristics alone, but must be construed as importantly conditioned by the culture-complex or social organization in which the particular masochistic woman has developed'.[10] But she never got far enough to see that she herself was a phenomenon of the same complex, making an imortant contribution to its maintenance at the expense of women.

Deutsch herself, despite her pretensions to intellectual stature, was deeply in love with the feminine stereotype. She drew an extraordinary picture of woman as the ideal life-companion.

. . . if they possess the feminine quality of intuition to a great degree, they are ideal collaborators who often inspire their men, and are themselves happiest in this role. They seem to be easily influenceable and adapt themselves to their companions and understand them. They are the loveliest and most unaggressive of helpmates and they want to remain in that role; they do not insist on their own rights – quite the contrary. They are easy to handle in every way – if one only loves them. Sexually they are easily excited and rarely frigid; but precisely in that sexual field they impose narcissistic conditions which must be fulfilled absolutely. They demand love and ardent renunciation of their own active tendencies.

If gifted in any direction they preserve the capacity for being original and productive, but without entering into competitive struggles. They are always willing to renounce their own achievements without feeling that they are sacrificing anything, and they rejoice in the achievements of their companions, which they have often inspired. They have an extraordinary need of support when engaged in any *activity directed outward,* but are absolutely independent in such feeling and thinking as relate to their inner life, that is to say, in their *activity directed inward.* Their capacity for identification is not an expression of inner poverty but of inner wealth.[11]

This is nothing more than a blueprint for the approved woman and as such it presents an artificial unattainable ideal. Such a woman cannot be a person, for she does not exist in her own terms at all. Her significance can only be conferred by the presence of a man at her side, a man upon whom she absolutely depends. In return for renouncing, collaborating, adapting, identifying, she is caressed, desired, handled, influenced and occasionally desired in vain. It is a bad bargain for a man for she makes no attempt to excite or interest him, so he cannot expect to be handled or influenced by her. The whole structure could be toppled by a wart on the nose, for Deutsch cannot keep words like lovely out of her prescription. What right can this creature have to demand ardent love and desire, seeing as she is powerless to offer it? She is a vain, demanding, servile bore. Nothing is more chilling than such a spectacle of unremitting self-sacrifice. This is a woman born to be abandoned by her ungrateful husband at the very pinnacle of the success she helped to make for him, for a shameless hussy of nineteen. And this is the norm described by the 'science' of psychoanalysis, a farrago of moralism and fantasy unillumined by any shaft of commonsense. Deutsch's crass prejudice has not been significantly questioned by more recent psychoanalysis: Bruno Bettelheim argues that 'we must start with the realization that, as much as women want to be good scientists or engineers, they want first and foremost to be womanly companions of men and to be mothers'.[12]

Erik Erikson invented the lunatic concept of an *inner space*

in a woman's *somatic design,* a hole in the head, as it were,
which harbours the commitment to take care of children.[13]
Joseph Rheingold restated the position of the mad captain in
The Father as recently as 1964.

When women grow up without dread of their biological functions
and without subversion by feminist doctrine and therefore enter on
motherhood with a sense of fulfilment and altruistic sentiment, we
shall attain the goal of a good life and a secure world in which to live
it.[14]

The women who do enter upon marriage and childbearing
with optimism and romantic sentiments are most vociferous
in their disappointments, and their children suffer most by
their mother's obsessive interest in them. Childbearing was
never intended by biology as a compensation for neglecting
all other forms of fulfilment and achievement. It was never
intended to be as time-consuming and self-conscious a
process as it is. One of the deepest evils in our society is
tyrannical nurturance. Feminists cherish a sanguine hope
that the conclusions of Masters and Johnson that the vaginal
orgasm is a myth have routed the Freudian fantasm forever,
when they established that all female orgasms originate in
the clitoris. It is not however beyond the scope of these
theorists to argue that all the women tested by Masters and
Johnson were infantile products of improper conditioning,
and that the fact that all the orgasms in their samples were
clitoral does not disprove that vaginal orgasm ever existed,
could exist or ought to exist. Basically it all comes down to the
same fact: the Freudian system describes the status quo as a
desideratum of the nineteenth-century middle class. Facts
are irrelevant to what is basically a value system. If we are to
place our strongest values in external reality, we can reject
the premises of Freudian psychoanalysis as extra weight in
the auto-repressive process, relying instead upon our own

observation, and the results of our own experiments with our environment. Not only is the Freudian construct arbitrary, it doesn't work as a pattern for living. We cannot have all the children we might need to arrive at the condition of mental health as understood by Freud, however much we might want to. If women were to be barefoot and pregnant all the time, as Mark Twain suggested, their number would have to be decimated.

There have been other statements by the fathers of psychology about the role of women, from the mumbo-jumbo of Jung to the notions of human normality derived from watching apes co-habiting in the battleground of the jungle. An anthropologist like Margaret Mead seeks the ratification of her academic theories of sex in her observation of primitive communities so that despite her apparent radicalism, she defends the concept of passive femininity. Her position is still that of Krafft-Ebing, who believes of woman that

If she is normally developed mentally, and well-bred, her sexual desire is small. If this were not so the whole world would become a brothel and marriage and family impossible. It is certain that the man that avoids women and the woman that seeks men are abnormal...nevertheless the sexual sphere occupies a much larger sphere in the consciousness of women than that of men, and is continual rather than intermittent.[15]

Freud would have told him how to interpret his latter observation in terms of the former. Women do have sexual desires and if it is a function of normal mental-health development and good breeding to destroy it, let us try some abnormal mental development, rejecting our breeding. If marriage and family depend upon the castration of women let them change or disappear. The alternative is not a brothel, for brothels depend upon marriage and family for their existence. If we are to escape from the treadmill of sexual fantasy, voracious need of love, and obsessiveness in all its forms we will have to reinstate our libido in its rightful function. Only then will women be capable of loving. Eternal Eros is imprisoned now in the toils of the sadomaso-chistic symbiosis, and if we are to rescue him and save the world we must break the chain. What after all was Deutsch describing in her impassioned rhetorical phrases but this?

The passive form of the symbiotic union is that of submission or...of masochism. The masochistic person escapes from the unbearable feeling of isolation and separateness by making himself part and parcel of another person who directs him, protects him; who is his life and his oxygen as it were. The power of the one to whom one submits may be inflated, may he be a person or a god, he is everything, I am nothing, except inasmuch as I am part of him. As a part, I am a part of greatness, of power, of certainty. The masochistic person does not have to make decisions, does not have to take any risks; he is never alone – but he is not independent; he has no integrity he is not yet fully born...the person who renounces his integrity, makes himself the instrument of somebody or something outside himself; he need not solve the problem of living by productive activity.[16]

In pushing the masochistic role as the proper role for woman, psychology reinforces the infantilization which has gone on ever since she was born. Her sufferings do not stem from her failure to grow up into mature womanhood, but from her striving against what prevents her from living and working with her own powers. From the time she was born she has been subjected to a pressure to return to the womb, from her first hour bound into a cot to her last strait-jacket. There is only one way to return to the womb, via death. The same pressures that bind with briars a woman's joys and desires are the pressures that will destroy the world. If half the world is to remain hostage to Death, then Eros must lose the battle to the total weapon. What is the arms race and the cold war but the continuation of male competiveness and aggression into the inhuman sphere of computer-run institutions? If women are to cease producing cannon fodder for the final holocaust they must rescue men from the perversities of their own polarization. The struggle may be long and even more painful than capitulation. It will be a struggle in the dark, for none of our vaunted knowledge, scientific or not, can describe the alternative possibility. Is it worth it?

The Raw Material

Despite all the arguments about the effect of conditioning on the developing woman, the suspicion might persist that women do have some congenital mental deficiency by reason of their sex. Given the bias of observers involved in testing for suspected or assumed tendencies we might not be surprised to find that there were 'proven' sexual differences in mind. The remarkable fact is that no such differences have ever been established. Methodical investigation into the sex

> Thus women's secrets I've surveyed
> And let them see how curiously they're made,
> And that, tho' they of different sexes be,
> Yet in the whole they are the same as we.
> For those that have the strictest searchers been,
> Find women are but men turned outside in;
> And men, if they but cast their eyes about,
> May find they're women with their inside out.
>   'The Works of Aristotle in Four Parts', 1822, p. 16

of mind has been going on for more than fifty years. It is known for example that sex hormones do enter the brain, but no correlation between that physiological fact and mental capacity or behaviour has ever been established, although it has been assumed. It was thought that the relative lightness of the female brain argued lesser mental powers, although it was pointed out that women have a heavier brain considered relatively to the total weight. In any case brain weight is irrelevant, as was swiftly admitted when it was found to operate to male disadvantage. If the frontal lobes are to be considered as the seat of intelligence, then it must also be pointed out that the frontal area of the brain is more developed in women. So we may discount that kind of statistic as well. The brain is so imperfectly understood that we simply do not know enough about its physiology and function to deduce facts about performance.

Rather than attempt to deduce behaviour from physiology it has seemed more logical to establish behaviour patterns from the observation of behaviour. There are problems attached to that too. It is impossible to control experiments which are conducted among subjects undergoing the continual chaotic conditioning of normal life. Unconditioned subjects do not exist, and the conditioned ones are not uniformly so. If such tests did reveal intellectual inferiority in women we could discount them; but in any case they do not.

In 1966 Eleanor Maccoby assembled the results of fifty years of testing in her book *The Development of Sex Differences* under an extraordinarily comprehensive range of subdivisions. Those relating to cognitive abilities were particularly interesting. According to Gesell and others (1940) and Terman (1925) girls speak before boys. All the further studies of the development of articulacy show that girls proceed faster than boys although boys performed better in situations requiring enterprise and lack of shyness, like speaking out in class, especially in the older age groups. Girls seem to have a wider vocabulary, although the differences do not seem very significant. Girls are better at grammar and spelling, although tests of reasoning produced a variety of results. Reading tests showed the same pattern. Non-verbal cognitive abilities like counting, mathematical reasoning, spatial cognition, abstract reasoning, set-breaking and restructuring, perceptual speed, manual, mechanic and scientific skills have all been tested, and no significant pattern of difference has emerged, except this slight pre-eminence of the girls, who may have this advantage for reasons connected with their enculturation, more time spent with adults, more sedentary habits, greater obedience and credulousness. Of the tests of total I.Q. eleven show no difference, three find a difference in favour of women, and three in favour of men. Given the amorphous nature of the faculties tested and the arbitrary character of the test situation itself, we must refrain from assuming anything about the female psyche from such evidence, except that the sex of mind is still to be demonstrated.[1]

There is a basic confusion in the test situations between creativity and getting good marks at school. In Lewis Terman's studies of genius, which consisted in following through the careers of a group of gifted children, he is very much hampered by his own limited concept of genius. One girl, Sarah, is highly praised by Terman, who includes this poem as evidence of her extraordinary gifts:

The Virgin

Her pride subdued by shyness, or by art,
The maiden walks; the whispers of her heart
Only betrayed by the elusive rose
Upon her cheek. Through all her being flows
A consciousness of happy innocence
And youth more sweet for its impermanence.

Eager to live, yet fearing to be caught
On life's rude turbulent flood, wise though untaught,
Aware of all she is designed to be,
She savours and delays her destiny.[2]

This pompous doggerel is not irradiated by one genuine insight. The tradition in which it is written perished ignobly a hundred years or more ago. All that such an opusculum can reflect is young Sarah's facility in emulation.

Nevertheless, the testers do distinguish some tendencies which may be of help to us in understanding what it is that happens to the girl when she is gradually outstripped by her male rivals, and finally leaves school before reaching any appreciable standard of literacy, or taking a job qualification. Despite the confusion between induction and education in the minds of the testers they were able to

> A Man ought no more to value himself for being wiser than a Woman, if he owes his Advantage to a better Education, than he ought to boast of his Courage for beating a Man when his hands were bound.
>
> Mary Astell,
> 'An Essay in Defence of the Female Sex', 1721, p. 18

observe a tendency which goes a long way to explain what eventually diddles girls:

For both sexes there is a tendency for the more passive dependent children to perform poorly on a variety of intellectual tasks, and for independent children to excel. . .[3]

Children who 'refuse to accept authority' do well in a variety of tasks, as do those who resist 'conformity pressures'.

Mothers who were less nurturant towards daughters during preschool years had the more academically successful daughters. . .
For girls by contrast [with boys] the crucial factor in the development of I.Q. appears to be relative freedom from maternal restriction – freedom to wander and explore.[4]

The failure of women to produce great works of art and all that can be explained in terms of this statement. Insofar as she escapes or rejects her conditioning, the little girl may excel in those kinds of intellectual activity that are called creative, but eventually she either capitulates to her conditioning, or the conflicts become so pressing that her efficiency is hampered. Maccoby does not see why the development of sexuality must have such a deleterious effect on girls' performance, although she has earlier quoted McKinnon's opinion on the relation between repression and mental capabilities.

Repression, McKinnon argues, has a generalized impact upon thought processes, interfering with the accessibility of the individual's own previous experience. An individual who is using

> **From all that has been said, it is apparent that we cannot speak of inferiority and superiority, but only of specific differences in aptitudes and personality between the sexes. These differences are largely the result of cultural and other experiential factors... the overlapping in all psychological characteristics is such that we need to consider men and women as individuals, rather than in terms of group stereotypes.**
>
> **Anna Anastasi,**
> **'Differential Psychology', 1958, pp. 497–8**

repression as a defence mechanism cannot be, to use McKinnon's term, 'fluent in scanning thoughts'. McKinnon has evidence that creativity is in fact associated with the absence of repression (as indicated through personality assessment tests) and Barron reports that originality is associated with 'responsiveness to impulse and emotion.'[5]

Certainly, McKinnon's view goes some way towards explaining the gradual fading of the young woman's hopes, as she takes over the repressive processes that her parents and superiors have demonstrated and continues them on her own behalf. What she began with cannot be proved to be in any way inferior to the raw material of which male genius is fashioned but from what we can observe it seems that girls can only prove that point by open intellectual rebellion.

Womanpower

The failure of specially designed tests to reveal any specifically sexual difference in intellectual capacity between males and females is irrelevant as far as those who challenge women's fitness for certain responsibilities and work are concerned. They think that the tests reflect more upon the testers and the method of testing than they do upon male and female. Dr Leavis believed that he could identify a woman writer by her style, even though necessarily all that she wrote must have been a parody of some man's superior achievement. After all, there was not much wrong with Virginia Woolf except that she was a woman. It could be argued that the tests were specially contoured in an attempt to counteract the effect of sexual conditioning, while real women in the real world are continually conditioned. No adjustment of our theoretical opinion of their basic capacity can alter the nature of their achievement. Men complain that they cannot handle women, that arguments with women must be avoided at all costs because they always get the last word mostly by foul means. How 'like a woman' they sigh, and all agree. The detection of sex in mind is not only the privilege of the most eminent literary pundits from Dr

> Women tend to make their emotions perform the functions they exist to serve, and hence remain mentally much healthier than men.
>
> Ashley Montagu,
> 'The Natural Superiority of Women', 1954, p. 54

Leavis to Norman Mailer,[1] it extends to the lowest levels of illiteracy – the schoolboy muttering about 'bloody girls'. Because the difference is so wholeheartedly believed in, it is also experienced. As a conviction it becomes a motive for behaviour and a continuing cause of the phenomenon itself. It is not to be put aside by rational means. There is of course no reason why women should limit themselves to logic: we might perversely decide to *exploit* the Ovarian Theory of Mind.[2]

One of the fullest statements of the theory of the female soul was set out in *Sex and Character,* a remarkably rigorous and committed book by a mere boy, Otto Weininger, who committed suicide some years after its publication. His brilliant, neurotic life can be taken as an illustration of what dimorphism must eventually accomplish. By disintegrating human nature and building boundaries between warring halves, Weininger condemned himself to perversion, guilt, and early death. He began by identifying women with the body, with unconscious sexuality, and thereafter with passive animalism. As a rational male he condemned such a bestial element. 'No men who think really deeply about women retain a high opinion of them; men either despise women or they have never thought seriously about them.'[3]

Like Freud, with whom he had much more in common, he thought of women as castrated by nature; because he thought so highly of the penis he thought women did too:

An absolute nude female figure in life leaves an impression of something wanting, an incompleteness which is incompatible with beauty...[4]
The qualities that appeal to a woman are the signs of a developed sexuality; those that repel her are the qualities of the higher mind. Woman is essentially a phallus worshipper...[5]

Weininger thought the dimorphism of the sexes right

through, and discovered that, given such a polarity, men could have no real communion with women, only a highly compromised shared hypocrisy. Valerie Solanas performed the same exercise for women, and found that men covet all that women are, seeking degradation and effemnisation at their hands.[6] She retaliated by shooting Andy Warhol in the chest. Weininger more honestly made his attempt upon himself and succeeded. Just as Solanas despises men as they present themselves to be and in their failure to live up to their own stereotype, Weininger despises women both because their image is passive and animalistic, and because they are not even genuinely so. Their pretence is brought about by the exigency of the sexual situation which they exploit, hence the duplicity and mendacity which characterize all their actions. Because woman lives vicariously she need take no moral responsibility for her behaviour: because she has no responsibility she has no morality and no ego. Because of the lack of ego and the variety of roles that women manipulate, they have no identity, as one may guess from their willingness to give up their names. Woman is never genuine at any period of her life.[7]

The most chastening reflection is that Weininger was simply describing what he saw in female behaviour around him. He could not see that these deformities were what women would one day clamour to be freed from. As far as he could see, women were like that and he did not know what

---

Political and civic equality of the sexes implies moral equality. It implies the perfectly appalling logical consequence that the morals of women shall in future be the same as those of respectable Christian Victorian man – at best. That, of course, means the total collapse of Christian morality.

Robert Briffault, 'Sin and Sex,' 1931, p. 132

came first, their condition or their character. He assumed that it must have been the latter, because he could not explain their condition any other way.

All the moral deficiencies Weininger detected masqueraded in Victorian society as virtues. Weininger is to be credited with describing them properly. Nevertheless his concepts of ego, identity, logic and morality were formed from observation of this same undesirable status quo, and women today might well find that what Weininger describes as defects might be in fact *freedoms* which they might do well to promote. For example:

With women thinking and feeling are identical, for man they are in opposition. The woman has many of her mental experiences as henids (undifferentiated perceptions) whilst in man these have passed through a process of clarification [8]

'Definitio est negatio.' We might argue that clarification is tantamount to falsification: if you want to know what happened in a particular situation you would be better off asking someone who had perceived the whole and remembered all of it, not just some extrapolated clarification. How sad it is for men to have feeling and thought in opposition: Eliot argued that the seventeenth century had seen a dissociation of sensibility, so that intelligence no longer served as a direct index of the intensity of feeling but rather undermined it.[9] Can it be that women have survived the process which debilitated the rest of male-dominated western culture? If we can make anything of such a seductive possibility, we must reflect that most educated women have simply been admitted to the masculine academic culture, and have lost their power to perceive in henids. According to Antonin Artaud, Anais Nin might have survived even that:

I brought many people, men and women, to see the beautiful canvas, but it is the first time I ever saw artistic emotion make a human being palpitate like love. Your senses trembled and I realized that the mind and body are formidably linked in you, because such a pure spiritual could unleash such a powerful storm in your organism. But in that universal marriage it is the mind that lords over the body and dominates it, and it must end up by dominating it in every way. I feel that there is a world of things in you that are begging to be born should it find its exorcist.[10]

Most of this is nonsense. We might expect the inventor of the theatre of cruelty to see the phenomenon of unified sensibility and spend a paragraph trying to prove the domination of the mind to the point of implying that she needed an exorcist! Artaud's manicheeism prevented him from seeing that the stimulus of the painting was sensual in the first instance. All that happened was that Nin responded with both mind and body to a sensible and intelligible stimulus. The painting was one and her response was equally integrated.

If women retain their experience in their original unclassified form they may escape the great limitation of scientific thought, which was pointed out by A.N. Whitehead in *Adventures of Ideas*.

In the study of ideas it is necessary to remember that insistence on hardheaded clarity issues from sentimental feeling, as it were a mist, cloaking the complexities of fact. Insistence on clarity at all costs is based on sheer supersitition as to the mode in which human intelligence functions. Our reasonings grasp at straws for premises and float on gossamers for deductions.[11]

At a banal level this functioning difference in male and female thought is easily demonstrated: we have only to think of Father mocking Mother for keeping the salt in a box marked Sago, or the frequently celebrated female intuition, which is after all only a faculty for observing tiny insignificant aspects of behaviour and forming an empirical conclusion which cannot by syllogistically examined. Now that most information is not disseminated in argumentative form on the printed page, but is assimilated in various non-verbal ways from visual and aural media, clarification and the virtues of disputation are more and more clearly seen to be simply alternative ways of knowing, and not the only or the principal ones. The take-over by computers of much vertical thinking has placed more and more emphasis on the creative propensities of human thought. The sudden increase in political passion in the last decade, especially among the generation which has absorbed most of its education in this undifferentiated form, bears witness to a reintegration of thought and feeling happening on a wide scale. In the circumstances any such pecularity of the female mind could well become a strength.

Unfortunately my own arguments have all the faults of an insufficient regard for logic and none of its strengths, the penalty after all for a Cartesian education. So much for privilege. Here I am, a negro who cannot do the lindy-hop or sing the Blues! Nowadays education itself is changing so that creative thought does not decline with the inculcation of mental disciplines, which are now not taught as ends but simply as means to other ends. Unfortunately, the chief result of the change so far seems to be the reluctance of children to study science, but eventually science itself will become a complete study.

Weininger has more serious charges though:

A woman cannot grasp that one must act from principle; as she has no continuity she does not experience the necessity for logical support of her mental processes... she may be regarded as 'logically insane'.[12]

It is true that women often refuse to argue logically. In many cases they simply do not know how to, and men may dazzle them with a little pompous sophistry. In some cases they are intimidated and upset before rationalization begins. But it is also true that in most situations logic is simply rationalization of an infra-logical aim. Women know this; even the best educated of them know that arguments with their men-folk are disguised real-politik. It is not a contest of mental agility with the right as the victor's spoils, but a contest of wills. The rules of logical discourse are no more relevant than the Marquess of Queensberry's are to a pub brawl. Female hardheadedness rejects the misguided masculine notion that men are rational animals. Male logic can only deal with simple issues: women, because they are passive and condemned to observe and react rather than initiate, are more aware of complexity. Men have been forced to suppress their receptivity, in the interests of domination. One of the possible advantages of infantilization of women is that they might after all become, in the words of Lao-Tse, 'a channel drawing all the world towards it' so that they 'will not be severed from the eternal virtue' and 'can return again to the state of infancy.'[13] If only the state of women were infancy, and not what we have reduced infancy itself to, new possibilities might be closer to realization than they seem. When Schopenhauer described the state of women as *moral infancy,* he was reflecting not only his prejudice against women, but also against babies. The failure of women to take logic seriously has serious consequences for their morality. Freud adds the gloss to Weininger's text:

I cannot evade the notion (though I hesitate to give it expression) that for women the level of what is ethically normal is different from what it is in men. Their superego is never so inexorable, so impersonal, so independent of its emotional origins as we require it to be in men. Character-traits which critics of every epoch have brought up against women – that they show less sense of justice than men, that they are less ready to submit to the great exigencies of life, that they are more often influenced in their judgements by their feelings of affection or hostility – all these would be amply accounted for in the modification of the formation of their super-ego.... We must not allow ourselves to be deflected from such conclusions by the denial of the feminists, who are anxious to force us to regard the two sexes as completely equal in position and worth.[14]

The circularity of this utterance is quite scary. After all, are the sexes equal in position and worth or not? What is position? What is worth? He promises to explain unsubstantiated modification in an unsubstantiated entity, the superego: if physiology is destiny Freud is anxious to invent a physiology of the mind. If judgement had not been separated from feeling so unnaturally in the Nazi officers presumably they would not have carried out orders so crisply. What kind of a criticism is it to say that women are less stoical than men? After two world wars stoicism seems to have outlived its value. If women have been denied moral responsibility by male 'justice' and dubbed angels while they were treated with contempt, it is likely that they will have formed their own conclusions about the monstrous superego and illusory morality of men. Protestant Europe has set for itself an unattainable morality of integrity in defiance of heavenly mercy, the unaided conscience bowed by full and unending responsibility for all actions, despite the partiality of knowledge and infirmity of will which characterize human action. Freud saw the results in his own community but he could not postulate an alternative to guilt and neurosis. The chief mainstay of such religion is the capacity of the ego to continue repression. Women may be bad at keeping up the cycle of the organism punishing itself, but that too may be an advantage which involves less delusion than its opposite.

The feeling of identity in all circumstances is quite wanting in the true woman, because her memory, even if exceptionally good, is devoid of continuity...women if they look back on their earlier lives, never understand themselves.[15]

> My colleague Nathan Leites, Ph.D., has concluded after a review of the literature that the term 'identity' has little use other than as a fancy dress in which to disguise vagueness, ambiguity, tautologies, lack of clinical data, and poverty of explanation.
>
> Robert Stoller, 'Sex and Gender', 1968, p. x

On Weininger's evidence the ego is ersatz, consisting of the memory of the self which exists at any particular time. He remarks with horror that if you ask a woman about herself, she understands it to be her body. She does not seek to define herself by asserting her image of her merit, her behaviour. Man has a temporal notion of identity, which is falsifiable, woman a simple spatial one. 'Here you are' said the white buttons Yoko Ono gave away at her exhibition. It seems important after all. Perhaps woman, like the child, retains some power of connecting freely with external reality. Weininger seemed to think so. 'The absolute female has no ego.'[16]

The primal act of the human ego is a negative one – not to accept reality, specifically the separation of the child's body from the mother's body...this negative posture blossoms into negation of self (repression) and negation of the environment (aggression).[17]

What a blossoming! If women had no ego, if they had no sense of separation from the rest of the world, no repression and no regression, how nice that would be! What need would there be of justice if everyone felt no aggression but infinite compassion! Of course I am taking advantage of the masters of psychology, bending and selecting their words like this, but what else can they be for? We cannot allow them to define what must be or change would be impossible. Whitehead and Needham looked forward to a new kind of knowledge which would correct the insanity of pure intelligence, 'a science based on an erotic sense of reality, rather than an aggressive dominating attitude to reality'.[10] If wisdom might not be incompatible with a low sense of ego, then charity seems in the mystical definitions of it to be dependent upon such a corrosion of separateness: the greatest myth of Christianity is that of the mystical body.

To heal is to make whole, as in wholesome; to make one again; to unify or reunify; this is Eros in action. Eros is the instinct that makes for union, or unification, and Thanatos, the death instinct, is the instinct that makes for separation or division.[19]

Weininger's disgust for Eros and his devotion to Thanatos drive him to state women's comprehensiveness more fully. Believing him we might think we had been saved already:

This sense of continuity with the rest of mankind is a sexual character of the female, and displays itself in the desire to touch, to be in contact with the object of her pity; the mode in which her tenderness expresses itself is a kind of animal sense of contact. It shows an absence of that sharp line that separates one real personality from another.[20]

Poor Weininger finally cut himself off altogether in a last act of fealty to death. The immorality of individualism is obvious in an age when loneliness is the most pernicious disease of our over-crowded metropolises. The results of parcelling families in tiny slivers living in self-contained dwellings has defaced our cities and created innumerable problems of circulation and cohabitation. The sense of separateness is vainly counteracted by the pressure for conformity without community. In most of the big cities of the world the streets are dangerous to walk upon. Woman's oceanic feeling for the race has little opportunity for expression; it is grotesquely transmogrified in organized works of charity, where her genius for touching and soothing has dwindled into symbolic attitudinizing. Weininger's repugnance for animal contact is still universal among the northern races. Even crushed against his brother in the Tube the average Englishman pretends desperately that he is alone. Psychoanalysis, the most obscenely intimate contact of all, is not hallowed by any physical contact. Latterly, special classes form in church halls in arty suburbs, so that men and women can recover their sense of reassurance by touch. Too late for Weininger.

> Might the cleavage between the subjective and objective have been badly made; might the opposition between a universe of science – entirely outside self – and a universe of consciousness – defined by the total presence of self to self – be untenable? And if realistic analysis fails will biology find its method in an ideal analysis of the psycho-mathematical type, in Spinozistic intellection? Or might not value and signification be intrinsic determinations of the organism which could only be accessible to a new mode of 'comprehension'?
>
> Maurice Merleau-Ponty,
> 'The Structure of Behaviour', p. 10

The intellectual pressure to make the whole world whole again has come from mystics like Lao-Tse, scientists like Whitehead and Needham and Merleau-Ponty, and as brilliant speculation from Norman O. Brown, Herbert Marcuse, Borges. Their words were not specifically addressed to women, because all of them felt that the polarity of the sexes was the basic alienation of man from himself, but none of them would reject the idea that their words were a special encouragement to women to undertake the work of saving mankind. Perhaps my treatment of their highly sophisticated arguments has been brutal, but reverence before authority has never accomplished much in the way of changing things. In inventing a new mythology one must plunder all sources, letting the situation into which the ideas fall serve as their crucible. Most of the defects pointed out by critics of women are simply the results of their having been sheltered from the subtler and more effective types of enculturation which their society lavished upon its male leaders. The strengths they have are of sheer ignorance.

Dominant ideas need not always be so obvious for them to exert just as powerful an organizing influence on the way a person thinks and approaches a problem. Old and adequate ideas, like old and adequate cities, come to polarize everything around them. All organization is based on them, all things are referred to them. Minor alterations can be made on the outskirts, but it is impossible to change the whole structure radically and very difficult to shift the centre of organization to a different place.[21]

Facing this problem, Edward de Bono devised a series of exercises to develop the faculty he called lateral thinking. Lateral thought is the kind which produces ideas and inventions, rather than demonstrable solutions to specific problems. It is the kind of problem solving which would not get you good marks for method in an examination, and is nevertheless right. It cannot be duplicated by a computer, which only has to learn what it is fed and a method to deal with it. In fact lateral thinking is a one-dimensional analogue of the child's modes of thought. A woman might claim to retain some of the child's faculties, although very limited and defused, simply because she has not been encouraged to learn methods of thought and develop a disciplined mind. As long as education remains largely induction ignorance will retain these advantages over learning and it is time that women impudently put them to work.

The prevailing criticism of the female soul can best be explained by the male battle to repress certain faculties in their own mental functioning. Women possessed in abundance those qualities which civilized men strove to repress in themselves, just as children and savages did. The value of such criticism is in the degree to which it reveals the severity of the contouring of the ideal personality, that is to say, male criticism of the female mind is revealing only of the male himself. Men in our culture crippled themselves by setting up an impossible standard of integrity: women were not given the chance to fool themselves in this way. Women have been charged with deviousness and duplicity since the dawn of civilization so they have never been able to pretend that their masks were anything but masks. It is a slender case but perhaps it does mean that women have always been in closer contact with reality than men: it would seem to be the just recompense for being deprived of idealism.

> For a Tear is an Intellectual thing,
> and a Sigh is the Sword of an Angel King,
> And the bitter groan of a Martyr's woe
> Is an Arrow from the Almightie's Bow.
>
> Blake, 'Jerusalem', pl. 52

If women understand by emancipation the adoption of the masculine role then we are lost indeed. If women can supply no counterbalance to the blindness of male drive the aggressive society will run to its lunatic extremes at ever-escalating speed. Who will safeguard the despised animal faculties of compassion, empathy, innocence and sensuality?

What will hold us back from Weininger's fate? Most women who have arrived at positions of power in a men's world have done so by adopting masculine methods which are not incompatible with the masquerade of femininity. They still exploit the sado-masochistic hook-up of the sexes, in which 'we have only the choice of being hammer or anvil.'[22] Wanda wore feminine clothes to add poignancy to her torture of Gregor, just as Mrs Castle made sure that she looked attractive when she went to berate the workers as a criminal and irresponsible element in society. It is up to women to develop a form of genuine womanpower against which the Omnipotent Administrator in frilly knickers cannot prevail.

> There is much to suggest that when human beings acquired the powers of conscious attention and rational thought they became so fascinated with these new tools that they forgot all else, like chickens hypnotized with their beaks to a chalk line. Our total sensitivity became identified with these partial functions so that we lost the ability to feel nature from the inside, and more, to feel the seamless unity of ourselves and the world. Our philosophy of action falls into the alternatives of voluntarism and determinism, because we have no sense of the wholeness of the endless knot and of the identity of its actions and ours.
>
> A.E. Watts, 'Nature, Man and Woman', 1958, p. 12

Womanpower means the self-determination of women, and that means that all the baggage of paternalist society will have to be thrown overboard. Woman must have room and scope to devise a morality which does not disqualify her from excellence, and a psychology which does not condemn her to the status of a spiritual cripple. The penalities for such delinquency may be terrible for she must explore the dark without any guide. It may seem at first that she merely exchanges one mode of suffering for another, one neurosis for another. But she may at last claim to have made a definite choice which is the first prerequisite of moral action. She may never herself see the ultimate goal, for the fabric of society is not unravelled in a single lifetime, but she may state it as her belief and find hope in it.

The great renewal of the world will perhaps consist in this, that man and maid, freed from all false feeling and aversion, will seek each other not as opposites, but as brother and sister, as neighbours, and will come together as human beings.[23]

Work

Women form thirty-eight per cent of the work force in England, which means that half the women between the ages of sixteen and sixty-four work outside their homes.[1] The average wage of women in administrative, technical and clerical work is less than £12 a week; men in the same industries earn an average wage of £28 a week. Male manual workers average £20 a week, females £10. However, equal pay for equal work will not make as great a difference in these figures as women might hope. The pattern of female employment follows the course of the role that she plays outside industry: she is almost always ancillary, a handmaid in the more important work of men. Of two and a half million women employed in manufacturing industry in 1967, 750,000 were described by the Ministry of Labour as semi-skilled, and 700,000 were employed in administrative, technical and clerical work, mostly we may be sure in the last category. By far the largest number of men working in manufacturing industry are skilled operatives, or in training to become so. In only three trades do the skilled women outnumber others – clothing, footwear and pottery. Of the nine million women in employment in this country only two per cent are in administrative position and only five per cent in professions. Only two million female workers are members of trade unions. Three times as many girls as boys leave school at fifteen: only one-third of A-level students are girls, and only a quarter of university students. Three-quarters of the eighteen-year-old girls in our society receive no training or higher education at all.[2] The pattern that emerges is that of an inert, unvalued female work force which is considered as temporary labour, docile, but unreliable. More than half the working women in this country are married, and the assumption is that the family is their principle concern, that work outside the home brings in a little extra for perks, that they have no ambition. By and large the assumptions are correct, but they prejudice the chances of the other half, the women who have to support themselves. Even where women do exactly the same work as men, the rate is from five per cent to two per cent lower, but righting this inequity will do little to ease the lot of the majority of female workers.

Possibly because of the mute significance of the fact that 1969 was the fiftieth anniversary of female suffrage in Britain the annual Conference of the Trades Union Council rang with stirring speeches by female delegates, and pledged itself to prosecuting the struggle for equal pay for equal work, even to the extent of supporting strikes by female workers, and indeed striking on their behalf. The then Prime Minister pointed out that the country could not afford the estimated cost of such a raise, that it would have to be awarded gradually year-by-year, while his cabinet racked its brains for a new kind of productivity deal to apply to this situation. The potential of female agitation had already been felt in the strike of women workers at the Ford Plant in Dagenham,[3] which Barbara Castle dealt with by the disgusting expedient of having a cuppa with the women and talking it over heart to heart. The working women were too polite to point out that Mrs Castle's £8,500 salary might have been equal to the pay of other Cabinet members but that women working in the House of Commons canteen were earning thirty shillings less than men doing the same work, but then nobody pointed out that the female clerks at T.U.C. headquarters were earning less than the men. The T.U.C. had the year before rejected the idea of a commission to investigate women's status and opportunities in industry, while Mrs Joyce

Butler's private members Bill for a Sex Discrimination Board had failed in the Commons for 'lack of time'.

The T.U.C. conference was panting for legislation but its naïve confidence was not echoed by more detached analysts of the situation. They could see that equal pay might mean that where women did not have the advantage of being cheaper they might not be employed at all, and women's work might become more and more segregated in the semi-skilled and unskilled categories.[4] The effect of breaking down the distinction in male and female appointments in the advertising of jobs is ultimately to drive discrimination underground, so that women apply for jobs which are not designated according to sex but which they have no chance of getting. The sad fact is that prejudice and discrimination cannot be legislated out of existence. Certainly laws will not bring women with training and constructive interest in their jobs into being. By and large women themselves are not interested in the problem. Their failure to unionize themselves and the failure of unionized women to be active within their unions is partly attributable to the claims of home, claims admitted by the T.U.C. which sought to institute safeguards against women being forced to work overtime and night shifts.

The small influence of women in State leadership is in large measure due to women's own inertia. . . . Not only do women show little desire to win a place in political leadership, but the great majority of them accept the system of justification invented by men to rationalize their standing aside from it. Curiously, they sometimes seem to be more uncompromising than men in this regard, and more anti-feminist.

Maurice Duverger, 'The Political Role of Women', UNESCO,' 1955, p. 126

The women argued that they were ready to accept the same inconveniences that men suffer but the men were unwilling to allow their own claims on the unpaid labour of housewives to be jeopardized.[5] There was even mention of setting up nurseries to be run by management and unions cooperatively at factories. The intrusion of sex and children adds a tinge of frivolity to the arguments: in fact, an employer who faces problems of organizing his employees' children as well as themselves might well be inclined to discriminate more and more, notwithstanding the sobering reflection that the mass rally of women workers organized by the national Joint Action Campaign for Women's Equal Rights on 18 May 1969 attracted no more than a thousand.[6] The activist women are forced in such an eventuality to make up for their rareness by an increase in raucousness invoking the mockery and sabotage of their own sex. The case of gallant Mrs Lillian Bilocca springs to mind: because of her agitation, Hull trawlermen sent out in fishing boats into the freezing gales of the North Sea in winter grew to the status of national martyrs. Her handsome angry face graced every national newspaper, and her vulgar rhetoric supplied rousing copy which eventually forced action on her menfolk's behalf. Nowadays Mrs Bilocca is unemployable, and the crowning insult was delivered on behalf of her sex by Skipper Laurie Oliver, secretary of the Hull Trawler Officers' Guild:

I have been asked by the wives of some of my members to state that the action of Mrs Bilocca has not enhanced the image the public may have of fishermen's wives. Women who have lost men in the three ships have had the least to say about it, which is what we admire. The idea of forming a women's committee to fight battles for the men is, to my mind, completely ludicrous.[7]

Conventions 110 and 111 of the I.L.O. Convention are to

be ratified by the British Government. They relate to
equality of pay and opportunity for women. The Prime
Minister excused this failure on the grounds that the
Government couldn't ratify the convention knowing that it
had failed to fulfil the conditions required by it. In such a
chicken-and-egg situation what can happen? As if that were
not enough in itself to fire indignation, it is unlikely that the
I.L.O. formulation will be accepted, for it stipulates *equal pay
for work of equal value*: our rulers have leapt at the loophole
supplied by the Common Market resolution that women
should be awarded equal pay for *identical* work, which means
that renaming a woman's job can justify unequal pay. One
of the most disheartening aspects of the situation for the
feminist is the reflection that in those unions where women
have won equal pay it has been awarded to them by men. At
the 1969 T.U.C. conference which demanded equal pay
there were only 51 women delegates and more than 1,200
men. Meanwhile, women working in banks have an
incremental scale which stops at £800 p.a., while men's rises
to £1,100: hardly more than one woman in thirty earns even
as much as the average man's wage. Bus conductresses were
lured into the industry by equal pay when staffing became a
problem, but they cannot become drivers, garage managers
or inspectors; when one-man buses come in they will be laid
off or employed at lower wages in the canteens. And yet
three thousand drivers are still needed. As long as Mr
Wilson said that women workers could have equal pay if
higher paid workers footed the bill he had the perfect formula
for involing male paranoia, and women will continue to
labour at home for nothing and in industry for a pittance.
We have yet to see what his decision to grant women equal
pay for equal work by gradual stages will mean in real terms.

In speaking of women in paid employment I am not
speaking of the greatest proportion of British women who are
housewives: sixteen million of them. The housewife is not

> The intention of your being taught needle-work; knitting
> and such-like, is not on account of the intrinsic value of
> all you can do with your hands, which is trifling, but to
> enable you to judge more perfectly of that kind of work,
> and to direct the execution of it in others. Another
> principal end is to enable you to fill up, in some tolerably
> agreeable way, some of the many solitary hours you must
> necessarily spend at home.
>
> Gregory, 'A Father's Legacy to his Daughters', 1809,
> p. 59

paid at all, although Lady Summerskill's Matrimonial
Property Bill of 1964 established her right to keep half the
housekeeping allowance. Such legislation could only benefit
the affluent, for it could not of course constrain husbands to
give an allowance which was double what the family actually
required. The number of wives who actually do earn and
save on their housekeeping allowance must be very small. In
fact all divorce legislation for the protection of abandoned
wives has the same curious character; it applies realistically
only to the affluent, who seem to be by far the minority if the
average wage of men and women in industry is anything to
go by. The less than affluent have no choice but to stay
married for their wives have no financial independence at
all; cohabitation is all that they can afford. The Tory
document 'A Fair Share for the Fair Sex' has hardly any
useful application to the majority of wives, although the
three thousand elegantly hatted delegates to the 41st Annual
Women's Conference of the Conservative Party may have
found it enthralling.[8] Likewise the Family Law (Reform) Bill
applies to a tiny minority, and the actions for Breach of
Promise, Restitution of Conjugal Rights and Enticement
and Seduction which it abolished were already anachronistic
and rare. This effect of the Matrimonial Property Bill, which

> The leisure rendered by the wife...is not a simple
> manifestation of idleness or indolence. It almost
> invariably occurs disguised under some form of work or
> household duties or social amenities, which prove on
> analysis to serve little or no ulterior end beyond showing
> that she does not and need not occupy herself with
> anything that is gainful or of substantial use...the taste
> to which these effects of household adornment and
> tidyness appeal is a taste which has been formed under the
> guidance of a canon of propriety that demands just these
> evidences of wasted effort...
>
> Thorstein Veblen,
> 'The Theory of the Leisure Class',
> 1899, pp. 81–2

enables wives to demand a settlement and restitution of
money invested in the conjugal home or business, was to
make divorce even more the prerogative of the rich. The
Law Commission has been investigating the possibilities of
an abandoned wife claiming damages from the Other
Woman: again in terms of hard fact it is a rare Other
Woman who has the wherewithal to pay damages. Marriage
could be more sordid than ever if such actions became at all
common. Most likely a sued Other Woman would have to
ask her husband to undertake payments for her, which
would be no different to alimony in effect. Just as the nation
cannot afford equal pay for equal work it cannot afford to
redeem women from the financial feudalism of marriage. If a
kind of national insurance for wives against abandonment
were instituted it would be seen by the Sunday papers as a
government sanction for immorality. In any case, despite the
heavy taxation of middle income groups in Britain, such a
scheme is economically unfeasible. Housewives must remain
economic casualties of the whole system, for all
disproportion between the cost of living and real earnings

must be buffered by them while they can expect no independence or freedom of movement to compensate.

More than half the housewives of Great Britain also work outside their homes. Some are professional women, who spend most of their earnings on home help, a car, superannuation and tax; for example, the married headmistress of a fairsized school earns £1,900 p.a., of which she pays £1,010 in tax, a further £110 superannuation, £200 for domestic help, £300 for her car, and £75 for extras like clothing and books, so that her net income is £205. A woman doctor found that her domestic help took home more money than she did. These women are treated very badly by the Inland Revenue officials, who refuse to discuss their husbands' tax returns with them.[9] If the country cannot afford to tax married women as independent individuals, it is also true that the country cannot afford the wastage of professional female labour. The greatest number of female professionals are teachers, and yet only one-third of them are still at work six years after their expensive state-paid training. The women doctors whose husbands cannot afford to subsidize their continued work cannot be spared.

The professional women who stuggle to continue in their vocation after marriage are a tiny minority; most of the working wives of Britain would sneer at their assumption that home help is necessary to their continued contribution to their profession, although obviously a teacher or a doctor cannot afford the ineffiency that fatigue would entail. Lower pay for female industrial workers might even be justified in a perverted sense if we reflect that more than half the female workers are working harder outside their employment than they are in it. For many women, sitting down to a machine, be it a typewriter or a power sewing machine, is a rest after the unremitting employment of all their physical strength and energy in service of a young family. The lunch-hour of a secretary who has to do the shopping and bill-paying for her family is the most strenuous part of her day. In July 1969 working wives marched on Epping Town Hall in protest against the increase of day nursery fees from £2 10s. to £6 or £7, because this meant that many trained nurses and teachers would no longer find it practicable to continue working. The teachers' strike of 1970 revealed that the indispensable function of teachers was baby-sitting for working mothers. Many working wives depend upon the labour of an unpaid relation to get to work at all. Many others pride themselves on the way they manage to run a home and hold their own in a job at the same time, accepting the patronizing title of 'working wonders' in a kind of unofficial Stakhanovism.[10] Some of the experience I have had first-hand of working wives has been dispiriting in the utmost. I once taught in a school where most of the teachers were married and staff-room conversation was strictly limited to the success or failure of their contraceptive methods, the expedients they adopted to keep home and children on an even keel, and their keen desire to give it all up as soon as their husbands were senior enough in their firms to afford idle wives. In another setting, I saw a working wife toiling as P.A. to a television director break down in the middle of taping simply because she was taxed beyond her strength.

The ancillary aspect of women's work is almost universal; in the home she must make her husband's lot easier and build up his confidence as breadwinner, and this is an aspect of the secondariness of female work outside the home which has not been evaluated. It is assumed that wives earn less than their husbands, and pity is evinced for men whose wives are more successful than they are. Even at work women must serve men; one reason why the P.A. broke down was that her boss was demanding and bullying and she was too anxious not to make any mistakes. The most overt kind of handmaidenship is practised by secretaries, part of whose function is to protect their bosses' egos, and even to cover their mistakes. The Alfred Marks secretarial bureau found that 80 per cent of secretaries earning more than £1,000 a year were prepared to run errands, 74 per cent were willing to do the shopping for their bosses and their wives, and 73 per cent were not averse to lying to protect him from trouble with his boss.[11] An answer to this article in the *Sunday Times* included instructions to the girl-in-a-million, the perfect private secretary; in reverse order of importance:

1. Always use a deodorant – you are not the girl in a thousand who doesn't need one.
2. Learn how to make good tea and coffee.
3. Don't give mother/boyfriend/husband/auntie the office phone number.
4. Use the powder room for applying lipstick, eyelashes, varnishing finger nails or changing stockings.
5. Do not put bad news on top of the incoming letters.
6. Always look beautiful but not provocative.[12]

A secretary is a boss's status symbol, like his wife: the more her duties are limited to his requirements the more her value. A switchboard/secretary/receptionist is a utility model: the private secretary is custom-built racing style. A glance at the appointment columns of a daily newspaper will provide an insight into the qualities of a perfect business acolyte: a secretary must be attractive, 'good organizer with calm temperament', lively, intelligent, tactful, 'efficient, well-groomed', bright; the tone of such soliciting may reach unbelievable depths:

No not nit but intelligent, efficient, possibly even pretty secretary for managing director.
I am leaving for Mauritius to join my fiancé. My boss, chairman of a small Mayfair consultancy group, mourns my departure. Do you think you could make the sort of personal secretary he would

appreciate? Company secretary bitterly regrets having allowed his bird to fly high. Please will somebody prove she is not irreplaceable?[13]

In almost every case the age is indicated, and the conflict between desire for an attractive woman and an efficient one sometimes produces interesting results. Nobody however ever wants a mature woman as secretary, for the filial relationship must be kept up. Thirty seems to be about the ceiling. If a private secretary wishes to become indispensable to her boss she must voluntarily increase her humility and servitude.

A good secretary is devoted to the single aim of furthering her boss's interests in every way she can... She is loyal, obedient, conscientious...she supports all his actions, never discusses with him other staff, and always backs him up in her relations with clients...

She must further 'apply subtle flattery' and 'never know better'. Her aim is to become 'a graceful and necessary piece of office furniture'.[14] Why should a woman serve a man so faithfully for a menial's wage and be actually increasing his earning power and cloaking his mistakes? Seeing as she must know his business pretty well, why should she not aspire to his job? Why should instructions not tell her how to flatter her boss's boss, and subtly undermine her boss, so that clients hope fervently that they might have to deal with her and not with him? The answer lies in the freemasonry of men: a girl who revealed the fact that her boss was an incompetent ninny would probably be sooner sacked than he was, and yet, given enormous guile and day-to-day treachery (although no more than is required to support him mendaciously) she might actually get the reward that she deserves. It is tempting to ponder just how many firms are actually run by secretaries. A nationwide strike of secretaries could have interesting results. At the lower levels of secretarial work an interesting phenomenon reveals that female liberation is carving out its own course. On 15 June 1969 Mr Harold Quitman, chairman of the City Affairs Committee, wrote to *The Times* complaining that there was 'an undoubted shortage of trained secretarial staff willing to fill permanent office vacancies' while agencies 'can offer temporary staff at a moment's notice'. Poor Mr Quitman.[15] It stands to reason after all that if a woman can expect no promotion, she has no incentive to immure herself permanently in any one firm. Much better to sample here and there, trying and tantalizing new bosses who have no opportunity to tyrannize over their fly-by-night aides. Priscilla Clemenson described her own system to *Petticoat*.

She works about seven or eight months a year in about twenty or thirty different jobs. She saves and plans during those months, then as soon as she is ready she packs her bags and is off, for Scandinavia if she's sailing, Switzerland if she's skiing. . .

'When I'm on the move, I'm a different person,' she explains. 'I'm so much more interesting and more interested in other people. . .'[16]

The success of agencies in deploying temporary labour can be assessed from the proliferation of them. Any girl bored with her job is assailed by repeated blandishments in the Tube on her way home, persuading her that she can command better money and have time off as well if she would only walk out of her typing pool and dare the harum-scarum world of the temp. In retaliation, prospective employers are forced to wheedle and coax with promise of young staff, pleasant offices, glamorous siting, the opportunity to meet interesting people, as well as a judicious mixture of flattery. Today's anarchistic young women seem to remain unmoved. Mr Quitman and his cronies cannot claim that they have not asked for it, but they will persist in explaining their present difficulties by the flightiness of the young female population, instead of seeing that what they offer is *no deal*. In desperation, employers are said to be turning to married women, whose home commitments will hopefully make them more reliable. At least they won't be rushing off to ski and sail. But they will have their hearts and minds at home. One way or another, women will win this struggle. There are retrograde steps: women in America are reported to be manipulating their menfolk by pussy-power, which is wheedling and caressing, instead of challenging. The covert caresses of secretaries are already squalid enough; the temps seem to have discovered an altogether more impressive and dignified method of bargaining. If a boss wants his temp to stay, he'll just have to find the incentive. One day, nothing short of his job is going to suffice. The effect of the know-how of girls who have experienced different kinds of office organization ought to be exploited by industry, but probably meanness and prejudice, and male incapacity to take criticism, will ensure that this never happens. Unfortunately the opportunities enjoyed by the London stenographer do not extend to provincial centres, where secretarial staff are immobilized and poorly paid, and live 'at home'.

The most depressing phenomenon in the pattern of women's work is the plight of the nurses. Nursing began when Florence Nightingale deployed the idle daughters of the Victorian middle class in a work of mercy which kept their hands from mischief, in the way that rich women still work for the Red Cross and Oxfam and what have you. The failure of this industry to evolve means that, today, 640,000 women are working for a travesty of a living wage, doing a vital work which requires skill, initiative and 'dedication'. Nursing and teaching have long been the most popular female professions, indeed, one might almost say the only female professions, but while the applicants for teacher training have more than doubled in ten years, trainee nursing has only attracted a further six thousand, an increase of a quarter. Meanwhile patient throughput has doubled in twenty years, and the cases retained in hospital are graver, seeing as the policy of home nursing is gaining hold. A trainee nurse earns £390 in her first year (£240 after deductions), a second year nurse £450, a third year nurse £480. Psychiatric nurses earn £100 more in each year. When nurses received a rise of thirty pounds a year, hospital residence fees were immediately increased so that the rise was instantly nullified. Ward Sister Elsa Farrier put the case to *The Times* in May, after the Orpington Hospital nurses had held a public meeting to warn the community they served that they could not continue in this way: 'We are not talking to patients as we should. We haven't the time to talk to relatives when they are worried. We have little time to be humane or kind.'[17]

The much vaunted emotional satisfactions of nursing have fallen foul of cuts in staffing. Nurses find that they have to do unskilled jobs like floorscrubbing, because even domestic staff will not consent to be bullied the way they, the professionals, allow themselves to be. Meanwhile, sophisticated methods of treatment require better educational preparation from nurses: the dangers of drug prophylaxis mean that a tired nurse can find herself a murderess. In fact, only one out of three nurses has more than three O levels, the same proportion have less than two, which is considered the lowest admissible level, because they have passed the General Nursing Council Test. One-third of trainee nurses drop out during their training, and the impression is that the wastage is not regretted because they form a valuable supply of cheap labour. When a nurse does complete her training there is no appreciable change in her condition: she wears a different colour belt and carries on. Nurses are, moreover, cloistered and disciplined in archaic uniforms on duty, and by prying and prurient regulations off duty. They tolerate the most arrantly maternal behaviour from matrons, who often treat them without respect and demand absolute obedience. The excuse for all this is the patient, but it is the patient who suffers at the hands of tired, resentful, and harried nurses. All the ludicrousness of the situation burst upon the British public in May 1969, when Sister Veal's United Nurses Association took to the streets, but even then Matron's iron hand was shown when nurses were ordered not to march in their uniforms, and they *obeyed*. Sister Veal has since been reviled in the gutter press for being a private nurse and advertising for patients, but she is doing no more than any one with skill and initiative is entitled to do. In fact Sister Veal can command only three hundred supporters: the usual argument, that she is damaging the public image of the profession, seems to dissuade most nurses from agitating. Trained nurses do not constitute a cohesive group: as a profession they are divided into health visitors, theatre sisters, psychiatric nurses, ward sisters, district nurses, matrons, state enrolled nurses. Not all of them belong to the Royal College of Nursing. On the Whitley Council, which negotiates pay and conditions, twelve separate organizations represent nurses; while in May 1969 the Whitley Council was awarding nurses £48 p.a. for their meals, in place of the iniquitous pay-as-you-eat scheme (it was immediately taxed), a mere twelve hundred hospital electricians did not scruple to strike for an extra shilling an hour, to bring them into line with outside labour. The point is clear. That nurses can be victimized by the essentialness of their work into accepting a shameful remuneration is an indictment of our society which is daring them to abandon the sick and dying, knowing that they will not do it. Must they wait until the sick and dying strike for them? It seems that the plight of academics will wait for attention until students support them in a strike and refuse to be qualified.

Perhaps patients ought to refuse to recover? In each case the state exploits the recipients of nurses' and teachers' services in order to oppress the nurses and teachers. New strategies must be devised. The recently awarded increase of twenty-six per cent sounds handsome until we consider what it is twenty-six per cent of: we have yet to see how the nurses will be forced to pay for their rise.

Nurses are skilled menials, and as such they fall into line with the dominant pattern of female employment. Salesgirls or 'vendeuses', waitresses, cleaners, packers, tea ladies, fill out the picture. The job of char is so tied to the female image that an amusing case was recorded in Vienna where one Alois Valkan, who needed to work for money to supplement his pension had to disguise himself as a woman to find work as a char. Eventually he was arrested when he went to a ladies' lavatory when he wasn't disguised and was questioned by police called to investigate thefts from the cloakroom.[18] Even in the trades dominated by women, the important posts are held by men; whoever heard of a head waitress or a *maîtresse d'hôtel?* Cutters and designers in the clothing industry are most often male. The women's branches of the armed forces are not soldiers in their own right, but clerical assistants and other kinds of handmaidens to the males. Even air hostesses, among the most envied of female employees, are no more than glorified waitresses, and often presided over by a steward. The most shocking cases of the exploitation of females for cheap labour are the *outworkers,* who were the subject of a *News of the World* scandal. Ostensibly such women must be registered with local authorities, but in practice the *News of the World* found this regulation was not observed, as the Prices and Incomes Board discovered when it conducted a survey. Of the sixty unions who covered industries likely to employ outworkers, only one had any regulations relating to them. Superfoam Ltd of Skegness farmed out aprons to be machined at 5d.

each. Brock's fireworks paid housewives one shilling a gross
for rolling and gluing cardboard cases. Women who made
sponge bags at 11s. a gross had the satisfaction of seeing them
retail in shops for 2s. 6d. each. To make the point clearer,
Conway Stewart farmed out ballpoint pens which had to be
assembled by putting in the refill, screwing a cap on, fitting
the clip cap at the other end and packing in packets of six, for
8d. or 9d. (depending on the pen) a gross, to spastic centres,
mental homes, prisons, detention centres and approved
schools, as well as housewives. Mrs Pollard who can
assemble a gross of plastic boats in five hours for eight
shillings, answered the *News of the World* reporter innocently:
'I regard it as a hobby to fill in my spare time...I like doing
it.' The women doing this work, who are also skilled in
machining in many cases, do not cost their employers anything
in lighting, heating or safety precautions, and can demand no
indemnifications or overtime, and their number is unknown.
In the clothing trade alone, it is believed that at least fifteen
thousand women are so employed. The manufacturers justify
their methods by pointing to competition from Japan and
Hongkong: an outworker is an Anglo-Saxon coolie.[19]

Girls who seek an alternative to ancillarism in a vocation
often dream of acting as a way out. Most of the few women
who shaped our century were actresses, if the *Sunday Times* is
to be believed. Michael Croft, director of the National
Youth Theatre, warned girls not to seek this alternative. In
new plays, he remarked, there are only two female parts to
every five male parts. In the profession as a whole there is
always four-fifths unemployment, and most of the
unemployed are women. And yet, of 4,150 applicants for the
Youth Theatre, which had only 200 places to offer, two-
thirds were girls.[20] For girls who want to exploit their
beauty, modelling may seem to offer another way out, but
even after training and deportment and the use of cosmetics
the aspiring model must get together a composite of good

photographs, and hawk it around the agencies.[21] The most successful models have been taken up by photographers, a profession dominated by men with a few remarkable exceptions. A model in work will find that she is paid months after she has done the work, no matter how diligently her agency works to collect the money for her; most often she will find that she is not in work, and must resort to more ignoble expedients to make ends meet. Nude modelling for girlie mags pays very well, but the indignities are almost insupportable. Bob Guccione of *Penthouse* boasts that his girls are put on the pill so that their breasts and buttocks swell, sent to Tangier to suntan, have their teeth capped, have moles removed, are clothed, coifed and manicured at the expense of the magazine, and then paid £200 a day for a week while they are photographed.[22] They are persuaded to pose by a mixture of flattery and gin. Ideally, film offers and further modelling ensue; if not, there you are, moleless, straight toothed, suntanned, and swelling, with a thousand pounds to lose through heavy taxation and further investment in the image.

Female entertainers are unionized, whether they be dancers, singers, or strippers,[23] but it is a long row to hoe, and no amount of unionization can guarantee work or regular recurrence thereof. Girls being appraised by prospective employers in these 'professions' have horrifying tales to tell, most of which are apocryphal, but I can remember humiliations myself which I had rather not undergo. When I went recently to present myself to the producer of a well-known TV series at his request, or so I supposed, he sneaked in a wet kiss and a clutch at my breasts in an exercise of his power, a privilege which he could not have extracted from any of the men who have appeared on the same programme. I have since instructed my agent to turn down any offer of work from him, but most girls would not be in a position to do that. Nevertheless, a gamble is probably better for the soul than ignominious servitude: a girl who thinks she has real talent for entertaining has really no option but to try it. Most of them eventually acquire a husband at their backs to keep them when they are 'resting.' The entertainment business has always been cheek-by-jowl with prostitution from the days when leading ladies of Drury Lane and the Comédie Française were also the leading courtesans. Many a prostitute, whether she calls herself a call-girl, a hostess, or a common whore, imagines that she is exploiting the male sex, and perhaps she is as long as she can retain her emotional independence, but the role of the ponce, the impresario of whoring, is too established for us to suppose that prostitutes have found a self-regulating lifestyle. The master ponce of Western Soceity is Hugh Hefner, who invented brothels where the whores are only to be looked at, which are brothels just the same. Every Bunny is a B-girl. As an alternative to nursing or outworking, waitressing in rabbit ears and a scut is not conspicuously preferable. The female entertainer is so often exploiting her attractiveness as a sexual object that her situation is a parallel to these. In seeking protection from sexual exploitation she may often find herself more tyrannized over by a minder than she ever would have been by a boss. She may be more than ever a valuable property for someone else, so that even her genuine talent may be obscured in the bally-hoo of the sexual object. It still comes as a surprise to most people to learn that Marilyn Monroe was a great actress, most pitifully to Marilyn herself, which is one of the reasons why she is dead.

There are, there must be, alternatives to such exploitation. As an academic, I daresay I have found one. I do receive equal pay; I was appointed in preference to male competition and nothing can prevent me from being promoted in the natural course of events. Guiltily I must also admit that I did not toil particularly hard to attain what academic distinction I have. As a female lecturer at a provincial university I have to tolerate the antics of faculty wives, but they are fairly easy to ignore. Probably I had to attain more striking academic distinctions than a man would have had to be awarded my present appointment but I cannot prove this. Perhaps if I had been a man I would have been offered a fellowship at Cambridge. The odds against the average pubescent girl pursuing her education are long, however, because of the loss of enterprise and energy which accompanies female puberty. The prejudice that academic women are neurotic is justified in actual experience if not in theory, but if a girl feels that she can make it there is no reason why she shouldn't. Teaching in other institutions is still the avocation favoured by intelligent girls, but it is, as teachers will be quick to tell although they are slow to take action about it, a difficult and unrewarding life. Men following this woman-dominated profession found conditions and salaries intolerable and the predominantly female membership of the National Union of Teachers so inert and apathetic that they founded the National Association of Schoolmasters in order to take militant action to improve their situation. The N.U.T. finally followed their lead and rejected the parity swindle, initiating a series of strikes in the winter of 1969–70. Needless to say, all the spokesmen for the union were male – of forty-four members on the executive only four were women.

A girl who studies medicine will qualify if she works hard enough – but it is true that women patients prefer male doctors and so do men. A girl may qualify as an architect or an engineer and if she can get employers to regard her seriously she may do well. Evidence is that women who learn a trade like electrical engineering or radio operating can find no employment.[24] Female chemists and scientists can win the Nobel Prize, if they are researchers, but they are unlikely to become heads of professional research establishments. In chasing all these asexual academic attainments a girl faces one relentless enemy – her family. The constant recriminations, the lamentations that she is missing out on what makes being a girl such fun, on dating and pretty clothes, that she will waste her training by getting married and so forth, the whole tiresome rigmarole, wears down her resistance from day to day. The pressure of home duties which are spared a boy in her situation is not relieved, unless she goes away to study at a distant university, an expedient which may meet with parental disapproval. A girl's emotional welfare is so much a matter of the demeanour of men towards her that she may jeopardize her academic chances by emotional involvement. I can testify to the wasteful effects of emotional involvement on studying women from personal experience as a tutor in universities. Men may take their pleasures how and where they will or not at all: girls feel rejected without male attention, and degraded by anything less than total involvement, and as long as this is the case they are highly likely to be academic casualties. Girls are seldom brilliant, and men sneak the top honours in the depressing majority of cases, while a girl who wants to enjoy equal opportunity with men in professional matters must not equal them but positively outstrip them because of the initial prejudice against her. If she feels that she must also retain her sexual identity by being feminine the conflict of desires can have radical effects.

There are success stories about women, and it is time, after such a depressing picture, to tell them. Asha Radnoti graduated with honours in Politics, Philosophy and Economics from Oxford, and was offered the usual female employment, teaching, by the Oxford appointments board. She turned down teaching, and jobs at I.B.M. and other management consultants, for a position as analyst in the investment research department of the Prudential. After eighteen months there she went to work for a Canadian investment banking firm as assistant to the investment director, and is now Portfolio manager for the Castle Britannia Unit Trust Group, with day-to-day responsibility for the investment of more than four million pounds. Miss Ishbel Webster spent twelve years working as a depilator in the Tao Clinic before she patented her own formula for an aerosol depilator called Spray Away. Jennifer Phillips sold her own comedy series *Wink to me Only*. Turi Wideroe is the first woman pilot to be employed by a commercial airline. Mrs Nora Rotheroe began as a housemaid in Camden Town, talked her way into a job as a mobile supervisor finding cleaning work and estimating costs for her firm, to the position of a director of Acme, Britain's largest firm of industrial cleaners, and finally chairman of Multi-Office Services Ltd. Mrs Margot Newlands is first woman director of Thomas de la Rue International. Mrs Margery Hurst is a millionairess and joint chairman of Britain's biggest secretarial agency, the Brook Street Bureau. Verite Collins invented her own firm of demonstrators and saleswomen for British goods overseas, the Union Jills, and became a company director of the agencies and firms that arrange such trade exhibitions. The clothing industry boasts many canny and creative women, like Mary Quant, Dorothy Tyoran, Sybil Zelker, Gina Fatini, Rosalind Yehuda, Marion Foale and Sally Tuffin, Fiona Browne (Spectrum), Janet Lyle (Annacat), Alice Pollock, Lee Bender, and the redoubtable Biba. Another field in which women have considerable success is journalism and writing generally; the number of female journalists and novelists who have achieved distinction in our age is too great and they are too well-known to need listing here. In television, women have been well-represented, although the present tendency is towards male replacements for Grace Wyndham Goldie, BBC TV Current affairs chief, Catherine Dove (Producer of Panorama), and Mary Somerville (Head of Schools Broadcasting). Female news readers have been supplanted by men, and even female producers have failed to proceed up the management ladder, but Yvonne Littlewood still produces light entertainment, Paddy Foy music, Margaret Douglas current affairs and Maggie Dale ballet. After Dame Ninette de Valois at Sadler's Wells, female producers have open opportunity, and Joan Littlewood is one of the most influential theatrical personalities of our age. Lloyd's have forty applications on their books after declaring women eligible for entry in February this year, and the Stock Exchange continues to debate the admission of women to the floor, while Miss Muriel Burley, a candidate since 1962, awaits the decision that will enable her to be a partner or begin her own brokerage firm. The first woman judge has been appointed. [25]

It seems that woman has more likelihood of success the higher she pitches her sights, and the more uncommon she is in her chosen environment. The highest value is placed by this society upon creativity, either in designing goods for large-scale consumption, or writing advertising copy or novels, or inventing forms of organization geared to current demand. British trade depends upon the export of ideas and expertise and men have no monopoly of either. Neither is incompatible with femininity for even Mary Quant has had her pubic hair shaved into a heart-shape by her adoring husband, if that is what you fancy. One of my favourite stories of female success is that of Mrs Pamela Porter, who owns her own car transporter and drives 1,500 miles a week with three spaniels in the cab for company. The onus is on women, who must not only equal men in the race for employment, but outstrip them. Such as incentive must ultimately be an advantage.

Love

The Ideal

If the God who is said to be love exists in the imagination of men it is because they have created Him. Certainly they have had a vision of a love that was divine although it would be impossible to point out a paradigm in actuality. The proposition has been repeated like a mantra in hate-filled situations, because it seemed a law of life. 'God is love.' Without love there could have been no world. If all were Thanatos and no Eros, nothing could have come into being. Desire is the cause of all movement, and movement is the character of all being. The universe is a process and its method is change. Whether we call it a Heraclitean dance or the music or the spheres of the unending galliard of protons and neutrons we share an idea in all cultures of a creative movement to and from, moved by desire, repressed by death and the second law of thermodynamics. Various methods of formulation approximate knowledge of it at any time because the laws which seek to control and formalize such dynamics for the reasoning mind must be reformulated endlessly. Energy, creation, movement and harmony, development, all happen under the aegis of love, in the domain of Eros. Thanatos trudges behind, setting the house in order, drawing boundaries and contriving to rule. Human beings love despite their compulsions to limit it and exploit it, chaotically. Their love persuades them to make vows, build houses and turn their passion ultimately to duty.

When mystics say that God is love, or when Aleister Crowley says 'Love is the law', they are not referring to the love that is woman's destiny. Indeed, many Platonists believed that women were not capable of love at all, because they were men's inferiors physically, socially, intellectually and even in terms of physical beauty. Love is not possible between inferior and superior, because the base cannot free their love from selfish interest, either as the desire for security, or social advantage, and, being lesser, they themselves cannot comprehend the faculties in the superior which are worthy of love. The superior being on the other hand cannot demean himself by love for an inferior; his feeling must be tinged with condescension or else partake of perversion and a deliberate self-abasement. The proper subject for love is one's equal, seeing as the essence of love is to be mutual, and the lesser cannot produce anything greater than itself. Seeing the image of himself, man recognizes it and loves it, out of fitting and justifiable *amour propre*; such a love is based upon understanding, trust, and commonalty. It is the love that forms communities, from the smallest groups to the highest.[1] It is the only foundation for viable social structures, because it is the manifestation of common good. Society is founded on love, but the state is not because the state is a collection of minorities with different, even irreconcilable common goods. Like a father controlling siblings of different ages and sexes, the state must bring harmony among the warring groups, not through love, but external discipline. What man feels for the very different from himself is fascination and interest, which fade when the novelty fades, and the incompatibility makes its presence felt. Feminine women chained to men in our society are in this situation. They are formed to be artificially different and fascinating to men and end by being merely different, isolated in the house of a bored and antagonistic being.

From the earliest moments of life, human love is a function of narcissism. The infant who perceives his own self and the external world as the same thing loves everything until he learns to fear harm.[2] So if you pitch him into the sea he will swim, as he floated in his mother's womb before it grew too confining. The baby accepts reality, because he has no ego.

> The Angel that presided o'er my birth
> Said 'Little creature, form'd of joy and mirth,
> Go love without the help of anything on Earth.'[3]

Even when his ego is forming he must learn to understand himself in terms of his relationships to other people and other people in terms of himself. The more his self-esteem is eroded, the lower the opinion that he has of his fellows; the more inflated his self-esteem the more he expects of his friends. This interaction has always been understood, but not always given its proper importance. When Adam saw Eve in the Garden of Eden he loved her because she was of himself, bone of his bone, and more like him than any of the other animals created for his delectation. His movement of desire towards her was an act of love for his own kind. This kind of diffuse narcissism has always been accepted as a basis for love, except in the male–female relationship where it has been assumed that man is inflamed by what is different in women, and therefore the differences have been magnified until men have more in common with other men of different races, creeds and colours than they have with the women of their own environment. The principle of the brotherhood of man is that narcissistic one, for the grounds for that love have always been the assumption that we ought to realize that we are the same the whole world over.

The brotherhood of man will only become a reality when the consciousness of alien beings corrects man's myopias, and he realizes that he has more in common with Eskimoes and Bengali beggars and black faggots than he has with the form of intelligent life on Solar system X. Nevertheless, we are discouraged from giving the name of love to relationships between people of common interests, like footballers and musicians, especially if they are of the same sex. In denying such a description we ignore the testimony of bodies and behaviour. If Denis Law hugs Nobby Stiles on the pitch we tolerate it because it is *not* love. If Kenny Burell blows a kiss to Albert King on stage we congratulate ourselves on knowing how to take it. The housewife whose husband goes to the local every night does not tell herself that he loves his friends more than he loves her, although she resents it despite herself as an infidelity.

The arguments about the compatibility of marriageable people stem from a working understanding of the principle of parity in love, but it is very rarely seen that compatible interests at the level of hobbies and books and cinema do not make up for the enormous gulf which is kept open between the sexes in all other fields. We might note with horror those counsels which advise girls to take up their boyfriends' hobbies in order to seduce them by a feigned interest in something they like. In any event, the man's real love remains centred in his male peers, although his sex may be his woman's prerogative. Male bonding can be explained by this simple principle of harmony between *similes inter pares,* that is, love. On the other hand, female castration results in concentration of her feelings upon her male companion, and her impotence in confrontations with her own kind. Because all her love is guided by the search for security, if not for her offspring then for her crippled and fearful self, she cannot expect to find it in her own kind, whom she knows to be weak and unsuitable. Women cannot love because, owing to a defect in narcissism, they do not rejoice in seeing their own kind. In fact the operation of female insecurity in undermining natural and proper narcissism is best summed up by their use of make-up and disguise, ruses of which women are infallibly aware. Those women who boast most fulsomely of their love for their own sex (apart from lesbians, who must invent their own ideal of love) usually have curious relations with it, intimate to the most extraordinary degree but disloyal, unreliable and tension-ridden, however close and long-standing they may be.

We can say the brotherhood of man, and pretend that we include the sisterhood of women, but we know that we don't. Folklore has it that women only congregate to bitch an absent member of their group, and continue to do so because they are too well aware of the consequences if they stay away. It's meant to be a joke, but like jokes about mothers-in-law it is founded in bitter truth. Women don't nip down to the local: they don't invent, as men do, pretexts like coin-collecting or old-schoolism or half-hearted sporting activities so that they can be together; on ladies' nights they watch frozen-faced while their men embrace and fool about commenting to each other that they are all overgrown boys. Of the love of fellows they know nothing. They cannot love each other in this easy, innocent, spontaneous way because they cannot love themselves. What we actually see, sitting at the tables by the wall, is a collection of masked menials, dressed up to avoid scrutiny in the trappings of the status symbol, aprons off, scent on, feigning leisure and relaxation where they feel only fatigue. All that can happen to make the evening for one of them is that she might disrupt the love-affair around her by making her husband lavish attention on her or seeing that somebody else does. Supposing the men do not abandon their women to their own society the conversation is still between man and man with a feminine descent. The jokes are the men's jokes; the activity and the anecdotes about it belong to the men. If the sex that has been extracted from the homosexual relationship were not exclusively concentrated on her, a woman would consider that she had cause for complaint. Nobody complains that she has sex without love and he has love without sex. It is right that way, appalling any other way.

Hope is not the only thing that springs eternal in the human breast. Love makes its appearance there unbidden from time to time. Feelings of spontaneous benevolence towards one's own kind still transfigure us now and then —not in relationships with the stakes of security and flattery involved, but in odd incidents of confidence and cooperation in situations where duty and compulsion are not considerations. This extraordinary case of free love appeared in the correspondence of the *People*:

Eighteen years ago my husband and I moved into our first house. Two weeks later our neighbours arrived next door. We thought they were rather standoffish, and they, in return, were not too keen on us.

But over the years we have blessed the day they came to live next door. We have shared happy times. They were godparents to our daughter. And when trouble was at its worst they were always at hand with help.

Now they have paid us the biggest compliment ever. My husband recently changed his job and we had to move 200 miles. The parting was just too much. Rather than say goodbye, my neighbour's husband has changed his job, and they have moved with us.

Although we are not neighbours, we are only five minutes away from each other. This is a friendship that really has stood the test of time.[4]

This remarkable situation is rare indeed, for it is the tendency of family relationships to work against this kind of extra-familial affection. Every time a man unburdens his heart to a stranger he reaffirms the love that unites humanity. To be sure, he is unpacking his heart with words but at the same time he is encouraged to expect interest and sympathy, and he usually gets it. His interlocutor feels unable to impose his own standards on his confidant's behaviour; for once he feels how another man feels. It is not always sorrow and squalor that is passed on in this way but sometimes joy and pride. I remember a truck driver telling me once about his wife, how sexy and clever and loving she was, and how beautiful. He showed me a photograph of her and I blushed for guilt because I had expected something plastic and I saw a woman by trendy standards plain, fat and ill-clad. Half the point in reading novels and seeing plays and films is to exercise the faculty of sympathy with our own kind, so often obliterated in the multifarious controls and compulsions of actual social existence. For once we are not contemptuous of Camille or jealous of Juliet we might even understand the regicide or the motherfucker. That is love.

The love of fellows is based upon understanding and therefore upon communication. It was love that taught us to speak, and death that laid its fingers on our lips. All literature, however vituperative, is an act of love, and all forms of electronic communication attest the possibility of understanding. Their actual power in girdling the global village has not been properly understood yet. Beyond the arguments of statisticians and politicians and other professional cynics and death makers, the eyes of a Biafran child have an unmistakable message. But while electronic media feed our love for our own kind, the circumstances of our lives substitute propinquity for passion.

If we could present an attainable ideal of love it would resemble the relationship described by Maslow as existing between self-realizing personalities. It is probably a fairly perilous equilibrium: certainly the forces of order and civilization react fairly directly to limit the possibilities of self-realization. Maslow describes his ideal personalities as having a better perception of reality – what Herbert Read called an innocent eye, like the eye of the child who does not seek to reject reality. Their relationship to the world of phenomena is not governed by their personal necessity to exploit it or be exploited by it, but a desire to observe it and to understand it. They have no disgust; the unknown does not frighten them. They are without defensiveness or affectation. The only causes of regret are laziness, outbursts of temper, hurting others, prejudice, jealousy and envy. Their behaviour is spontaneous but it corresponds to an autonomous moral code. Their thinking is problem-centred, not ego-centred, and therefore they most often have a sense of commitment to a cause beyond their daily concerns. Their responses are geared to the present and not to nostalgia or anticipation. Although they do not serve a religion out of guilt or fear or any other sort of compulsion, the religious experience, in Freud's term, the *oceanic feeling*, is easier for them to attain than for the conventionally religious. The essential factor in self-realization is independence,

> His word pronounced 'selfishness' blessed, the wholesome healthy selfishness that wells from a powerful soul – from a powerful soul to which belongs the high body, beautiful, triumphant, refreshing, around which everything becomes a mirror – the supple, persuasive body, the dancer whose parable and epitome is the self-enjoying soul.
>
> Nietzsche, 'Thus spoke Zarathustra'

resistance to enculturation; the danger inherent in this is that of excessive independence or downright eccentricity; nevertheless, such people are more capable of giving love, if what Rogers said of love is to be believed, that 'we can love a person only to the extent we are not threatened by him.' Our self-realizing person might claim to be capable of loving everybody because he cannot be threatened by anybody. Of course circumstances will limit the possibility of his loving everybody, but it would certainly be a fluke if such a character were to remain completely monogamous. For those people who wanted to be dominated or exploited or to establish any other sort of compulsive symbiosis, he would be an unsatisfactory mate; as there are many fewer self-realizing personalities than there are other kinds, the self-realizer is usually ill-mated. Maslow has a rather un-looked for comment on the sexual behaviour of the self-realizer:

Another characteristic I found of love in healthy people is that they have made no really sharp differentiation between the roles and personalities of the two sexes. That is, they did not assume that the female was passive and the male active, whether in sex or love or anything else. These people were so certain of their maleness or femaleness they did not mind taking on some of the aspects of the opposite sex role. It was especially noteworthy that they could be both passive and active lovers . . . an instance of the way in which common dichotomies are so often resolved in self-actualization, appearing to be valid dichotomies only because people are not healthy enough.[5]

What Maslow expresses may be little more than a prejudice in favour of a certain kind of personality structure, merely another way of compromising between Eros and civilization, nevertheless we are all involved in some such operative compromise. At least Maslow's terms indicate a direction in which we could travel and not merely a theoretical account of what personality might be like if psychoanalysis accomplished the aim which it has so far not even clearly declared itself or justified to the waiting world, 'to return our souls to our bodies, to return ourselves to ourselves, and thus to overcome the human state of self-alienation'.[6]

It is surprising but nevertheless it is true that Maslow included some women in his sample of self-realizing personalities. But after all it is foreseeable, even if my arguments about the enculturation of women are correct. In some ways the operation of the feminine stereotype is so obvious and for many women entirely unattainable, that it can be easily reacted against. It takes a great deal of courage and independence to decide to design your own image instead of the one that society rewards, but it gets easier as you go along. Of course, a woman who decides to go her own way will find that her conditioning is ineradicable, but at least she can recognize its operation and choose to counteract it, whereas a man might find that he was being more subtly deluded. A woman who decided to become a lover without conditions might discover that her relationships broke up relatively easily because of her degree of resistance to efforts to 'tame' her, and the opinion of her friends will usually be on the side of the man who was prepared to do the decent thing, who was in love with her, etcetera. Her promiscuity, resulting from her constant sexual desire, tenderness and interest in people, will not usually be differentiated from compulsive promiscuity or inability to say no, although it is fundamentally different. Her love may often be devalued by the people for whom she feels most tenderness, and her self-esteem might have much direct attack. Such pressures can never be utterly without effect. Even if a woman does not inhibit her behaviour because of them, she will find herself reacting in some other way, being outrageous when she only meant to be spontaneous, and so forth. She may limit herself to writing defences of promiscuity, or even books about women. (Hm.)

For love's sake women must reject the roles that are offered to them in our society. As impotent, insecure, inferior beings they can never love in a generous way. The ideal of Platonic love, of Eros as a stablizing, creative, harmonizing force in the universe, was most fully expressed in English in Shakespeare's abstract poem, 'The Phoenix and the Turtle', who

> Loved, as love in twain
> Had the essence but in one
> Two distincts, division none:
> Number there in love was slain.

> Hearts remote, yet not asunder;
> Distance and no space was seen
> 'Twixt the turtle and his queen:
> But in them it were a wonder.

The poem is not a plea for suttee, although it describes the mutual obsequies of the phoenix and the turtle. It states and celebrates the concept of harmony, of fusion, melting together, neither sacrificed nor obliterated, that non-destructive knowledge which Whitehead learned to value from the writings of Lao-Tse.

> Property was thus appall'd
> That the self was not the same;
> Single nature's double name
> Neither two nor one was called.
>
> Reason in itself confounded,
> Saw division grow together;
> To themselves get either neither
> Simple were so well compounded.[7]

The love of peers is the spirit of commonalty, the unity of beauty and truth. The phoenix and the turtle do not necessarily cohabit, for they are the principle of sympathy which is not dependent upon familiarity. The phoenix renews itself constantly in its own ashes, as a figure of protean existence. The love of the phoenix and the turtle is not the lifelong coherence of a mutually bound couple, but the principle of love that is reaffirmed in the relationship of the narcissistic self to the world of which it is a part. It is not the fantasy of annihilation of the self in another's identity by sexual domination, for it is a spiritual state of comprehension.

Spirituality, by which I mean the purity of a strong and noble nature, with all the new and untried powers that must grow out of it – has not yet appeared on our horizon; and its absence is a natural consequence of a diversity of interests between man and woman, who are for the most part brought together through the attraction of passion; and who, but for that, would be as far asunder as the poles.[8]

In fact, men and women love differently, and much of the behaviour that we describe by the term is so far from benevolence, and so anti-social, that it must be understood to be inimical to the essential nature of love. Our life-style contains more *thanatos* than *eros,* for egotism, exploitation, deception, obsession and addiction have more place in us than eroticism, joy, generosity and spontaneity.

Altruism

'Love seeketh not Itself to please,
Nor for itself hath any care,
But for another gives its ease,
And builds a Heaven In Hell's despair.'

So Sung a little Clod of Clay,
Trodden with the cattle's feet...[1]

I have talked of love as an assertion of confidence in the self,
an extension of narcissism to include one's own kind,
variously considered. And yet we are told, 'Greater love hath
no man than he lay down his life for his friend.' At our
school we were encouraged to deny ourselves in order to give
to others. We ate no sweets and put our pennies in a red and
yellow box with a piccaninny on the front for the missions, if
we were holy that is. That understanding of love was that it
was the negation by abnegation of the self, the forgetfullness
of the self in humility, platience, and self-denial. The
essential egotism of the practice was apparent to many of us
in the demeanour of the most pious girls, for the aim of the
exercise was ultimately to earn grace in the eyes of the Lord.
Every such act had to be offered up, or else the heavenly
deposit was not made to our account. And yet it was a
seductive notion. It picked up on our masochistic tendencies
and linked with fantasies of annihilation. This is the love, we
were told, of the mother who flings her body across her
child's when danger threatens, of the mother duck who
decoys the hunters from her nest. Noble, instinctive and
feminine. All our mothers had it, for otherwise they would

177

not have dared pain and illness to bring us into the world. Nobody could tell the greatness of a mother's sacrifices for her children, especially for us who were not even getting free education. Every mother was a saint. The Commandment was of course to love thy neighbour as thyself, but the nuns were fired by the prospect of loving their neighbours more than themselves.

The ideal of altruism is possibly a high one, but it is unfortunately chimeric. We cannot be liberated from ourselves, and we cannot act in defiance of our own motivations, unless we are mother ducks and act as instinctive creatures, servants of the species. We, the children who were on the receiving end, knew that our mothers' self-sacrifice existed mostly in their minds. We were constantly exhorted to be grateful for the gift of life. Next to the redemption, for which we could never hope to be sufficiently grateful, although we had no very clear idea of why we needed anyone to die for us in the first place, we had to be grateful for the gift of life. The nuns pointed out that the Commandment to love our parents followed immediately upon the Commandments about loving God, and because they themselves were *in loco parentis* and living solely for God and their neighbour we ought to be grateful for that too. But children are pragmatic. We could see that our mothers blackmailed us with self-sacrifice, even if we did not know whether or not they might have been great opera stars or the toasts of the town if they had not borne us. In our intractable moments we pointed out that we had not asked to be born, or even to go to an expensive school. We knew that they must have had motives of their own for what they did with and to us. The notion of our parents' self-sacrifice filled us not with gratitude, but with confusion and guilt. We wanted them to be happy yet they were sad and deprived, and it was our fault. The cry of Portnoy's mother is the cry of every mother, unless she abandons the role of martyr absolutely.

When we were scolded and beaten for making our mothers worry, we tried to point out that we did not ask them to concern themselves so minutely with our doings. When our school reports brought reproach and recrimination, we knew whose satisfaction the sacrifice was meant to entail. Was there no opportunity for us to be on the credit side in emotional transactions? As far as the nuns were concerned we were fairly sure that in giving up the world to devote their lives to God and to us they had not given up anything that they had passionately wanted, especially not for us whom they did not know.

But while boy-children might remain relatively detached and cynical about their parents' motivation little girls eventually recapitulate. Their concepts of themselves are so confused, and their cultivated dependency so powerful, that they begin to practise self-sacrifice quite early on. They are still expiating their primal guilt for being born when they bravely give up all other interests and concentrate on making their men happy. Somehow the perception of the real motivation for self-sacrifice exists alongside its official ideology. The public relations experts seek to attract girls to nursing by calling it the most rewarding job in the world, and yet it is the hardest and the worst paid. The satisfaction comes in the sensation of doing good. Not only will nurses feel good because they are relieving pain, but also because they are taking little reward for it; therefore they are permanent emotional creditors. Any patient in a public hospital can tell you what this exploitation of feminine masochism means in real terms. Anybody who has tossed all night in pain rather than ring the overworked and reproachful night nurse can tell you.

In sexual relationships, this confusion of altruism with love perverts the majority. Self-sacrifice is the leit-motif of most of the marital games played by women from the crudest ('I've given you the best years of my life') to the most sophisticated ('I only went to bed with him so's he'd promote you'). For so much sacrificed self the expected reward is security, and seeing that a reward is expected it cannot properly speaking be called self-sacrifice at all. It is in fact a kind of commerce, and one in which the female must always be the creditor. Of course, it is also practised by men who explain their failure to do exciting jobs or risk insecurity because of their obligations to wife and/or children, but it is not invariable, whereas it is hard to think of a male/female relationship in which the element of female self-sacrifice was absent. So long as women must live vicariously, through men, they must labour at making themselves indispensable and this is the full-time job that is generally wrongly called altruism. Properly speaking, altriusm is an absurdity. Women are self-sacrificing in direct proportion to their incapacity to offer anything but this sacrifice. They sacrifice what they never had: a self. They cry of the deserted woman, 'What have I done to deserve this?' reveals at once the false emotional economy that she has been following. For most men it is only in quarrels that they discover just how hypocritically and unwillingly their women have capitulated to them. Obviously, spurious altruism is not the monopoly of women, but as long as women need men to live by, and men may take wives or not, and live just the same, it will be more important in feminine motivation that it is in male. the misunderstood commandment of Aleister Crowley to _do as thou wilt_ is a warning not to delude yourself that you can do otherwise, and to take full responsibility to yourself for what you do. When one has genuinely chosen a course for oneself it cannot be possible to hold another responsible for it. The altruism of women is merely the inauthenticity of the feminine person carried over into behaviour. It is another function of the defect in female narcissism.

Egotism

But a pebble of the brook
Warbled out these metres meet:

'Love seeketh only Self to please,
To bind another to its delight,
Joys in another's loss of ease,
And builds a Hell in Heaven's despite.

If altruism is chimeric, it does not follow that all love behaviour is basically egotistical. The narcissism that I pointed to as the basis for love is not a phenomenon of the ego, which is only the conscious, self-conscious part of the personality, but a function of the whole personality. Egotism in love is not the love of one for another of its own kind, but the assumption of a unity existing between two people which must be enforced and protected against all attempts to socialize it. If a person loves only one other person, and is indifferent to the rest of his fellow men, his love is not love but a symbiotic attachment, or an enlarged egotism.[2] Freud assumed that sexual passion was elusive because jealousy seemed so integral a part of it, and indeed we shall see that most experiments in group marriage founder upon the difficulties that almost everybody experiences when trying with the best will in the world to conquer sexual egotism. The jealousy of a man about his woman is obviously egotistical in a way which differs markedly from female jealousy. A woman becomes the extension of a man's ego like his horse or his car. She can be stolen, and the offence rests with the thief not with the possession. And so men attempt to restore their damaged image when they offer violence to men who dance with or ogle their wives. It is not usually the assumption that women are promiscuous which provokes male jealousy in our society but rather the assumption that they are merely acquiescent in sexual relations. It would appear that men most often flirt with other men's women because of a desire to get at the men, not desire for the women, and hence the cock-fighting syndrome which is even in twentieth-century Anglo-Saxon society ludicrously prevalent. For some people love relationships define themselves in terms of jealous exclusivity. 'I just like being near her. I don't particularly want to have great conversations with her. I just feel awful when I see her with somebody else.'[3] The terms of such passion are all negative. 'I never wanted anyone but you: you're the only woman I've ever loved' is taken as sufficient justification for undisputed possession. Because the lover cannot live without his beloved she must remain with him even against her will. And this is most often recognized as love. As long as the beloved stays she may be treated with great generosity but once she leaves she is an object of hatred and reprisal. The connotations of such a symbiosis are summarized in a macabre story which appeared in Italian newspapers. Meo Calleri stole Maria Teresa Novara from her parents' house at Asti in Piedmont and installed her in an underground room unknown to anyone. There he kept her supplied with food and fumetti, in the margins of which she kept a kind of journal which described her days waiting for her lover to come to her. But one day he was drowned in a car accident. Nobody knew of his love-nest, and his unfortunate hostage suffocated slowly, lying heavily made up waiting for him on the narrow bed. Too true she could not live without him.[4]

And yet the affirmative answer to the questions 'Do you feel that you cannot live without him?' and 'If you lost him tomorrow would you feel that life had no further meaning, and that you would never feel the same for anyone else?'[5] is assumed by one contemporary sentimental counsellor to be evidence that a woman is in love, truly in love. If men regard women's fidelity as a necessary prop to their ego and cuckoldom as the deepest shame, and they do even in England, women are prepared to tolerate infidelity because they so badly need actual security, and not apparent security. They suffer torments of jealousy because they are terrified of abandoment, which seems to them mostly to be all too probable. No man expects to be abandoned until he is

---

Envying stood the enormous Form, at variance with
   Itself
In all its Members, in eternal torment of love &
   jealousy,
Driven forth by Los time after time from Albion's
   cliffy shore,
Drawing the free loves of Jerusalem into infernal
   bondage
That they might be born in Contentions of Chastity & in
Deadly Hate between Leah and Rachel, Daughters of
   Deceit & Fraud
Bearing the Images of various Species of Contention
And Jealousy & Abhorrence & Revenge & Deadly
   Murder,
Till they refuse liberty to the Male, & not like Beulah
Where every Female delights to give her maiden to her
   husband.

                    Blake, 'Jerusalem', pl. 69, II. 6–15

---

faced with evidence that he is being cuckolded or left. As Compton Mackenzie made one of his *Extraordinary Women* observe:

Voltaire had said that no man could ever imagine why any woman should wish *coucher* with anybody except him; but I think he could have said also that after a certain age no man can ever be quite sure that the woman *qui couche avec lui veut coucher avec lui.* But from the first moment that a woman *couche avec un homme* she is always thinking that he is wanting *coucher avec une autre femme.*[6]

Man is jealous because of his *amour propre*; woman is jealous because of her lack of it. Once a boy who wanted me to live with him assured me when I asked him whether or not he would be possessive that he would make love to me so much that I shouldn't be capable of wanting anybody else. This kind of arrogance is what makes actual betrayal so unbearable for men: its utter impossibility for women, who imagine that they have no way of controlling the sexuality of the menfolk, is what makes for feminine insecurity. A woman is so aware of being appreciated by her husband as a thing, and a stereotyped thing at that, that she herself can see no reason why he should not covet the bosom exposed to him by another guest at dinner, especially if she is miserably afraid that in terms of the stereotype the exposed bosom shapes up better than hers. Of course, many women do assume control of their mates' sexuality and one of the easiest ways of doing it is by perverting them so some practice to which they become addicted. I remember a woman boasting to me once that she had something in bed that I did not have therefore a mutual friend of ours must have loved her better than he did me. I eventually found out that what she had in bed was a desire to be beaten and humiliated, which forced our mutual friend to recapitulate to a tendency in himself that he had always mistrusted, which made him very unhappy. Women are happy to replace spontaneous association for pleasure's sake with addiction because it is more binding. There are hundreds of cases in England where wives consent to dress up in leather or rubber, and beat their husbands or shit upon them or what-ever they require, because the compulsivity of the activity is their security.

This kind of abasement may be justified by the woman to

herself as an extreme form of altruism, when it is obviously like most other forms of feminine altruism, disguised egotism. When abandoned women follow their fleeing males with tear stained faces, screaming *you can't do this to me,* they reveal that all that they have offered in the name of generosity and altruism has been part of an assumed transaction, in which they are entitled to a certain payoff. The ultimate expression of this kind of love-egotism is the suicide attempt, and it is practised by both sexes. Our society encourages the substitution of addiction for spontaneous pleasure and specifically encourages women to foster dependencies which will limit their mates' tendencies to roving and other forms of instability. But, while popular moralists encourage a wife to cope indirectly with her husband's infidelities using his guilt to cement the marital symbiosis, they allow the man considerable power of surveillance and limitation, even over apparently innocent activities, as far as his wife is concerned. Almost any woman's magazine will supply an example of this mechanism. This example comes from a letter addressed to 'Evelyn Home' of *Woman*:

A party a year ago is still a volcanic topic between my wife and me.

A week after it, one of the male guests who'd danced with my wife visited her while I was at work. Rightly or wrongly I called at his home where his wife laughed and said her husband was just friendly. My own wife made a stormy scene and said I could trust her; if not, she will jump into bed with the next caller and give me something real to worry about.

I insist that, once married, neither partner should have such visitors. Should I stand by this or copy my wife's brand of conduct?

For a year this poor wretch has pondered this question. His wife has a male visitor in the daytime, and he broods for a year. Indeed, he thinks so little of her that he takes the matter up with the other man's wife, who laughs at him, his disloyalty, his insecurity and his presumption. His wife though shows no great love, for she threatens him, and does not take up the issue of principle. This is marriage, the foundation of society! But Evelyn Home does not reject his morality. She endorses his basic suppositions about the friends of his wife and dignifies the relationship with the name love.

As you don't admire your wife's brand of conduct, don't copy it –but do ask yourself why she welcomed another man's attentions. I don't doubt that his visit was merely social, but your wife was clearly delighted at the compliment.

Do you tell her often that you love her? If not, start now, for she needs reassurance. And think over the kind of life she leads. Would you be bored in her place? Would you need extra mental activity or interests? Maybe your wife needs them too, if she's to stay happily faithful.[7]

People who buy books may laugh at such views, dismiss them as typical of a certain civilization, but this is to set aside the fact that the moral attitudes of a concept like 'Evelyn Home', whose name sweats domesticity, are computer-proven to be the ones that the great majority of female readers find acceptable.

The love that one can fall into is exclusive; all other loves, including the love for the offspring of such love, cause jealousy. Hence the proverbial hatred for the mother-in-law, another example of how the single-couple household pulls away from the larger social fabric. It is itself a repetition of the Oedipal situation and it reproduces the Oedipus complex in the offspring, so that the family is the battleground of the house of Atreus, all caught in the net and all being hacked piecemeal to a lingering death. Lovers live only for each other, dead to the outside world. A dead man makes a good employee and his dead wife sits obliterated in her red-brick mausoleum waiting for her husband to come home so that they can continue their game of ritual murder – whether by caresses or taunts and blows makes little difference, for each man kills the thing he loves, as Oscar Wilde remarked with characteristic irresponsibility. The techniques which are employed to keep young children at the level of dolls and cripples are employed in the marital love situation to seal off the egotistical unit. Baby-talk, even to the extent of calling the husband 'daddy' or 'poppa', and the wife 'momma' or 'mother' and both partners alike 'baby', keeps the discourse to a correctly fatuous level.

Even between lovers who would shy at baby-talk the accumulation of little sentimentally significant objects and rituals is a part of the mutual egotism of love. Objects, places, droll words, games, presents are hung about as charms warding off the intrusion of the outside world. Women's egotism operates more completely in this than man's, for women regard the disregard of their toys and rituals as the greatest heartlessness. To give away a pet object or to call another person by a pet name is to signify the end of the affair; it cannot be forgiven. Ultimately many of the expedients of *égoisme à deux* bring about the separation of lovers, for where there are no visible ties none can be visibly broken. (If you don't give me your fraternity pin I can't send it back.)

One of the most chilling aspects of love egotism is the desire of males and females to feel proud of their partners. Most men desire women who can be shown off to the boys, women desired by other men, although evidently subjugated

---

It would shame me to return her to her parents: I will make a covering for my head from her hair and grind her bones for mortar. I will not release her, but I will wed another.

Disappointed groom, Battak, Sumatra

to the desire for their owners alone. Much of the outrage that men feel when the wives have flirted with other men is due to the fact that kudos of having a pretty and desirable wife has been dissipated by the impression that she is not content and happy with her master. The number of teenage songs which mourned the fickleness of beautiful women and yearned for paper dolls which other fellas couldn't steal is evidence about the prevalence of this kind of egotism. When a man commits himself to his dream girl one of his most urgent desires is to show her to his friends, while women are less concerned, for they are prepared to neglect all their own acquaintances and acquire that of their mate. There is a parallel egotism in female attitudes towards men only when a woman is a member of a group which may declare some men simply too wet, too corny, too *bleahh* to go out with, and no assurances about their deep-down lovableness or riches or whatever will serve to counteract this uneasiness about the public impression. A woman shows her own value to her sisters by choosing a successful and personable man. It is probably a part of the process of natural selection, operating at the very outset of the courting game, and a healthy egotism at that, if only the criteria involved in such judgements were not so ersatz and commercial, and so trivial. One man of my acquaintance, explaining why he was besottedly in love with his secretary, to the utter detriment of his marriage, explained that his secretary had had famous lovers, had been a hippie when it was still the done thing and moved out of Haight Ashbury when it ceased to be okay to live there. She had long legs, blonde hair, and a fashionable figure, who knew all about acid and had been initiated by Leary and Kesey: how could he not love her? His wife, who had been a trendy catch ten years before, was not making it so well (partly because she had been married to him) so it was better for everybody that he go with the trend. Women too bask in the reflected glory of their chosen mates. It would be nonsensical to marry a celebrated and artistic man while remaining indifferent to his achievement: everyone wants to be recognized and rewarded but it might be a better world if achievement was more variously regarded, and if people did not think in terms of catching people's love but of loving them. 'I got him' is nonsense in terms of love relationships, and so is 'I lost him.' If we could stop thinking in terms of capture, we would not have to fear the loosening of the captives' bonds and our failing beauty, and he would not have ulcers about being outstripped or belittled. Lillian Hellman loved Dashiel Hammett all her life, and continues to do so although he is dead. Her love for him did not militate against her love for other people, did not force itself upon him when he did not invite it, did not belittle or destroy him, even by mendacious praise. When he was dying she was there to help him. This strange distant love affair is only one example of how many forms love might take if we had the foresight and the imagination to rescue it from the stereotypes of our dying consumer culture.

(I know as little about the nature of romantic love as I knew when I was eighteen, but I do know about the deep pleasure of continuing interest, the excitement of wanting to know what somebody else thinks, will do, will not do, the tricks played and unplayed, the short cord that the years make into rope, and in my case, is there, hanging loose, long after death.)

And so he lived with me for the last four years of his life. Not all of that time was easy, indeed some of it was very bad, but it was an unspoken pleasure that having come together so many years before, ruined so much and repaired a little, we had endured. Sometimes I would resent the understated or seldom stated side of us and, guessing death wasn't too far away, I would try for something to have afterwards. One day I said, 'We've done fine, haven't we?'

He said, 'Fine's too big a word for me. Why don't we just say we've done better than most people?'[8]

The hallmark of egostistical love, even when it masquerades as altruistic love, is the negative answer to the question 'Do I want my love to be happy more than I want him to be with me?' As soon as we find ourselves working at being indispensable, rigging up a pattern of vulnerability in our loved ones, we ought to know that our love has taken the socially sanctioned form of egotism. Every wife who slaves to keep herself pretty, to cook her husband's favourite meals, to build up his pride and confidence in himself at the expense of his sense of reality, to be his closest and effectively his only friend, to encourage him to reject the consensus of opinion and find reassurance only in her arms is binding her mate to her with hoops of steel that will strangle them both. Every time a woman makes herself laugh at her husband's often-told jokes she betrays him. The man who looks at his woman and says 'What would I do without you?' is already destroyed. His woman's victory is complete, but it is Pyrrhic. Both of them have sacrificed so much of what initially made them lovable to promote the symbiosis of mutual dependence that they scarcely make up one human being between them.

Obsession

In Love, as *in* pain, *in* shock, *in* trouble.

Thus love is a state, presumably a temporary state, an aberration from the norm.

The outward symptoms of this state are sleeplessness, distraction, loss of appetite, alternations of euphoria and depression, as well as starry eyes (as in fever), and agitation.

The principle explanation of the distraction, which leads to the mislaying of possessions, confusion, forgetfulness and irresponsibility, is the overriding obsession with the love object, which may only have been seen from a distance on one occasion. The love object occupies the thoughts of the person diagnosed 'in love' all the time despite the probability that very little is actually known about it. To it are ascribed all qualities considered by the obsessed as good, regardless of whether the object in question possesses those qualities in any degree. Expectations are set up which no human being could fulfil. Thus the object chosen plays a special role in relation to the ego of the obsessed, who decided that he or she is the *right* or the *only* person for him. In the case of a male this notion may sanction a degree of directly aggressive behaviour either in pursuing the object or driving off competition. In the case of a female, no aggressive behaviour can be undertaken and the result is more likely to be brooding, inexplicable bad temper, a dependence upon the telephone and gossip with other women about the love object, or even acts of apparent rejection and scorn to bring herself to the object's attention.

Formerly this condition was believed to afflict the individual acutely from the first contact with the object:

Whoever loved that loved not at first sight?[1]

However, the sudden and acute nature of the affliction seems to have been a characteristic of the illicit form, and since obsession has been made the basis of marriage, more gradual chronic states have also been recognized. The cause of the malady was supposed to have the infective glance from the eyes of the love-object, which was commonly referred to metaphorically as Cupid's arrow striking the beholder to the heart and leaving a wound which rankled and would not heal. In more extreme cases of destructive passion even more farfetched pseudo-explanations were invented, like Phaedra's belief that she was being specifically tormented by Venus:

> Ce n'est plus qu'une ardeur dans mes veines cachée:
> C'est Vénus toute entière a sa proie attachée.[2]

Such imagery makes great use of images of burning, implying both the heat of lust and the chafing of frustration. Ironically it was supposed that any attempt to control this condition, either by avoiding the object which caused it or seeking to exert the will over the passions, has the effect of banking a fire, which is to increase it so that eventually it leaps forth more violently than before. 'Love will find a way. Love laughs at Locksmiths.' Thus to 'fall in love' was a terrible misfortune, which inevitably involved the break-up of any stable ménage and self-immolation in irrational ardour. Racine used a French equivalent to describe love, both as an evil and an illness, by calling it *un mal*. The belief that love is a disease, or at least as haphazard and damaging as disease, survives in terms like *lovesick,* and in the imagery of popular corn.

Some of the longest lived popular song themes make direct use of the traditional imagery. The muzack which dulls the apprehensions of tea-drinkers in fashionable hotels and thrills through the pump-rooms in faded resorts is still based upon the staple of the great songs of the thirties and forties. The words may be less well-known than the tunes, especially as Iriving Berlin and his ilk are understandably loth to allow them to be quoted, nevertheless it is a rare tea-drinker or spa visitor who cannot croon absently along about moon and June. These 'classics' are as overstuffed with references to hearts going thumpety-thump, eyes dazzled with starlight, blinded with the smoke and fumes from the furnace of passion which is the heart, as any of the extravagant poems of the quattrocento-secentisti. Lovers don't slip, they aren't pushed, they fall, hopefully if pathetically, right into the middle of a warm caress. They feel very strange but nice, afflicted it would seem by a pleasant ache, or even rubbed down with a velvet glove. They sigh, they sorrow and they get dizzy spells, or perhaps they do not, but then they just love to look in their beloved's eyes.

The supreme irony must be when the bored housewife whiles away her duller tasks, half-consciously intoning the otherwise very unforgettable words of some pulp lovesong. How many of them stop to assess the real consequences of the fact that 'all who love are blind' or just how much they have to blame that 'something here inside' for? What songs do you sing, one wonders when your heart is no longer on fire and smoke no longer mercifully blinds you to the banal realities of your situation? (But of course there are no songs for that.)

Another song ironically denies that the singer is in love because he does not sigh or sorrow, or get dizzy spells. Are we so very far after all from Romeo's description of his conventionalized passion for a woman he did not know, who was utterly indifferent to his advances?

> Love is a smoke rais'd with the fume of sighs;
> Being purg'd a fire sparkling in lovers' eyes;
> Being vex'd, a sea nourish'd with lovers' tears.
> What is it else? a madness most discreet
> A choking gall, and a preserving sweet.[3]

This attitude, which is an eminently consistent way of regarding adulterous passion, survives in the imagery of the state of 'in love' as the proper one for spouses. It is still ironically maintained for example that love is blind, just as Cupid was represented in the courtly love tradition as blind-folded. However, this blindness is usually taken to mean only the refusal of the lover to see his beloved in any way realistically, and especially to discern his faults.

The impotence of will and rationality to deal with this mania are recognized in the common terms 'madly', 'wildly', 'deliriously', 'head-over-heels' in love, while it would be oxymoronic to claim to be gently, reliably or sensibly in love. There is some disagreement about the self-immunizing propensities of the disease, for some claim that one is only ever really in love once in a lifetime, others that it is better the second time around, others that the first time is the only genuine manifestation, still others that they fall in love every week or even every day.

> Sex is a momentary itch,
> Love never lets you go.[4]

It is an essential quality of the disease that it is incurable; this has meant that in cases where young people in love must be weaned off each other because they are too young or ill-assorted the only method is to deny that they are so afflicted. The 'love' must be proved to be false on the grounds, say, that it cannot happen to people so young...

I can remember Nat King Cole topping the charts (sometime during my unspeakably dreary teens) with a heart-rendingly bland number about a couple surrounded by enemies forever trying to tell them they were too young to reallee bee in luv, because love was only a word that they had heard (like all the other concepts that they knew). The argument of the kill-joys was manifestly invalid, for if they were to try the truth of the notion of love by experience, then presumably they would have to go ahead and love. However invalid the argument, the counter-conclusion of the song, that their love will last through years may go, hardly seems to constitute relevant refutation.

As love cannot actually be demonstrated to be present, so it cannot be demonstrated to be genuine. The advantage of denying its existence in a particular case, is that the denial cannot be refuted, although, as the song insinuates, it is likely to give rise to an enduring pose of young love persecuted by the world, an Aucassin and Nicolette fantasy which endures chiefly to refute the critics.

Methods of diagnosis of this condition vary. External observers will base a judgement upon observation of agitation, impairment of concentration and efficiency, or an undue preoccupation with the love object expressed in curiosity or speculation. However, it must be noticed that such observers have a vested interest in the detection of love affairs because of the particular voyeurist pleasures they afford, and often precipitate such situations. 'All the world loves a lover.' The sufferer may diagnose himself as having contracted the disease because of the intensity of his reactions when the love-object is expected or in sight or fails to make an anticipated appearance. He will also suffer the omnipresence of a mental image of the beloved in dreams, at meals, during completely irrelevant discussions. If the love remains unrequited the symptoms either fade gradually or become transferred to a new object or intensify until they become agonizing. Which of these alternatives ensues is largely dependent upon the attitude of the sufferer to his affliction. The greater the degree of masochism and the inherent doubt of competence in actually prosecuting a love-affair, the more he will resign himself to isolation and barren suffering. The unconscious love-object then has to bear the brunt of responsibility for his self-induced condition and may be accused of cruelty or trifling with a good person's heart. If the lover enacts some outrage upon the object to revenge himself for its cruelty, he will find that it is treated with special consideration by the lawmakers who allow a special status to those who are 'in love', especially if the object be considered unworthy. If his passion is denied this privilege, it will be justified by refusing it the status of 'love' and relegating it to mere vengeful lust or some such.

Generally it is considered proper for women not to arrive in this state of obsession unless induced thereto by a man. Unfortunately the presentation of the state of being in love as a desirable, and indeed consummate human experience is so powerful that adolescent girls seem to spend much more time in its throes than their male counterparts. However, the social fiction is kept up by the popular imagery of girls responding to male wooing and the contagion of love. The acid test of the experience is the astonishingly potent kiss. 'It was my first kiss, and it filled me with such wild thundering rapture. I had been crazy about Mark so long, and now, with our kiss, I knew that he loved me too!'[5]

Love is *being crazy about someone* (Oh Ah'm jes' wil' about Harree!) and the extraordinary effects of the contact of the lip with lip and tongue with tongue bring on wild thundering rapture. However, in the case quoted the love was spurious although its symptoms were identical with the genuine ones: Betsy has just been kissed by Mark, 'the best athlete in school and the wealthiest boy in town! Gosh, I am lucky,' but she has a better friend in Hugh, the boy-next-door, who warns her about Mark and his fast, arrogant ways. In the second encounter Hugh plucks up courage to make a declaration and sweeps Betsy into his arms... 'His kiss set my heart to pounding and a feeling swept over me that I couldn't name...a feeling that brought a carpet of clouds under my feet...' This, it appears, is the real thing, or so the conclusion tells us: 'I had made a mistake and had that for comparison! Love is not always what it seems, and kisses can be false!'[6]

The sensations caused by the two kisses are not genuinely distinguishable. Both are described in terms more appropriate to the abnormal experiences of the organism under drugs – pounding of the heart, roaring in the ears and cottony legs; in fact *love* is also the drug which makes sexuality palatable in popular mythology. Sex without love is considered a crude animal evacuation: with love it becomes ecstatic and transcendental. Obviously it is meant to perform an autosuggestive function in affecting cortical sexual responses, and it probably does. The fact still remains that Betsy can only distinguish between two kisses on some kind of political ground: it is in fact desirable for Betsy to marry into her own class, and one would not object if the policy were openly stated instead of cloaked in the mumbo-jumbo of the comparison between two identical kisses. In both cases the terms of reference are more apt to hallucination than to motivation for marriage; the emphasis is all on egotistic response, not at all on communication between the persons indulging in such osculation.

This confusion typifies all literature on the diagnosis of true love. Sentimental bias militates against the subjugating of love to any rational or wilful control, while anarchic passion is regarded with deep suspicion. Generally, as in the above sample, the most appropriate match must be trans- mogrified into the most gratifying. The real difference between true and false love, which are both compounds of lust and fantasy, is that true love leads to marriage. Provided it does that, a significant downgrade in the level of excitement is tolerated but not admitted. Adultery and fornication are still more exciting than marriage, but our culture is committed to maintaining the contrary. We are actually committed to the belief that this mania is an essential precondition to marriage... IS IT A SIN TO MARRY BEFORE FALLING IN LOVE! was the banner of an advertisement for Taylor Caldwell's *Let Love Come Last.*[7] Paradoxically love sanctifies both marriage and illicit encounters. 'Love conquers all.'

The irrationality of love is fondly celebrated in those pulp stories of women who gave up cold career and ambition for the warmth of a husband's pressing love. Efficient career woman X holds out against junior buyer Y's love for her for months until he acts cold and she gets jealous, or until he has an accident and she rides in the ambulance with him. After all 'When love calls – who can really deny it?'[8]

Love is here either compared to a necessary human function (*cf.* Nature calls!) or to a person summoning to a pleasant duty, another survival of older forms of analogue. Nevertheless the crises in such a story were aimed to reveal to the unconscious sufferer that she was in fact in love, just as the leper finds out by pouring boiling water over his numb feet. Some such testing is allowable, and even prescribed for those who doubt that they are really truly in love. 'Love is never really love until it is reality-tested.' Trial separations can be useful in proving the durability of an obsession. Some experts in this kind of homeopathy have devised questionnaires which the patient must apply for himself, a fairly unreliable procedure at best. The questions may range from 'If he left you, could you bear to go on living?' to 'Do you find his breath unpleasant?' A more common procedure is to advise the love-lorn, a term which has sinister connotations if only anyone ever understood it, what love is *not,* which is no guide to what it *is*.

Love is not mere thrill or passing pleasure. It is not escape from loneliness or boredom, nor is it a comfortable adjustment for practical convenience or mutual benefit. It is not a one-way feeling, and it can't be made two-way by wishing or willing it so.

The adolescent lover following this rule of thumb may be excused for feeling a little confusion. Certainly, many poets and others have burnt with one-way love; the establishment of parity in love is quite impossible. It is impossible to know if pleasure is passing before it is past, and if it is not an escape from loneliness and boredom, or a comfortable mutual arrangement, there would seem to be little point in setting it up as a desideratum at all. The positive description supplied by the same author is not less daunting:

Love is many things. It's a little child's satisfied response to attention and tenderness and it's also the older child's affectionate curiosity. It's the playfulness of adolescents and their romantic flight of imagination. Then again it is the earnest, mature devotion of mature marriage...

Love is delicate, elusive and above all spontaneous. It thrives on honesty and sincerity and naturalness combined with mutual responsibleness and concern. At the beginning it just 'happens' but to flourish and endure it requires the full capacity for giving of the open heart and soul.[9]

This is one man's attempt to counteract the dangerous mythology of falling in love as a basis for marriage, but it is not convincing. Such a vague but deeply committed view never inspired a single love poem. The lure of the psychedelic experience of love which makes the world a beautiful place, puts stars in your eyes, sweeps you off your feet, thumps you in the breast with Cupid's bird-bolt is not lessened by such bad prose. The magical mania still persists as a powerful compulsion in our imagination. 'Was he very much in love with her?' the second wife asks of her dead rival. 'He was crazy about her,' they say of the man who killed his faithless wife, and the jury recommends mercy. 'I knew he was a murderer but I was in love with him,' says the lady who married the man in the condemned cell. Love, love, love – all the wretched cant of it, masking egotism, lust, masochism, fantasy under a mythology of sentimental postures, a welter of self-induced miseries and joys, blinding and masking the essential personalities in the frozen gestures of courtship, in the kissing and the dating and the desire, the compliments and the quarrels which vivify its barrenness. 'We were not made to idolize one another, yet the whole strain of courtship is little more than rank idolatry.'[10] It may seem that young men no longer court with the elaborate servilities that Mary Astell, the seventeenth-century feminist, was talking about, but the mystic madness of love provides the same spurious halo, and builds up the same expectations which dissipate as soon as the new wife becomes capable of 'calmly considering her Condition'. In the twentieth century a feminist like Ti-Grace Atkinson makes a similar point more crudely: 'Love is the victim's response to the rapist.'[11]

Not all love is comprehended in such a description, but the sickening obsession which thrills the nervous frames of the heroines of great love affairs whether in cheap 'romance' comic-papers or in hard-back novels of passionate wooing is just that. Women must recognize in the cheap ideology of *being in love* the essential persuasion to take an irrational and self-destructive step. Such obsession has nothing to do with love, for love is not swoon, possession or mania, but 'a cognitive act, indeed the only way to grasp the innermost core of personality.'[12]

Romance

Perhaps it is no longer true that every young girl dreams of being in love. Perhaps the pop revolution which has replaced sentiment with lust by forcibly incorporating the sexual ethos of black urban blues into the culture created by the young for themselves has had a far-reaching effect on sexual *mores*. Perhaps young girls have allowed an actual sexual battle to replace the moony fantasies that I certainly fell for in my teenage years. Nevertheless, it is only a perhaps. Dr Peter Mann's researches at the University of Sheffield show that twenty-five to forty-five-year old women are avid readers of romantic fiction, especially housewives and secretarial workers. Some buy as many as eighty books a year. The market is bigger than ever before.[1] *Romance still lives!* cried the *Woman's Weekly*, 'famed for its fiction', as recently as August 1969.

For all their new freedoms, the majority of 'young people of today' still dream the same dreams, find life as adventurous and appreciate the best values as have the generations before them.

...Kathy, on the lawn that evening might have been modelling an illustration for a Victorian love story. Her white dress, of some filmy material, was high at the throat and went down to her black satin slippers. She had a black velvet ribbon round her small waist and wore an old gold chain with a locket, and her black hair was parted in the middle... 'She's going to her first ball,' her mother said to me... 'She's wildly excited.'

...For every sad daughter whiffing in marijuana in some darkened discotheque, there are thousands like Kathy, 'wildly excited' in their first formal dance frock.[2]

This apparently is romance. The stress placed by the male author of this piece on the dress which is appropriate to romance is typical of the emphasis which characterizes such lore. The dance is the high mass in which Kathy will appear in her glory, to be wooed and adored. Her young man will be bewitched, stumbling after her in his drab evening dress, pressing her cool hand, circling her tiny waist and whirling her helpless in his arms about the floor. He will compliment her on her beauty, her dancing, thank her for an unforgettable evening.

Debutantes still come out every year, in their virginal white, curtesying to the Queen, the Mayor, the Bishop, or whomever, pacing their formal patterns with downcast eyes. The boys ask politely for dances while the girls accept prettily, or try to find pretexts for refusing in the hope that someone nicer will ask. Their beaux ought to have given them flowers. But every girl is hoping that something more exciting, more romantic than the expected sequence of the social event will happen. Perhaps some terrifyingly handsome man will press a little closer than the others and smell the perfume of her hair. Perhaps after supper, when they stroll upon the terrace, he will catch his breath, dazzled by the splendour of her limitless eyes. Her heart will pound, and her cheeks mantle with delicious blushes. He will say wonderful things, be strangely tender and intense. She may be swept into his masterful arms. Nothing more sexual than a kiss, no vulgar groping embraces, only strong arms about her protecting her from the coarseness of the world, and warm lips on hers, sending extraordinary stimuli through her whole body.

In the romantic world, kisses do not come before love, unless they are offered by wicked men who delude innocent girls for a time, for they will soon be rescued by the omnipotent true lover. The first kiss ideally signals rapture, exchange of hearts, and imminent marriage. Otherwise it is a kiss that *lies*. All very crude and nonsensical, and yet it is the staple myth of hundreds of comics called 'Sweethearts', 'Romantic Secrets' and so forth. The state induced by the kiss is actually self-induced, of course, for few lips arc so gifted with electric and psychedelic possibilities. Many a young man trying to make out with his girl has been surprised at her raptness and elation, only to find himself lumbered with an unwanted intense relationship which is compulsorily sexless.

When it happens it will be wonderful, unforgettable, beautiful. It will be like Mimi and Rodolfo singing perfect arias at their first meeting. Perhaps they will not fall in love all at once but feel a tenderness growing until one day POW! that amazing kiss. The follow-through would have to be the constant manifestation of tenderness, esteem, flattery and susceptibility by the man together with chivalry and gallantry in all situations. The hero of romance knows how to treat women. Flowers, little gifts, love letters, maybe poems to her eyes and hair, candlelit meals on moonlit terraces and muted strings. Nothing hasty, physical. Some heavy breathing. Searing lips pressed against the thin stuff of her bodice. Endearments muttered into her luxuriant hair. 'Little things mean a lot.' Her favourite chocolates, his pet names for her, remembering her birthday, anniversaries, silly games. And then the foolish things that remind him of her, her perfume, her scarf, her frilly underthings and absurd lace hankies, kittens in her lap. Mystery, magic, champagne, ceremony, tenderness, excitement, adoration, reverence –women never have enough of it. Most men know nothing about this female fantasy world because they are not exposed to this kind of literature and the commerce of romanticism. The kind of man who studies this kind of behaviour and becomes a ladies' man whether for lust or love or cupidity is generally feared and disliked by other men as a gigolo or even a queer. Male beauticians and hairdressers study the foibles of their customers and deliberately flirt with them, paying them compliments that they thirst for, hinting that they deserve better than the squalid domestic destiny that they bear.

If *Sweethearts* and the other publications of the same kind with their hallucinated love imagery are American, it is unfortunately true that they find a wide distribution in England. There are also trash weeklies called *Mirabelle, Valentine, Romeo* and, biggest of all, *Jackie* selling upwards of a million copies a week to girls between ten and sixteen years of age, which set forth the British ideals of romance. The girls are leggier and trendier, with tiny skirts, wild hair and sooty eyes; mostly they avoid the corniness of the psychedelic kiss. The men are wickedly handsome on the lines of the Regency Buck, more or less dapper and cool, given to gazing granite-jawed into the glimmering eyes of melting females. The extraordinary aspect is the prominence given to fetish objects. Romance appears to hinge on records, books, knick-knacks, and, in one case which appears to the detached observer to be almost surreal, a park bench. Kate and Harry are sweethearts. They sit on a bench in the park and exchange dialogue thus:

'Oh, Kate, I love you more than anything on earth.'
'And I love you more than anything in the whole universe, darling.'

The bench becomes enormously important in their relationship and when the council decides to move it Kate dashes to Harry's office in the Town Hall with a demand that they sit in, on it. Harry does so until his boss, the borough surveyor, tells him he'll lose his job if he holds out any longer. He gives in, leaving Kate to defend her bench alone. She takes it as an indication of the shallowness of his love for her. But one of the people involved in the moving of the bench, obviously a lover because of his granite jaw and Byronic hair, takes his place beside her. 'We'll save this bench for you, for the past and all the lovers to come.' The last frame shows our heroine peering dewily at him through tear-dimmed eyes, her baby pouting lips a hair's breadth from his rugged prognathous contours. 'But you'll lose your job for nothing. Do...do you really think we can beat them,' says her balloon. 'I know we can beat them,' his balloon rejoins. 'People can do anything if they try hard enough and love well enough. Let's try...'[3] *The end,* to say the least.

The lover in romance is a man of masterful ways, clearly superior to his beloved in at least one respect, usually in several, being older or of higher social rank and attainment or more intelligent and *au fait*. He is authoritative but deeply concerned for his lady whom he protects and guides in a way that is patently paternal. He can be stern and withdrawn or even forbidding but the heroines of romance melt him by sheer force of modesty and beauty and the bewitching power of their clothes. He has more than a hint of danger in his past conquests, or a secret suffering or a disdain for women. The banked fires of passion burn just below the surface, muted by his tenderness and omnipotent understanding of the heroine's emotional needs. The original for such characters is in fact romantic in the historical sense for perhaps the very first of them are Rochester, Heathcliff, Mr Darcy and Lord Byron. However, the sense of Austen and Brontë is eclipsed by the sensibility of Lady Caroline Lamb. Exploiting the sexual success of the Byronic hero in an unusually conscious way Georgette Heyer created the archetype of the plastic age, Lord Worth, the Regency Buck. He is a fine example of a stereotype which most heroes of romantic fiction resemble more or less, whether they are dashing young men with an undergraduate sense of humour who congratulate the vivacious heroine on her pluck (the most egalitarian in conception) in the adventure stories of the thirties, or King Cophetua and the beggar maid.

He was the epitome of a man of fashion. His beaver hat was set over black locks carefully brushed into a semblance of disorder; his cravat of starched muslin supported his chin in a series of beautiful folds, his driving coat of drab cloth bore no less than fifteen capes, and a double row of silver buttons. Miss Taverner had to own him a very handsome creature, but found no difficulty in detesting the whole cast of his countenance. He had a look of self-consequence; his eyes, ironically surveying her from under world-weary lids, were the hardest she had ever seen, and betrayed no emotion but boredom. His nose was too straight for her taste. His mouth was very well-formed, firm, but thin-lipped. She thought he sneered...

Worse than all was his languor. He was uninterested, both in having dexterously averted an accident, and in the gig's plight. His driving had been magnificent; there must be unexpected strength in those elegantly gloved hands holding the reins in such seeming carelessness but why in the name of God, why must he put on such an air of dandified affectation?[4]

Nothing such a creature would do could ever be *corny*. With such *world-weary lids*! With the patrician feature and aristocratic contempt which first opened the doors of polite society to Childe Harold, and the titillating threat of *unexpected strength*! Principally, we might notice, he exists through his immaculate dressing – Beau Brummell is one of his friends – but when he confronts this spectacle –

She had rather have had black hair; she thought the fairness of her gold curls insipid. Happily, her brows and lashes were dark, and her eyes which were startlingly blue (in the manner of a wax doll, she once scornfully told her brother) had a directness and fire which gave a great deal of character to her face. At first glance one might write her down a mere Dresden china miss, but a second glance would inevitably discover the intelligence in her eyes, and the decided air of resolution in the curve of her mouth.[5]

Of course her intelligence and resolution remain happily confined to her eyes and the curve of her mouth but they provide the excuse for her naughty behaviour towards Lord Worth, who turns out to be that most titillating of all titillating relations, her young guardian, by an ingeniously contrived mistake. He, confronting her in this charming dress – 'a plain round gown of French cambric, frilled around the neck with scalloped lace; and a close mantle of twilled sarsenet. A poke bonnet of basket willow with a striped velvet ribbon...'[6] – and most compromisingly placed shaking a pebble out of her sandal, and so having to hide her stockinged foot in her skirts, sweeps her up into his arms and hurls her into his curricle (for at this point neither of them knows their relationship) where he 'took the sandal from her resistless grasp, and calmly held it ready to fit on to her foot'. Then to provoke her charming indignation still further he kisses her. At such a rate of conquest the novel would be merely twenty pages long, if it were not that as her guardian Worth is too much of a man of principle to pay his addresses to her. She becomes, with his help, given sternly and diffidently, the belle of the season, wooed by all but loving none (but him). She has eighty thousand pounds a year, which is the motive for one sort of suitor; lustful desire for her is the motive of the rest, the most remarkable being the Prince of Wales, whose advances are so repugnant that she faints dead away to be brought around and carried home by her masterful father–lover, who alone loves her without greed or self-interest (being fabulously wealthy), steadfastly and strong. He protects her all the time, even though most of the time she is unaware of it, until her majority when, after a moment of looking down into her face, he sweeps her into his arms. Georgette Heyer has a streak of discretion, or perhaps prudery, which prevents her from exploiting the sexual climaxes in the writing: Barbara Cartland, on the other hand, overwrites the imagery of embracements and thereby reveals much more of the essential romantic preoccupations. In *The Wings of Love* she divides the love interest into with

Lord Ravenscar the forty-year-old lecher who coverts tiny
Amanda's lovely body and forces his hideous attentions on
it...

His hold on her tightened; his lips fastened to hers were like a vice
[sic]. She felt his passion rising within him like an evil flame; and
then suddenly he lifted her in his arms.

'Amanda!' he said hoarsely, 'Damme! Why should we wait?' He
was carrying her to a large sofa in the corner of the room; and as she
struggled, fighting with every ounce of her strength, she knew how
small and ineffectual she was and that her resistance was merely
exciting him.

'Amanda! Amanda!'

His thick lips were on her eyes, her cheeks, her throat. She felt
him lay her down on the sofa, while she fought fruitlessly to regain
her feet, knowing as she did so that she was quite powerless. She
heard the fichu of her gown tearing beneath his hands.[7]

The utterly ineffectual heroine is the most important part
of the story, ineffectual against ravishment (for how could
such a delicate thing kick a peer of the realm in his rising
passion?) and against more agreeable forms of sexual
conquest, at the hands of the other male, the hero who will
protect her from his own animal passions and the crimes and
follies of the world.

She turned towards the door and then suddenly Peter Harvey had
dropped on one knee beside her. She looked at him wonderingly as
he lifted the hem of her white muslin gown and touched his lips with
it. 'Amanda,' he said, 'that is how a man, any man, should
approach you. No one – least of all Ravenscar – is worthy to do
more than to kiss the hem of your gown. Will you remember that?'[8]

That's the kind of man you marry. On his knees chewing
her muddy hem and still her moral tutor. Miss Cartland's
taste for titillation as far exceeds Heyer's as Heyer's
researches into historical colour exceed her own. By a series

of preposterous contrivances the lovers meet in a brothel bedroom where he is engaged in rescuing her. Amanda confesses her love in a more decorous setting.

'Amanda, you are making it unbearable for me,' Peter said, and his voice sounded as if it was strangled.

'You do not want me,' she said.

'One day I will make you apologize for that,' he said. 'Just as one day I will kiss you until you cry for mercy. Until that day comes – and pray God it will come soon – take care of yourself, my little beloved.'

He took both her hands and raised them to his lips. Instead of kissing the back of them he turned them over. She felt him kissing the palms with a reverence, and, at the same time, a hungry passion that made her thrill until her whole body trembled with a sudden ecstasy.[9]

They have not actually kissed yet because Peter has said 'If your lips touched mine I should not be answerable for the consequences.' Indeed when handkissing results in orgasm it is possible that an actual kiss might bring on epilepsy. She is at the altar repeating the vows which will bind her to Ravenscar for life when her lover unmasks him as a traitor, duels with him, and takes his place at her side.

She felt her love rise up in her like a flame. She felt her whole body tremble with the *excitement and the ecstasy of the thrill* that swept over her, because she knew that in a few seconds she would be his wife and belong to him forever.[10]

Both these books I bought for three and sixpence in a supermarket, but it could not claim to have been a random choice, because I remembered these names, Heyer and Cartland, from my fantasy-ridden teens. Indeed I met Miss Cartland in a cascade of aquamarines at a university debate were the topic was 'Be good sweet maid and let who will be clever', Miss Cartland of course taking the affirmative, as if it were possible to be good without being clever! Nowadays she seems to have set up as a sentimental counsellor and purveyor of honey-based aphrodisiacs and may point to her daughter's success in happily marrying into the peerage. If women's liberation movements are to accomplish anything at all, they will have to cope with phenomena like the million dollar Cartland industry. The third book bought on that same day was bought on spec. It was called *The Loving Heart*, and described as 'another great romantic story of the Australian outback'. All the well-tried paraphernalia of romance were there. In inventing Grant Jarvis, Lucy Walker availed herself of the feudal paternalism of the sheep-station set-up. Not only is her hero wealthy, he directly rules a society of loyal retainers, white and relatively infantile, as well as black and totally infantile.

In order to bring the elements of her story unto the juxta-position that will provide the maximum in sentimental thrills Lucy Walker devises a situation so intricate and unlikely that it would take as long to summarize as it did to invent. All we need to know is that Elizabeth Heaton is posing as Grant Jarvis's fiancée to protect him from designing women who desire him for motives of alliance and ambition. They are fast, energetic and gorgeous, but she has an English complexion and purity, as well as a trick of imitating the queen in carrying out her functions as lady of the worse-than-feudal manor. Her modesty is so excessive that she suffers acutely when, on her first night on the station, the resolution of a crisis involves her in sleeping in her slip on the ground beside the fire, with Grant's body shielding her on the cold side. When Grant visits her bedroom in broad daylight, despite the fact that she is not alone she cannot 'for the life of her' prevent 'the tell-tale blush that crept up her cheeks'. She is thankful that 'the breakfast tray lay across her knees...some kind of symbolic shield.'[11] Physically Grant is well-constructed as the father-phallus, 'extremely handsome', 'with cold grey-blue eyes', which coupled with his straight mouth and firm jaw 'gave an impression of hardness...and indifference.'[12] All her efforts in the book are expended to earn his approval, and in her quiet moments when not teaching the children, or washing the Union Jack (truly!), she falls to contemplation of his hard masculine beauty, and to masochistic reverie.

Yet as she looked at Grant, leaning on that balustrade, staring out over the plain, with that fine white scar showing on his arm, she felt he was, for all his wealth and power, a lonely man. Whether he was isolated by his personal tragedy or by his great wealth Elizabeth did not know. If he required her to stay on she would not raise difficulties. She had a strange compulsive inclination to serve him.[13]

All romantic novels have a preoccupation with clothes. Every sexual advance is made with clothing as an attractive barrier; the foot fetish displayed in Miss Walker's descriptions is an optional extra.[14] The book has been through four impressions in the Fontana edition, and the authoress has written eleven others at least. The climax of the titillation comes when Grant Jarvis joins the ship in which Elizabeth is travelling home to London at Colombo.

She knew he was real because the tweed of his coat hurt her nose, and she could feel the great power of his arms as he crushed her to him...

The incredible had happened. Someone in the world had crossed continents and flown oceans to get *her*...Elizabeth Heaton, typist...

He bent his head and his lips met her lips. For a long moment Elizabeth had the taste of heaven on her mouth.[15]

This is the hero that women have chosen for themselves. The traits invented for him have been invented by women cherishing the chains of their bondage. It is a male common-place that women love rotters but in fact women are hypnotized by the successful man who appears to master his fate; they long to give their responsibility for themselves into the keeping of one who can administer it in their best interests. Such creatures do not exist, but very young women in the astigmatism of sexual fantasy are apt to recognize them where they do not exist. Opening car doors, manoeuvring headwaiters, choosing gifts, and earning money, are often valued as romantic attainments: in search of romance many women would gladly sacrifice their own moral judgement of their champion. Many a housewife thrills to the story of Charmaine Biggs, and in telling her story to the dailies the train-robber's wife or her ghost has known just which aspects of a relatively sordid and confused life to delineate and emphasize.[16] Biggs's size, physical strength and daring are reiterated, along with his impudence in courtrooms and remand centres, his cavalier attitude to money and his prowess in bed. Even an adultery has been taken in stride.

Although romance is essentially vicarious the potency of the fantasy distorts actual behaviour. The strength of the belief that a man should be stronger and older than his woman can hardly be exaggerated. I cannot claim to be fully emancipated from the dream that some enormous man, say six foot six, heavily shouldered and so forth to match, will crush me to his tweeds, look down into my eyes and leave the taste of heaven or the scorch of his passion on my waiting lips. For three weeks I was married to him. The impression that women dress to please men must be understood as meaning that women dress to create an impression which corresponds they think to the devastation wrought on Peter Harvey by Amanda in white muslin. Ballroom dancing is an extraordinary capitulation on the part of society to the myth of female submissiveness; the women travel backwards, swept along in a chaste embrace, their faces close to the men's but not actually touching. Such dancing which is only as old as Heyer's Regency Buck may be seen as the expression of middle-class manners, for the aristocratic modes of dancing were formal while the lower orders allowed an independent part to the woman, involving greater or lesser exertion. There is no folk dance or native dance that I have ever heard of in which the man takes over the automotion of the woman. The favourite spectacle of the middle-class female is ballet; all the romantic stereotypes are embodied in it, as the female, although her solo exhibitions demand great power and discipline, *leaps* but *appears to be lifted* like a leaf or a pile of swansdown. Even at the merely social level successful ballroom dancing involves the same contradiction. The woman must exercise physical control so that she appears to be guided weightless about the floor.

The most significant operation of the romance myth, however, is in the courting situation. Boys, unless they are consciously exploiting female susceptibility, have little idea what the kiss means in the romantic canon. For them it is a beginning, a preliminary to intimacy; for the girls it is the crown of love to be staged at climactic points. While a girl does not really believe this, she does not understand the boy's attitude to it either. Reverent intensity is most frequently lacking from adolescent embraces although maturer men might fake it, and fake it almost unconsciously. The best behaved teenager necks, even if nobody ever does in *Valentine, Mirabelle* or *Sweethearts,* but even acknowledging this fact a teenage girl yearns for love and romance as things that could happen to her, but which she cannot bring about. The impulse to yield militates against the impulse to impose the right form on the circumstances, and most often a girl breathing out her soul on the lips of her callow lover seduces herself with an inflated notion of what is really happening. She offers at one time both more and less than he is asking.

The baffling scenes that ensue when boys violate sentimental protocol testify to the fantasy operations of romance. It is such a simple role that more cynical young men fake it deliberately: the veriest tyro soon learns the best line is the suppressed-but-almost-uncontrollable-desire line, which a little heavy breathing and significant glancing can put over. How about the Cartland line, 'If I kiss you I won't be answerable for the consequences'? Such dialogue could be dynamite. For all their prudish insistence on blushing and the excision of any suggestion of less intense and less decorous human contact, Cartland and Heyer are preparing the way for seducers – not lovers, seducers. But while they make the handsome man's job easier they put even more obstacles in the way of the homely male. Although the romantic male is not so invariable a stereotype as the characterless, passive female, he has certain indispensable qualities. He is never gauche, although he might be insolent or even insulting; he is never nervous or uncertain or humble, and he is always good-looking. In the tribal teenage situation there are some boys with whom one does not go out; they are not acceptable, being homely, or corny, or eager. Actual debauchery is less of a disqualification than any of these.

Settings, clothes, objects, all testify the ritualization of sex which is the essential character of romance. Just as the Holy Communion is not a real meal and satisfies no hunger, the Almighty Kiss stands for a communion which cannot actually be enjoyed. Cartland's imagery of hem-kissing and lilies gives away the fact that we are dealing with a kind of sexual religion. Devotion is what is demanded, not love. For some women these rituals are necessary even in married life to make sex acceptable. Without such observances, sexual intercourse is another household duty and some such need of glamour is very often closer to the heart of wifely reluctance than mere sordid sexual bargaining. The desire to have sex built up into an important occasion has a curious relationship with the alleged slowness of feminine respone, for many women seek in sex not physical release but exaltation, physical worship as promised in the marriage service. Some of the sexual demand women make is actually the demand for the enactment of the sexual ceremony of togetherness, which men recoil from because they misinterpret it as a demand upon their potency.

I whined and tried to coax him. He said I was a 'nympho'. I'll love you the way I loved you at Saint-Remy in the story... He gave way, I was in despair.

I began with arabesques. All my hope was in my hand. Frivolous, light, aerial, adventurous, simple, complicated, coaxing, surprising, deceptive, hesitant, precise, rhythmical, unending, subtle, lively, slow, dragging, conscientious. Do you like this, this long circling round your nipple? There is a swallow back from the warm-south, Gabriel, fluttering from your thigh down to your ankle, listen to it on the outlines of your body. Moving carelessly, diligently, attentively, curiously, watchfully, I traced the name of Saint-Remy over my lover's flesh. I also wrote down the old woman picking up the rotting flowers when the market was closing. I twined a long paragraph of honeysuckle around his haunches, around his wrist, around his ear. My slow lotus stream flowed into his blood, but it didn't make Gabriel go to sleep. A shiver across his shoulder blades, token of my power. Dance-hall bowers, potatoes frying in the open air, his armpits, his groin. Hunched inside the chaos of my love, my hand followed the outline of his leg as I fed like a baby at my husband's heel. Dear teacher, you encouraged me, I listened at the sounds of the clearing: his shoulder as I gambolled around it. My fingers and my nails told about a very fragile moon intimidated by a cloud, about a sunset being massacred, about the trills and the waterdrops of a shadow bird. A heavy walk we went on then. Oh God, how well I wrote from his knee up to his groin; oh God, that was my religion.[17]

In the work of Violette Leduc vulgarity is a strength. Here

cheap romance joins the superior variety called romanticism to create a pantheistic ritual of love. Following the romantic notion of togetherness *La Bâtarde* embarks on an egotistical sentimental journey over her husband's helpless body. One could imagine any man feeling a deep disgust for this kind of preciosity, craving some straight dirt, some gusto in the business instead of this neurasthenic need. Some inferior version of this amalgam of vanities and devotion is at the bottom of feminine refusal to tolerate certain sexual acts which are unmistakably specific and mechanical, and tolerance of perversions, conversely, because they are ritually apparelled. Much can be accomplished sexually by flattery, which is a version of prayer. The act of adoration of a woman's nakedness is not overlooked by the most extrovert lovers, and much caress is in fact ritual observance, not to mention the ritual repetition of the phrase 'I love you' demanded by some of the most dissolute of women. The recurrent terminology in sexual magazines of orgasm as the 'supreme' experience is another reflection of romanticism and the belief in a kind of mystic immolation in sex.

Like most young girls, I had always been vaguely longing for my 'Prince Charming' to come and awaken me with his magic kiss. But when I had my first kiss and many more without the promised results, I was deeply disappointed. It was not until much later when, after a deep and satisfying orgasm, I suddenly realized the true meaning of the fairy tale and the nature of the magic kiss of which it speaks.[18]

As a cynical young sexual reformer I often observed that the mystical kiss of the romance was more properly to be under-stood as orgasm, but I have come to think that that was wrong. What happens in the romantic view of sex is that the orgasm comes to signify the kiss, or vice-versa. The fairy-tale conditioned mind is translating the phenomena into terms of popular pulp culture. No boy who has ever masturbated,

whether into a baseball mit in a burlesque show or on to a
clean sheet of white paper, would be tempted to describe
orgasm in such a *silly* way. Maxine Davis does not see the
pomposity of her own prose in this statement.

A girl may have studied marriage manuals diligently and tried to
absorb any instructions made available by objective, responsible
people. But if she has never kissed or petted or masturbated or
dreamed to the point of climax, she has not the faintest idea of what
the supreme experience might be like.[19]

I have always been troubled by the same kind of quality in
D.H. Lawrence's writing about actual sexual experience.
He couples a strange reluctance to describe what his protago-
nist is actually doing with the most inflated imagery of
cosmic orgasm. It is a short step from the more familiar

Slowly, very slowly, and with a wonderful tenderness, his lips found
hers. Just for a moment their mouths touched; the petal of a flower
against the petal of a flower... His mouth sought her once more
and it was as if the whole world was swept away from them and they
stood alone above the clouds in the glory of the sunshine, which had
something divine about it.[20]

with all its fairy-tale religious elements to

She seemed to faint beneath, and he seemed to faint, stooping over
her. It was a perfect passing away for both of them, and at the same
time the most intolerable accession into being, the marvellous fullness of immediate gratification, overwhelming, outflooding from
the source of the deepest life-force, the darkest, deepest, strangest
life-source of the human body, at the back and the base of the
loins.[21]

This is the same romanticism that would have Elizabeth
Heaton protecting her lap with the breakfast tray, the notion
that the penis is a mighty fountain forced momently out by

some mysterious dynamism. Nevertheless, I was not sure what was wrong with it until I paid attention to the sexual imagery of urban blues which seems to escape all the prudery and false mysticism of the sex prophet. Perhaps that might explain the emergence in America of writers who can talk of sex with enthusiasm and clarity. However, one could not class Hemingway amongst them, for his description of successful orgasm is when *the earth moves* and the older tradition seems still to be by far the better represented.

The prudery, excitement and 'poetry' of Lawrence's and Hemingway's writing places them in the tradition of the sexual romantics, even if their wares are sold to a more literate readership. Their vocabulary is larger than Cartland's but the structures of titillation are the same, provided we accept the fuck as the end of the story and not the kiss. As indications of a sexual life-style they are as misleading. The female role is still one of passing mysteriously, with all proper delay, from state to state of feverish exaltation. It is perhaps worth notice that both Lawrence and Hemingway have been accused of impotence. Now that the sexual role of women is being admitted the masochistic postures of the feminine romance are being complicated and enhanced but they remain essentially the same. Women are now expected to enjoy sex but not to descend from imprisonment in the bourgeois temple. Instead sex is being brought into the temple as a part of ritual observance, a mystical experience which is a grace from men, as Teresa of Avila was granted ecstasy by God.

A woman is never so happy as when she is being wooed. Then she is mistress of all she surveys, the cynosure of all eyes, until that day of days when she sails down the aisle, a vision in white, lovely as the stefanotis she carries, borne translucent on her father's manly arm to be handed over to her new father-surrogate. If she is clever, and if her husband has the time and the resources, she will insist on being wooed all her life; more likely she will discover that marriage is not romantic, that husbands forget birthdays and anniversaries and seldom payed compliments, are often perfunctory. Nobody flatters, nobody makes her feel desirable. She realizes that her husband's susceptibility is much more sexual than personal, or at least she feels it is, because he is so careless of the rituals that she established as a blushing bride. In the courting phase her relationship was all glamour (spellbinding as the preliminary to imprisonment in the glass

---

Women are told from their infancy and taught by the example of their mothers, that a little knowledge of human weakness, justly termed cunning, softness of temper, 'outward' obedience and a scrupulous attention to a puerile kind of propriety, will obtain for them the protection of man....

Mary Wollstonecraft,
'The Vindication of the Rights of Women', 1792, p. 33

---

mountain) for she met her husband only when she was being taken out, wined and dined and dated and fêted, looking pretty, talking only of herself and her love. If her need for the old adulation grows desperate she may be seriously affected. Romance had been the one adventure open to her and now it is over. Marriage is the end of the story. Women's magazines exhort her not to let the romance die out of her marriage. She tries not 'to let herself go', keeps young-looking, pretty, tries not to ask her husband every single day if he loves her, wishes his morning kiss before leaving her alone for the day were a little less mechanical. Sooner or later she sees her courting as a seduction; she may blame her husband for it but in fact she engineered the seduction herself. What love seemed to be in her head, all electric lips and dreaming of him wide awake in her bed it never really was at all. She sees that she was a silly romantic girl. Now she finds that marriage is a hard job. Her romanticism becomes, if it has not already become, escapism. She treats herself to little romantic things like perfumes which her husband does not even notice. Romance is now her private dream.

Felice – a summer affair that will last forever.

Miss Lentheric is a love affair. It really is the most romantic new perfume and you'll never know what you've missed if you don't try some.

Aqua Manda. Two words to change your life.

Now that she must flatter herself, the market throngs with products with which she can caress herself.

From clove-spiced Zanzibar...to the early dew of Burma...the world over, more girls use Lux than any other soap. Beautiful girls, with beautiful complexions. Lux lather, you see, is specially enriched with the cream of natural oils...made milder to keep your skin soft and smooth the natural way. So join the world's most beautiful women...

The advertising for hair colouring is always made with an eye on the escapism of women, *a new, crazy you* will result, new possibilities will open up. Even your bath can become a romantic ritual:

New Dew brings Alpine magic to your bath. Like a flower, newly awakened by the dew. Fresh, lovely and ready to greet the day. That's how you feel each time you bath in New Dew... Just two capfuls of this fragrant green essence is all you need to drift lazily away to nature's world of flowers and freshness.[22]

But the supreme adventure is still falling in love; although that unworldly excitement is past women still insist on reliving it. It is the only story they really want to hear. I saw a young wife, of a few months at the most I should judge, on a vaporetto in Venice with her husband, intently reading a fotoromanzo while her husband tried vainly to chat with her and caress her. The fantasy was even then more engrossing than the reality. Women's magazines treat the same story over and over again, changing the setting, inventing more and more curious combinations of circumstances to vary the essential plot; but falling in love, the kiss, the declaration and the imminent wedding are the staple of the plot. Other stories treat ancillary themes, of adultery, of delusion and disappointment, or nostalgia, but the domestic romantic myth remains the centrepiece of feminine culture.

Sexual religion is the opiate of the supermenial. A particularly naïve letter to a women's magazine made this unusually clear.

Have you ever thought how much modern inventions are ruining romance? There's no need for her to darn his indestructible nylon socks or iron his drip-dry shirt. What man will pick up a dropped paper hanky or wheel an overloaded trolley basket? There's no need to help a mini-skirted girl on to a bus, and her gas cigarette lighter always works.[23]

Romance sanctions drudgery, physical incompetence and prositution (for the cigarette lighter situation is more likely to incommode street walkers than anybody else). If Miss S.A. of Rhiwbira is right romance must be doomed, but there is not as much indication of that as I would demand if it is to serve as a ground for optimism. Female clothes are much more romantic now than they were in the years of austerity, and if mini-skirts have increased mobility, false hair and eyelashes and false modesty in the way of wearing those mini-skirts have inhibited it again. Even a book as flat and documentary as *Groupie* embodies the essential romantic stereotype in Grant, the masterful lover who supplants all Katie's other fucks. He tells Katie when she may call, how long she may stay, commands her to make the bed and perform all his other requirements without demur and she loves it.[24] She persuades herself that this is love-in-disguise, like it was with Lord Worth and Grant Jarvis, and ends the book on a hopeful note, waiting for him to return from America and go on ordering her about. The book is based on experience, and often positively dreary in its fidelity, but the character of Grant is a genuinely unconscious falsification of the original. If female liberation is to happen, if the reservoir of real female love is to be tapped, this sterile self-deception must be counteracted. The only literary form which could outsell romantic trash on the female market is hard-core pornography. The titillating mush of Cartland and her ilk is supplying an imaginative need but their hypocrisy limits the gratification to that which can be gained from innuendo: by-pass the innuendo and you short-circuit the whole process. I and my little friends swapped *True Confesions* back and forth because we were randy and curious. If you leave the *Housewives' Handbook*[25] lying about, your daughter may never read Cartland or Heyer with any credulity.

The Object of Male Fantasy

Little children of both sexes read adventure stories. The very little ones read unisexual adventure with both heroes and heroines. The older read segregated stories of all girl or all boy exploit. Verisimilitude means that the writers of girls' stories cannot exclude male characters, but they do exclude all sexual or love interest, from their pre-pubescent readers. For boys the exclusion of sex entails the exclusion of all female characters. I can still remember the disgust felt by all of us in the eighth grade when the films of the Biggles stories included a love interest as a concession to dating couples. Puberty ends the young girl's hearty fantasies of being, say, Pony rescuing Colonel Buffalo Bill Cody by skipping a stone across a river on to the pate of an Indian archer only to snatch the archer from alligators' jaws two frames later,[1] and initiates her in the passive excitements of the infantilized heroine of romance. For boys broaching manhood the dominant fantasy of adventure simply expands to include woman as exploit: sex is admitted as a new kind of prowess or hazard. Because novelty is an essential character of adventure so we may expect the sex interest to be superficially diversified, racially, physically, and perhaps socially, but nevertheless the patterns of gratification are simple, and seem to fall into two patterns, the Great Bitch and the Poison Maiden.

The Great Bitch is the deadly female, a worthy opponent for the omnipotent hero to exercise his powers upon and through. She is desirous, greedy, clever, dishonest, and two jumps ahead all the time. The hero may either have her on his side and like a lion-tamer loose her on to his enemies, or he may have to battle for his life at her hands.

...unconditional surrender was her only raw meat. A Great Bitch has losses to calculate after all if the Gent gets away. For ideally a Great Bitch delivers extermination to any bucko brave enough to take carnal knowledge of her.[2]

Mailer's Deborah Caughlin Mangaravidi Kelly is carefully constructed to embody as many of the features of the type as possible in one single manifestation. In describing her Mailer is not entirely detached, his narrator still murmurs in the heavy American dream; the power of the book is derived from this tension between the surgeon and his wound. The deadly strain of sex as exploit, the tireless self-proof which makes communication impossible, the imaginary but genuinely killing battle of the sexes is what Stephen Rojack escapes from, but his escape makes continuation of the book impossible. In contemporary sexual myth there are no alternatives, unless we heed the thin self-satisfied voice of the hippies. The most important fact about Deborah is the aspect mentioned first: all the descriptions of Spillane's and Fleming's women as expensive, classy, rich, top-drawer and so forth are eclipsed by Mailer's insane hyperbole. The context and the understatement ought to give the game away, although feminists like Kate Millett persist in assuming that Mailer is a cretin.[3]

I met Jack Kennedy in November 1946. We were both war heroes, and both of us had just been elected to Congress. We went out one night on a double date and it turned out to be a fair evening for me. I seduced a girl who would have been bored by a diamond as big as the Ritz.[4]

Which must be taken to mean that Rojack is an all-American hero moving in the Grace Kelly/Jacqueline-Lee-

Bouvier enclosure, with a cock more interesting in every way than anything Scott Fitzgerald could put words to. The imagery of war and sex is inextricably confused. The enemy is a faggot to be blasted to a bloody pulp below the waist; pain is a clean pain, a good pain, evidence of good clean destruction, no rot, for of rot life is born. The womb smells of rot, for the source of life is despair for barren Rojack, whose very mind is an arsenal. Deborah is not only war, she is sport.

> . . . she'd been notorious in her day, picking and choosing among a gallery of beaux: politicians of the first rank, racing drivers, tycoons, and her fair share of the more certified playboys of the western world, she had been my entry to the big league.[5]

The physical attributes of this creature are those of the opulent tigresses of thriller literature. Barbara Cartland and Georgette Heyer would not recongize the lithe, full-breasted, very tall, amazing-haired female toughs who blast the heroes at a mere flash. Mailer is less stilted but the attributes are typical.

> She was a handsome woman, Deborah, she was big. With high heels she stood at least an inch over me. She had a huge mass of black hair and striking green eyes. . . . She had a large Irish nose and a wide mouth which took many shapes, but her complexion was her claim to beauty, for her skin was cream-white and her cheeks were coloured with a fine rose . . .[6]

We are not far from those extraordinary springing women with slanting eyes and swirling clouds of hair who prowl through thriller comics on the balls of their feet, wheeling suddenly upon the hero, talons unsheathed for the kill. Their mouths are large, curved and shining like scimitars: the musculature of their shoulders and thighs is incredible, their breasts like grenades, their waists encircled with steel belts as

narrow as Cretan bull-dancers'.[7] Ian Fleming devises
women who drive cars well or are clever horsewomen or
marksmen.[8] Deborah is the most exciting kind of female
competent, a killer.

> . . . She was an exceptional hunter. She had gone on Safari with her
> first husband and killed a wounded lion charging ten feet from her
> throat, she dropped an Alaskan bear with two shots to the heart
> (30/06 Winchester). . . . Often as not she fired from the hip, as
> nicely as pointing a finger.[9]

What is the fate of Deborah's tribe of deep-chested, full-
breasted, narrow-hipped, dancer-legged anti-heroines? In
less self-conscious mythology they submit to the hero's iron
cock to be battered by his animal vigour into dewy softness
and submission, even if they are man-haters like Pussy
Galore. This is Tiger Mann subduing Sonia Wutko:

> Her mouth was a hot, wet thing of such demanding passion that it
> itself was a fuse that ignited one explosion after another. Her mouth
> melted against mine, a torch that could nearly scream unless it was
> choked off, her entire body an octopus of emotion that demanded
> and demanded and when it was satisfied for a short time was almost
> content in a relaxation close to death itself.
> But I wouldn't give her that relaxation. She asked, she got. She
> wanted to see what a tiger was like, and now she had to find out.
> She knew the depth of the canines and the feeling of being absorbed
> because she was only a woman in the lust of a horrible hunger and
> in that frightening sunlight she knew for the first time what it was
> like to live as one.[10]

Adventure-sex is a matter of pyrotechnics, explosives,
wild animals, deep-sea diving, rough riding. The ideal
sexual partner gives promise of a good tussle and the more
animosity she harbours the better. It is clear from the
imagery of the Spillane passage that the proper fate of the
Great Bitch is death, either the metaphoric death of orgasmic

frenzy and obliteration, or actual death, which Mailer's hero metes to his savage wife by strangling. She asked, she got.

She smiled like a milkmaid and floated away and was gone. And in the midst of that Oriental splendour of landscape, I felt the lost touch of her finger on my shoulder, radiating some faint but ineradicable pulse of detestation into the new grace. I opened my eyes, I was weary with a most honourable fatigue, and my flesh seemed new. I had not felt so nice since I was twelve. It seemed inconceivable at this instant that anything in life could fail to please.[11]

Killing your woman is like killing a bear or a legendary monster: manhood sneaks out from under the domination of sex, escapes from addiction. It is a man's world once more. The culture of a nation in which men are segregated and educated in a Spartan regime of exertion, sport and cleanliness is bound to reflect this element, but it is frightening to consider what its repercussions must be in ordinary unwritten day-to-day transactions between the sexes. Mike Hammer's Velda is a Great Bitch, but she runs (something currishly) for her master and kills for him, bringing her prey home to lay at his feet. Her reward is Hammer's sexual abstention from her: ostensibly she is being saved up for a proper reward in some future realm where even Hammer might accept domesticity, but actually sexual intercourse with Velda would mean her destruction. Hip filmgoers laughed at the extraordinary collection of phallic weaponry which James Bond carried with him, catching the director's joke that every gadget was another form of cock, but they might not have laughed so hard if they had reflected that the converse is equally true, that the penis has become a weapon.

The penis-weapon is used aggressively on the Great Bitch: in the case of the Poison Maiden it is used defensively. The Poison Maiden of *An American Dream* is called, appropriately enough, Cherry. She is pure, to all intents virgin as her name implies:

I had an orgasm with you. I was never able to before. . . . Never before. Every other way, yes. But never, Stephen, when a man was within me, when a man was right inside me.[12]

Achieving first love with the Poison Maiden is like the Siege Perilous. Cherry is surrounded by threatening creatures, mostly the nightclub heavies who sit around her as she sings in a dive in the Village, negroes, prizefighters of ill-repute, detectives and harpies, who are killed by the bullets fired at them from Rojack's brain. Here apartment was inhabited before her by her sister, killed because of the maleficent supermale, Shago (!) Martin. The precious moments Rojack spends with her there are threatened by the imminent return of the black enchanter. He is ostensibly a singer, but what a singer! '. . . you were glowing when he was done, the ear felt good, you had been dominated by a champion.'[13]

Other knights who had frequented this lady had run; only Rojack will make a stand, nothing but his mighty penis against a crazy nigger with a switchblade. He wins, of course. The Poison Maiden has conceived by him, and is plumb ready to enter the divine category of mother, only one last fiend clubs her to death. The final clinch of male romanticism is that each man kills the thing he loves; whether she be Catharine in *A Farewell to Arms,* or the Grecian Urn, the 'tension that she be perfect' means that she must die,[14] leaving the hero's status as a great lover unchallenged. The pattern is still commonplace: the hero cannot marry. The sexual exploit must be conquest, not cohabitation and mutual tolerance.

The extent to which the traits of adventure sex can be found in real life, or rather injected into life because they are part of a man's preoccupations, can be judged from the fantastic out-pourings of that sexual Munchhausen, John

Philip Lundin. The authenticity of his book, *Women,* as in some sense an autobiography is attested by an introduction signed by R.E.L. Masters. The first chapter delineates a favourite male fantasy, the cash value of female charms. Whether they be married to rich men, working as hostesses in high-class clubs, as 'models' or simply walking the streets, women are believed to be cashing in all the time. Lundin's exploit is the getting of what other men must buy, and dearly, for free. Of course, he is no ponce sweating over a prostitute's pleasure for his keep. He is a lover equal to the expectations of professionals. Husbands are paying customers or, more tersely, suckers. As a permanent free-loader Lundin is always in peril, and his women all have the excitement of the Poison Maiden as well as the sporting prowess of the Great Bitch. His greatest affair, accepting his own criteria, was with Florence, the boss's wife, and it follows the classic pattern of sexual exploit which we find in male literature. The flash is struck at first sight and the symptoms are typical.

No electric spark that ever hit me when I got into the way of an electric short ever hit me as powerfully as seeing Florence. My heart was pounding, my blood shot through my veins as if I had a fever, and a lump squeezed itself between my windpipe and my aorta. My stomach was going down an elevator shaft, as if I were afraid for my life. And I felt a stirring of the testicles as if they knew independently that this woman would swing them into action.[15]

The risks of a clandestine adultery are deliciously exacerbated by Florence's extraordinary heat and the fact that the gross cuckoldy husband has certain 'boys' who protect his interests. Lundin is eventually driven off. Because she is universally desirable many other men are in love with her, a prime requisite of male fantasy, for the exploit must be hailed by other men. Florence manages to persaude her husband's boys to drive her to see Lundin, and they have a passionate reunion in the back seat of the car. When the boys demand similar favours and threaten blackmail, she hotfoots to Mexico, where she marries another sucker, a millionaire, naturally. She leaves him to fly to yet another savage guardian, her harpy mother. Her enduring position as Lundin's only love is ensured when she finds she has cancer and goes back to her first rich husband: 'Somehow I've known ever since I was told she was dead that my life will never be complete without her.'[16]

> **Love, for too many men in our time, consists of sleeping with a seductive woman, one who is properly endowed with the right distribution of curves and conveniences, and one upon whom a permanent lien has been acquired through the institution of marriage.**
>
> **Ashley Montagu,**
> **'The Natural Superiority of Women', 1954, p. 54**

The quite ersatz notion of the complete life is essential to male notions of falling in love. Men do not hope to find a daughter in the way that women hope to find a new father, nor do they hope to find a mother. They hope for a woman who will be the 'answer to it all', who can fulfil my needs for understanding, companionship and excitement'. Basic to the demand is an inflated notion of the capacity of the man in question for desire (need), excitement, companionship, and understanding. The man is the given: his mate must be equal to him, or adaptable. The exciting woman of fantasy is the one who creates the desire and releases virile potential by the mere sight of her, and the sight of all the men in the room gaping at her. One aspect of the fantasy is reflected almost invariably in behaviour in the pleasure which men get from being seen with a woman whom other men covet. The extent to which this pleasure may be developed is indicated by the extremity of the device invented by James Jones in *Go to the*

Widowmaker to reveal Lucky Videndi's superlative desirability and Grant's security in holding her. Having refused to join a nude bathing party, she waits until the others and her husband are all out of the water and then

Lucky suddenly got up and walked down into the water. She lay down and half-crawled, half-paddled out a short distance, all of her under but her head...suddenly she stood up, her arms over her head in a classic ballet pose. She had taken off her suit and was completely nude. The water seemed to pour off her in slow motion as it were, and there she was in all her glorious sensuality, the lovely white breasts and lean rounded hips making the other, skinnier girls look mechanical and asexual. Her arms still up, and not quite knee-deep in the water she did a series of classic ballonné fouetté, a real pas de bourrée directly toward them, all beautifully done. It was a movement which...gave the impression of opening the crotch up completely, and she must have chosen it deliberately. There was a hush of stillness from the shore.... The champagne-coloured hair had not gotten wet and it flashed about her as she moved like white gold.[17]

It is small wonder that Grant is besotted with such a creature, especially as she has the added athletic grace of being able, when love-making, to put both feet behind her head. It is certainly some kudos to be able to *need* a woman

> Has anyone else a husband like mine? He was attracted to me because I am a long-legged brunette. Now, after six years of marriage, he feels like a change and pines for a bosomy blonde. He has not run off or been unfaithful. Instead, I now have a long, silky blonde wig, and a chest-expander for daily exercises. – V. Ladbrooke, Essex.
> P.S. If I get a guinea I shall put it towards a 'pop-singer' wig for him!
>
> Petticoat, 15 November 1969

like that. To make the point clearer, Lucky Videndi describes herself as an author-fucker, and the man she falls in love with is an author, so her continued presence by his side enchances his profesional prestige.

In Mailer's words she is his entry *into the big league*. As long as we have these patterns of woman as challenge, we are dealing with subpornographic literature pandering to an impossible fantasy, which, because of the intimate relationship between potency and fantasy, has a tendency to obtrude into actual sexual behaviour. Women may be frigid because the requirements of romance are not satisfied but men too quail at the lack of excitement which domesticity affords.

> I cannot live with you,
> It would be life,
> And life is over there
> Behind the shelf.[18]

The Middle-Class Myth of Love and Marriage

Loveless marriage is anathema to our culture, and a life without love is unthinkable. The woman who remains unmarried must have missed her chance, lost her boy in the war or hesitated and was lost; the man somehow never found the right girl. It is axiomatic that all married couples are in love with each other.

> The art of managing men has to be learned from birth. It is easier as you acquire experience. Some women have an instinctive flair, but most have to learn the hard way by trial and error. Some die disappointed. It depends to some extent on one's distribution of curves, a developed instinct, and a large degree of sheer feline cunning.
> Mary Hyde, 'How to Manage Men', 1955, p. 6

Sympathy is often expressed for those people, like kings and queens, who cannot be solely directed by Cupid's arrow, although at the same time it is tacitly assumed that even royal couples are in love. In the common imagination nuns are all women disappointed in love, and career-women are compensating for their failure to find the deepest happiness afforded mankind in this vale of tears. But it was not always believed even if the normality of the idea persuades us that it must have been. The mere mention of Cupid's arrow ought to remind us that there was a far different concept of love which prevailed not so long ago, a concept not only separate from pre-nuptial courtship, but quite inimical to marriage. Even in the brief lifetime of the concept of nuptial love it has not always been the same idea: many of the defenders of marriage for love in the sixteenth century would be horrified if they could know the degree of romanticism and sexual

---

I am 39 and have been submitting to corporal punishment from my husband ever since we married 15 years ago. We have both treated this matter of punishment as a normal sort of proceeding. It was not until recently, when we saw some letters in 'Forum' that we realized there were people who had guilt complexes about spanking their mates.

Our ideas are quite simple. My husband happens to believe that in marriage the husband should be the boss. I agree with him and I recognize that wrong-doing should be punished. We both think that the simplest, most convenient, most effective and most natural way for a man to punish the faults of his woman is to spank or whip her; but not too severely, certainly not brutally.

Letter in 'Forum', Vol. 2, No. 3

---

passion with which their ideal is now invested. Gradual changes in basic assumptions have obscured the traces of the development of the myth of falling-in-love-and-getting-married; demographic information about its early stages is hard to come by. Acknowledging all these uncertainties with due humility we may embark upon a speculative exploration.

It is by now commonplace to point out that in feudal literature romantic love was essentially anti-social and adulterous. The discussions of de Rougemont and his ilk are well-known, at least in their gist.[1] The term 'courtly love' has become a cliché of historical criticism. The tales of Guinevere and Iseult were the product of the minority culture of the ruling class, at which the serfs and yeomen must have marvelled when they heard them recounted in song and folk-tale. They were the product of the feudal situation in which a noble wife was a wife only when her warrior husband was at home (which with any luck was seldom), otherwise she ruled a community of men, many of them young and lusty, with the result that they entertained fantasies about the unobtainable to whom they could not even address their advances. She exploited their servility, which was the original of chivalry, and may or may not have served her own lusts by them. To her husband she was submissive and offered him her body as a fief. Victorian scholars exclaimed in horror at the description of marital love given in tracts like *Hali Maidenhad,*[2] and joyously acclaimed the protestant reformers for bringing the first breath of 'fresh air into the cattle shed' of marital theory.[3] The monkish author of the fourteenth-century tract *Hali Maidenhad* put it to the virgins he was addressing that if they really liked reading in Latin, illuminating manuscripts, embroidering (not antimacassars and guest towels but precious vestments and magical tapestries which are now among the finest art treasures of European museums), and writing poetry and music, then they were better off in the all-female society of a convent, where they were not surrounded by the bustle and brutality of a barracks, condemned to dangerous childbirth and the rough caresses of a husband too used to grappling with infidel captives and military whores to be aware of their emotional and sexual needs. He did not say but we might infer that the loves of clerks and nuns were more likely to be satisfying than the infatuation of young squires and the endless exacerbation of unfulfilled desire which is the whole motive force behind Provençal minstrelsy. Rabelais combined the elements of medieval humanist fantasy of sexual and intellectual adjustment in his jolly secular monastery of Thelème.[4] Rattray Taylor has listed the period as a matrist one, and however dubious his classification may ultimately be it is true that the influence of women upon the character of medieval civilization was great,[5] and appears greater when we consider that all culture which was not utterly ephemeral was the culture of a tiny minority. It is perhaps significant that most of the women who made a valuable contribution to medieval culture were either religious or women living in celibacy within or after marriage, like Hilda, Queen Edith, the sainted Margaret, her daughters Matilda and Mary, and Lady Margaret Beaufort.

The amorous character in the feudal castle was the young squire, not eligible for knight-service until he was twenty-one. His beardless youth and beauty were most often described as effeminate for he was long-haired, dressed in embroideries, skilled at musical performance with voice and instrument, and at dancing, and penning poetry. It was inevitable that a lad torn from his mother's breast to serve first as page and then as squire should yearn for the affection of his liege-lord's wife. The exigencies of adolescent flesh ensured that he would suffer sexual aches and pains and naturally he attached them to his beloved lady-image. It was a submissive, tearful, servile posture; once he attained his majority and came to know the permissive society of the battle-field, this compulsive feeling became more intellectual and less immediate as he became more manly, less effeminate and perforce less sexually obsessed. The situation was full of hazards: the lord's wife was often closer to her fellow vassal in age and temperament; he was certainly more attractive to her physically than her gruff stranger husband. If she should fall from grace and compromise the legitimacy of her heirs the only outcome was disaster. Divorce was impossible, adultery was punishable by death be it the husband's *crime passionel* or the sentence of the law. The community attempted to exorcize this deep fear by externalizing it. Stories of ill-fated passion were cautionary tales. Love was a blight, a curse, a wound, death, the plague.

Sex itself was outlawed, except in desire of issue. The chastity belt and its attendant horrors are reminders of the intense pressure built up in such a situation. The body-soul dichotomy which characterizes medieval thought operated to protect the status quo. Servant girls and country bumkins were debauched without mercy, while the passion for the lady of the manor became exalted into a quasi-religious fervour. The literature of adulterous passion was, like the modern stories of obsession, fetishism and perversion, a series of vicarious peeps into a region so fraught with dangers that only a lunatic would venture there. Every young clerk learnt from his dominies what *love* was:

Set before thyne eyen howe ungoodly it is, how altogether a mad thing, to love, to waxe pale, to be made leane, to wepe, to flatter and shamefully to submyte thyselfe onto a stynkyng harlot most filthy and rotten, to gape and synge all nyght at her chambre wyndowe, to be made to the lure & to be obedyent at a becke, nor dar to do anything except she nod or wagge her head, to suffre a folyshe woman to reigne over the, to chyde the, to lay unkyndnesse one against ye other to fall out, to be made at one agayne, to gyve thyselfe wyllynge unto a Queene that she might mocke, knocke, mangle and spoyle the. Where I beseche amonge all these thinges the name of a man? Where is thy berde? Where is that noble mynde created unto most beautyfull and noble thynges?[6]

But the more he strove to heed their teachings and disdain love, the more likely he was to be struck down unsuspecting by the bright glance of another man's chaste wife, which is what happened one fateful day to Francesco Petrarca. The effect on European letters was to last five hundred years. Petrarch was, besides a genius, very astute and he understood pretty clearly the nature of his passion. He managed to integrate it into his whole philosophical system, sublimating it by a thoroughly conscious and meticulous process. Laura became the mediatrix of all love and all.

knowledge of which God himself is the only Begetter. Her
death made the process easier. Love of Laura, the lady of the
laurel, the topaz and the ermine, the white deer, the
madonna, was his greatest cross and his greatest blessing. By
bearing it conscientiously all his life he made it his salvation.
In almost every sonnet Petrarch achieves a reconciliation
between his joy and his pain, his body and his soul but his
myriad followers were neither so intelligent nor so fortunate.
Probably only Dante achieved the same sort of dynamic
equilibrium with his Beatrice, consciously demonstrating it
in the *Purgatorio* and the *Paradiso* when she takes over from
Virgil and leads him to the beatific vision. For lesser men
Petrarchism became a refinement of adulterous sensuality.
One of the factors in the survival of Petrarchism was that
Petrarch was not living in a feudal situation. Laura was not
the wife of his lord but of a peer, the citizen of a city-state
which was bureaucratic and not hierarchic in structure. He
managed singlehanded the transfer of courtly love from the
castle to the urban community in a form which enables it to
survive the development of the mercantile community and
centralized government.

With the breakdown of the feudal system came the
corrosion of hierarchic, dogmatic religion. Medieval
Catholicism had based its authority upon the filial station of
the celibate clergy. Celibacy was incessantly promoted by
edicts of the Church in favour of sexual abstemiousness not
only in the clergy but even in the married. It would be
tiresome, if shocking, to relate the prohibitions which the
Church laid upon intercourse within marriage, before
communion, during Advent and Lent and on rogation days
and fast days, or the prurient interrogatories which priests
were instructed to conduct in the confessional. Marriage was
a station in life inferior to vowed celibacy and infantile
virginity and the abstention of widows. Second marriage was
not allowed a blessing in the Catholic rituals. It was

considered better for a priest to have a hundred whores than one wife. Mystics and saints compelled to be married by their station in life, like Edward the Confessor, made vows of celibacy within marriage. The second-class status of marriage became one of the principal issues in the Reformation. Martin Luther, the Augustinian friar, had barely posted his ninety-five theses on the door of the church in Wittenberg when he took himself a wife.

Perhaps the best way of understanding the Reformation is to connect it with the decline of the feudal system in those northern countries where it took place. In England its course seems to reflect pretty clearly the impact of lower-class values on upper-class culture. The poor do not marry for dynastic reasons, and they do not marry out of their community in alliances with their peers. Goings-on in the castle have never been based upon practice in the cottage, except when a lord decided to take unto himself a supermenial as he does in the story of Patient Griselda, told by Boccaccio in the thirteenth century and taken up by the Renaissance in a big way[7]; possibly the fascination that this story of the lord who married a peasant girl had for the Renaissance throughout Europe was an indication of the rethinking about marriage that is insensibly and unofficially going on. Griselda, taken from her hovel, is installed as her lord's humble and uncomplaining wife. Even when he takes a new, young and noble wife, she does not abate her servility, for she welcomes her and dresses her for the wedding, and as a result wins her lord back. He of course claims he was testing her. The story reflects the general effect of the impact of lower-class *mores* on the attenuated and neurotic sexuality of the ruling class, albeit in a distorting mirror. When Adam delved and Eve span there was little point in lady-worship. Nostalgic and probably mythical accounts of marriage and giving in marriage in Merrie England are unanmimous in their praise of the young folk who grow up working side by side in the tight-knit agricultural community. A boy made his choice from the eligible girls of his own village, lovingly steered by his parents and hers, indulgently watched during permitted revels at Maying and nutting, pursuing a long courting process of token-giving and kiss-stealing, until there was space in his home for his bride, and need of a new hand in the butter and cheese making, the milking, the brewing, the care of lambs and chickens, at the spinning wheel and the loom. Books of husbandry listed the qualities he should look for in a wife – health, strength, fertility, good-will and good-humour as well as her proper complement of household skills.[8] He respected her as a comrade and provided they were both healthy and strong they desired each other. The obsession of romantic love was simply irrelevant. Provided they agreed in age and social standing (a condition guaranteed by dowry and jointure) there was no obstacle except the tiresome caprice of the church laws against affinity, which had to be bought off by dispensations seeing as by the sixteenth century they disqualified nearly all the members of a village from marriage through either blood relationship or the imaginary ties of gossipry, the spiritual relationships incurred by baptismal sponsors.

By the sixteenth century this placid picture, which resembles the courting situation which still pertains in the extended kinship systems of feudal Calabria and Sicily, was broken up by the effects of enclosures, the increased exactions of the Church, and the rise of urban centres. Increased mobility, especially of the young men, increased the likelihood of marriage outside the known community. Changes in land tenure came to mean that a young man could not marry until his parents died and left him master of his own small property. By the seventeenth century a new pattern was established in England; late marrying was combined with betrothal followed by cohabitation. Peter Laslett found that parish registers showed christenings following hard of weddings, while marriage at thirty must be construed, in terms of the average life-span, as senile marriage.[9] The Church had long since lost control of the parish and her own courts were inadequate to deal with the results of her unrealistic laws about affinity and kinship. Too many parishes were left without competent clergy, and common law marriage was on the increase. The religious reformers began to forge a new ideology of marriage, as public and holy, so holy that it had first been celebrated by God in heaven. It was extolled as the highest state of life and the condition of attainment of the status of citizenship and manhood. The increase in literacy and the advent of printing gave new scope to theory and literary example. The first tales of courtship and marriage found their way into written forms, now printed for the new, semi-literate readership. Much of this was didactic and set out ways and whys of marrying; some of it was cautionary, some escapist, and some direct polemic. Ballads appeared, containing the exempla of the marriageable girl; possibly based on old songs of wooing like *Jone can call by name her cowes*.

Any girl who was personable, healthy and good-natured,[10] was likely to be heartily wooed, but love was always subject to firm considerations of suitability and advantageousness. Her husband must not be old or disfigured or cruel or a whoremaster. She was not married away vilely for money, for the heroes of ballads and their admirers strongly condemned the practice of the nobility in disposing of their children like stud cattle; on the other hand a girl could not be married out of her father's house until a suitable groom presented himself in a proper manner. She agreed to treat him well, respect him and joyfully to do his will in bed, but there is no indication that she expected her life to be transfigured by love. She considered herself to be as others thought her, a sexual creature ready for mating, and her husband was chosen as *likely* in this fashion too. On her marriage day she would be wakened by her bride knights and maidens, dressed in her best gown, stuck over with rosemary and crowned perhaps with ears of wheat, and taken in procession to the village church, where she would be assured of her husband's protection and a share in his fortunes. The blessing would promise children and freedom from nameless fear and jealousy. Feasting would last all day while the young couple chafed to be alone, for weddings were held in midsummer when the sun does not set until eleven; then they would be escorted to bed and left alone.

This is what happened according to the folklorists of the sixteenth century. Too often it did not, but it supplies the justification for the boast of the country to the court, that it alone knew the secrets of 'true love', based on familiarity and parental control.[11] But the legacy of Petrarchan passion, with the invention of printing, became more and more accessible as an idea and reacted on the sensibilities of young folk whose brains were already inflamed by the sexual abstinence imposed by a system of late marrying. Schoolmasters, preachers and reformers raged and wept over the prevalence of lecherous books and plays; prose works spun out long tales of chivalry debased into adventure, poems sang of adultery and the delights of sexual titillation, plays set forth images of juvenile infatuation and clandestine marriage. Young men in search of uncontaminated women, for the arrival of venereal disease at the beginning of the sixteenth century had complicated many things, rode up and down the country wooing country girls of substance with snatches of Serafino, Marino and Anacreon, justified in the name of the great Petrarch whom few Englishmen had ever read.[12] The Elizabethan press thundered with denunciations of the lewd seducers of silly country girls. Elizabeth and Mary both brought out the severest edicts against young men who charmed country wenches, lured them into marriage, wasted their dowries and then cast them off.[13] The church authorities insisted on the reading of the banns in the parishes of both parties, but often they were read in quite the wrong places and more often not read at all. Religious turmoil added to the confusion. Parishes left without incumbents depended upon hedgepriests to legitimize children; the preposterously ramified laws which could nullify marriage were unknown until invoked by an interested and better informed party. We will probably never know how many people suffered from the confusion about ecclesiastical law, which dealt with all questions of marriage and inheritance, and the changes of official religion in the sixteenth century. Perhaps it was only the reforming clergy persecuted by Mary, and disappointed by Elizabeth's refusal to recognize clerical marriage, who created the myth of perfect marriage, but minorities change the culture of majorities and certainly a change was occurring.

By the end of the sixteenth century love and marriage was already established as an important theme in literature. The nuclear household was certainly typical of urban households, and a greater proportion of the total population now lived in cities, but even the agricultural majority was also following the trend to triadic families. But it was still a developing argument, and not yet an escapist theme. The town took its cue from the country, where marriage was tolerance and mutual survival in a couple of rooms, where winter was longer than summer and dearth more likely than plenty. The disastrous step to marriage as the *end* of the story, and the assumption of 'living happily ever after' had not yet been taken. One of the most significant apologists of marriage as a way of life and a road to salvation was Shakespeare. It is still to be proved how much we owe of what is good in the ideal of exclusive love and cohabitation to Shakespeare, but one thing is clear – he was as much concerned in his newfangled comedies to clear away the detritus of romance, ritual, perversity and obsession as he was to achieve happy endings, and many of the difficulties in his plays are resolved when we can discern this principle at work. Transvestism is a frequently discussed Shakespearean motif, but it is rarely considered as a mode of revelation as well as a convention productive of the occasional frisson. Julia (in *Two Gentlemen of Verona*) and Viola (in *Twelfth Night*) are both transvestite heroines, on close terms with the audience, who are explicitly contrasted with Petrarchan idols living on another plane of ceremony and imagery, Silvia and Olivia. These goddesses are debased in the course of the play by their own too human tactics, and even in the case of Silvia by an attempted rape. The girls in men's clothing win the men they love by a more laborious means, for they cannot use veils and coquetry; they must offer and not exact service, and as valets they must see their loves at their least heroic. In *As You Like It* Rosalind finds the means to wean Orlando off his futile Italianate posturing, disfiguring the trees with bad poetry; love at first sight for a stranger lady who addressed kind words to him on a day of victory becomes the love of familiarity for a sexless boy who teaches him about women and time, discovering her own role as she teaches him his, thereby leaping the bounds of femininity and tutelage. In *Romeo and Juliet* the same effect is got by Romeo's overhearing Juliet's confession of love, so that she cannot dwell on form, however fain. Because their love is not sanctioned by their diseased society they are destroyed, for Shakespearean love is always social and never romantic in the sense that it does not seek to isolate itself from society, family and constituted authority. In *Midsummer Night's Dream* obsession is shown as a hallucination and a madness, exorcized by the communal rite. Portia in *The Merchant of Venice* only manages to show Bassanio the worth of what he really found in his leaden casket when she dons an advocate's gown to plead for Antonio, her husband's friend and benefactor, so that her love is seen to knit male society together, not to tear it apart.

When the choice lies between the ultra-feminine and the virago, Shakespeare's sympathy lies with the virago. The women of the tragedies are all feminine – even Lady Macbeth (who is so often misinterpreted as a termagant), especially Gertrude, morally unconscious, helpless, voluptuous, and her younger version, infantile Ophelia, the lustful sisters, Goneril and Regan opposed by the warrior princess Cordelia who refuses to simper and pander to her father's irrational desire. Desdemona is fatally feminine, but realizes it and dies understanding how she has failed Othello. Only Cleopatra has enough initiative and desire to qualify for the status of female hero.

The opposition between women who are people and women who are something less does not only rest in the vague contrast between the women of the comedies and the women of the tragedies. There are more explicit examples of women who may earn love, like Helena who pursued her husband through military brothels to marriage and honour in *All's Well,* and women who must lose it through inertia and gormlessness, like Cressida. In *The Taming of the Shrew* Shakespeare contrasted two types in order to present a theory of marriage which is demonstrated by the explicit valuation of both kinds of wooing in the last scene. Kate is a woman striving for her own existence in a world where she is a *stale,* a decoy to be bid for against her sister's higher market value, so she opts out by becoming unmanageable, a scold. Bianca has found the women's way of guile and feigned gentleness to pay better dividends: she woos for herself under false colours, manipulating her father and her suitors in a perilous game which could end in her ruin. Kate courts ruin in a different way, but she has the uncommon good fortune to find Petruchio who is man enough to know what he wants and how to get it. He wants her spirit and her energy because he wants a wife worth keeping. He tames her like he might a hawk or a high-mettled horse, and she rewards him with strong sexual love and fierce loyalty. Lucentio finds himself saddled with a cold, disloyal woman, who has no objection to humiliating him in public. The submission of a woman like Kate is genuine and exciting because she has something to lay down, her virgin pride and individuality: Bianca is the soul of duplicity, married without earnestness or good will. Kate's speech at the close of the play is the greatest defence of Christian monogamy ever written. It rests upon the role of a husband as protector and friend, and it is valid because Kate has a man who is capable of being both, for Petruchio is both gentle and strong (it is a vile distortion of the play to have him strike her ever). The message is probably twofold: only Kates make good wives, and then only to Petruchios; for the rest, their cake is dough.

There is no romanticism in Shakespeare's view of marriage. He recognized it as a difficult state of life, requiring discipline, sexual energy, mutual respect and great forbearance; he knew there were no easy answers to marital problems, and that infatuation was no basis for continued cohabitation. His lifetime straddled the decay of the ancient state and the development of the new, the collapse of Catholicism and the solidification of English Protestantism, and the changes in the concept of the created universe, of ethics and science and art which we call the English Renaissance. Much of his writing deals expressly with these changes and their meaning, balancing notions of legitimacy and law with cooperation, spontaneity and moral obligation, nature and mercy against authority and vengeance.

The new ideology of marriage needed its mythology and Shakespeare supplied it. Protestant moralists sought to redeem marriage from the status of a remedy against fornication by underplaying the sexual component and addressing the husband as the wife's friend.[14] It was unthinkable to them that children should marry without consent of their parents, but unthinkable also that parents should oppose a match which was suitable in the sense that the parties were of the same social standing and wealth, of an age and not disqualified by illness or criminality. Now that the property to be parcelled and transferred in marriage was more divisible and portable, girls may have had more freedom of choice but by the same token the old safeguards had ceased to apply. Parents demanded the right to know something of a bridegroom's background, and feared marriage with a stranger who might prove to be bigamous or a pauper. The country still taunted the city with the differences between their marryings but now the urban community was growing at the expense of the agarian, and the rural community was losing its cohesiveness.

Where a wife is actively employed in production, helping with planting out and harvesting as well as minding the women's work, she was naturally not the family's chief consumer in circumstances of vicarious leisure. She was not primarily chosen for her obvious charms, not used to manipulating them for her own ends, had no opportunity to gad about, wear fine clothes and make mischief. The subjects of popular farces about marrying and cuckoldry were the town-wives who were not employed in running their husband's business with them, who sat about with their gossips all day, flirting, drinking, flaunting new fashions and making mischief by carrying assignations and rumours, or entertaining the priest. Antoine de la Sale's very circumstantial account, *Les Quinze Joies de Mariage,* enjoyed several centuries of popularity and was even translated and adapted by Dekker at the end of the sixteenth century.[15] This was no mere misogynist's account, but the heart-felt cry of a man who felt that he had been exploited by women all his life. In the larger community of the town there was more sexual competition and girls learnt early to enhance their chances by the use of cosmetics and other forms of sexual display, laying forth their breasts and padding their buttocks. Their mothers superintended the process and instructed their daughters in the arts of sexual bargaining; if the worst came to the worst, and dalliance with a lusty young buck menaced an advantageous match with untimely progeny, mother arranged for an abortion or for the patching up of a hasty wedding with a more or less wealthy gull. The tensions in the situation were exaggerated by the laws which prevented apprentices from marrying until their long articles were over: many a master craftsman free at last to wive picked out a juicy young thing only to find that he had some soldier's or apprentice's leavings. Many of the city wives were idle, but, unlike women in other countries where urban dwelling had developed at an earlier epoch, they were not chaperoned and supervised and kept indoors, but allowed to walk forth freely and salute their acquaintance. The staple of French and English farce was the unwitting cuckoldom of the hardworked and henpecked husband whose wife will not keep house or cook for him.[16] The miserable husband reflected that her lust seemed to fire at the sight of every man but him, that she nagged, wheedled for fine clothes to attract strangers, that the first pregnancy meant the decline of her health and the assumption of permanent valetudinarianism. Obviously, such a dismal picture is an exaggeration, but the characteristics of middle-class marriage are already present: the wife is chief consumer and showcase for her husband's wealth: idle, unproductive, narcissistic and conniving. She had been chosen as sexual object, in preference to others, and the imagery of obsession became more appropriate to her case. This is the class who were most exposed to the popular literature of escapist wedding which grew out of the collision of upper-class adulterous romance and the simple stories of peasant wedding. As long as literature kept the essential character of marriage in sight, stories of love and marriage remained

These London Wenches are so stout,
   They are not what they do;
They will not let you have a Bout,
   Without a Crown or two.

They double their Chops, and Curl their Locks,
   Their Breaths perfume they do;
Their tails are pepper'd with the Pox,
   And that you're welcome to.

But give me the Buxom Country Lass,
   Hot piping from the Cow;
That will take a touch upon the Grass,
   Ay, marry, and thank you too.

Her Colour's as fresh as a Rose in June
   Her temper as kind as a Dove;
She'll please the Swain with a wholesome Tune,
   And freely give her Love.

                            English Ballad, c. 1719

vibrant, ambiguous and intelligent, but true love was quick to become a catch-phrase: the country had used it to mean their innocent couplings leading to a life of shared hardship and endeavour; the religious reformers added the notion which they culled from the scripture, 'Rejoice in the wife of thy youth, may her breasts delight thee always.' Sexual pleasure within marriage was holy, nevertheless marriage was also meant to be a remedy for lechery in that a good wife restrained her husband's passion and practised modesty and continence within marriage, especially when breeding. Unrestrained indulgence was thought to lead to illness, barrenness, disgust, and deformity of issue. For this reason it was considered particularly horrible when a woman married against her better judgement.[17] It was originally considered to be a mistake to marry a woman with whom you had been 'in amors', at whose feet you had grovelled and wept, to whom you had made flattering poems and songs. Shakespeare made his comment on the disparity between what is promised to the courted woman and what the wife can realistically expect in his picture of Luciana and Adriana in *The Comedy of Errors*. The divine mistress was to dwindle into a wife within hours of her wedding: the goddess was to find herself employed as supermenial.

Despite all pressures to the contrary from religious reformers, intelligent poets and playwrights, and the desperate interest of propertied parents in retaining control of marriage behaviour, love-and-marriage took over, ending in that triumph of kitsch, the white wedding. Part of the explanation can be found in the story of what happened to Petrarchism in Protestant England. The English sonnet sequences of the 1590s were either frankly adulterous like Sir Philip Sidney's or totally honorific like Daniel's artificial passion for the Countess of Pembroke. Wyatt had been unable to keep a note of genuine physical tension out of his dramatic and colloquial translations of Petrarch, but he never ceased to battle with this irrelevant sensuality. Sidney makes no such effort. His sexual successes with Penelope Rich are chronicled in the poetry.[18] Reaction to this licence in a society crusading for marriage as a sacred condition and deeply conscious of the differences in the practice of the nobility after a half-century of scandals was not slow in making an appearance on the same literary level. The Puritans were agitating for severer punishments for fornication as standing at the church door in a white sheet was treated by some blades as a sign of prowess and prestige. The reaction to the adulterous element in the courtly literature of the nineties can be found in the epithalamia which were written as public relations work for marriage. Spenser's, the best of them, was also virtually the first, for its precedents were mainly fescennine and Latinate. In it he combined reminiscences of the rural modes of celebrating bridals with imagery from the Song of Songs and a platonic injection of veneration for intellectual beauty. The result is a poetical triumph, although the sonnet sequence of which it is the climax is a failure. The adoption of the Petrarchan mode to describe the methodical steps of Spenser's very proper wooing is simply a mistake, but it is a mistake which continues to be made. The anguish and obsession of the Petrarchan lover is artificially stimulated by his lawful betrothed in fits of pique or capriciousness: the lawful wooer lashes himself into factitious frenzies at her father's frown.[19] William Habington followed the new pattern of Petrarchan wedding in a dreary sequence called *Castara*,[20] which ought to have proved beyond further dispute that adultery provided greater inspiration than marriage. Playwrights succeeded better than poets at establishing marriage as the *non plus ultra* of romantic love, but the real source of the marrying-and-living-happily-ever-after myth is that art-form invented to while away the vacant hours of idle wives, the love-novel.

Richardson's *Pamela* is the source of all, but it had various founts to draw upon for its own being. The invention of printing had meant that literature was no longer the prerogative of the nobility, and developments in education under the Tudors, buttressed by the Protestant anxiety that all should be able to read the Bible, led to the development of a market for all forms of escapist literature, many of which treated marriage as an adventure. The daughters of up and coming burghers learnt romance from the same sources that they learnt to use knives and forks and how to avoid farting in public. The notion of marriage as exploit first appears in stories like those told to the gentle craft of shoemakers, stories of the abduction of princesses by humble cobblers.[21] Bit by bit the archetypal story of the winning of the nobleman by the virtuous commoner like the Fair Maid of Fressingfield was developed.[22] The novels of Nashe, Defoe and other writers of the picaresque, were not proper reading for ladies. Moll Flanders and Fanny Hill were not fit heroines for the gentle sex. The pattern of the trials of *Pamela* is the pattern of the *Golden Legend,* in which virgin saints fought off all the machinations of the devil and his earthly agents to present themselves as unsullied spouses to Christ himself in heaven.[23] Pamela's divine spouse is the squire, and heaven is several thousand pounds a year. Richardson continued the story, but its proper ending, if the story is to correspond to the structure of sexual fantasy, is entry upon married life and unimaginable bliss. Richardson's followers did not attempt to describe the indescribable. The great bulk of the novel industry has been maintained until our own age by the lending libraries, which depend largely upon the category called *romance,* escapist literature of love and marriage voraciously consumed by housewives. Now the market is contested by the cheap paperback and the cinema, women's magazines and love comics and fotoromance. Gillian Freeman was offered work by one women's magazine which set out her staple plot in these terms.

The girl in the story should be a secretary...the boyfriend must be elevated above her socially – he could be the son of the boss, an advertising executive, a student or a serviceman...or a young doctor. The story had to have a happy ending, there was to be no mention of religion or race, and lovemaking must be restricted to a kiss.[24]

The myth is still as widely dispersed as it ever was, although permissiveness is loudly argued to have made great inroads upon it. It has no demonstrable relation to what actually happens in the majority of cases but this fact itself reflects nothing upon its sway as a myth. The myth has always depended upon the riches, the handsomeness, the loveliness, the considerateness of a man in a million. There

---

Chances are, when a fellow asks you out for dinner, you're someone pretty special in his life. A dinner-date means he doesn't mind spending a wallet-full of wampum on you – and more important, a great deal of time just sitting across at table from you with nothing to do but eat and talk. And it also means he expects to be proud of you as he follows you and the head waiter to the table.

'Datebook's Complete Guide to Dating', 1960, p. 115

---

are enough women prepared to boast of having got a man in a million to persuade other women that their failure to find a man rich enough, handsome enough, skilled enough as a lover, considerate enough, is a reflection of their inferior deserts or powers of attraction. More than half the housewives in this country work outside the home as well as inside it because their husbands do not earn enough money to support them and their children at a decent living standard. Still more know that their husbands are paunchy, short, unathletic, and snore or smell or leave their clothes lying around. A very high proportion do not find bliss in the conjugal embrace and most complain that their husbands forget the little things that count. And yet the myth is not invalidated as a myth. There is always an extenuating circumstance, the government, high taxation, or sedentary work, or illness, or perhaps a simple mistake or a failure in the individual case, which can be invoked to explain its divergence from the mythical norm. Most women who have followed in the direction indicated by the myth make an act of faith that despite day-to-day difficulties they are happy, and keep on asserting it in the face of blatant contradiction by the facts, because to confess disappointment is to admit failure and abandon the effort. It never occurs to them to seek the cause of their unhappiness in the myth itself.

The women of the lower classes have always laboured, whether as servants, factory hands or seamstresses or the servants of their own households, and we might expect that the middle-class myth did not prevail as strongly in their minds. But it is a sad fact that most working-class families are following a pattern of 'progress' and 'self-improvement' into the ranks of the middle class. In too many cases the wife's work is treated as a stop-gap, a contribution to buying or furnishing a house, and the omnipotent husband looks forward to the day when she will be able to stay at home and have the babies. They too consider even if they cannot exactly manage it that mum *ought* to be at home keeping it nice for dad and the kids. In extreme cases a husband may even object to the sight of his wife scrubbing the floor as an affront to his male romanticism. Too often his wife's work merely supplies him with the property or the mortgage necessary to admit him once and for all to the middle class; behind it the myth lurks secure and unthreatened.

The wedding is the chief ceremony of the middle-class mythology, and it functions as the official entrée of the spouses to their middle-class status. This is the real meaning of saving up to get married. The young couple struggles to set up an image of comfortable life which they will be forced to live up to in the years that follow. The decisions about the cost of the celebration are possibly less important than the choice of a shop whereat to place the *list*. The more class the families can pretend to the more they can exact in the way of presents at showers, kitchen teas and the like. A list placed at the most expensive store in town embeds the couple and their interlacing families in the high-consumption bracket. The result is big business and mutual satisfaction. Harrods assures the bride that all she needs to do is 'find the groom, we'll do the rest'. Some stores bombard girls whose engage-

> ...when through man's social and economic organization
> she became dependent, and when in consequence he
> began to pick and choose...women had to charm for her
> life; and she not only employed the passive arts innate
> with her sex, but flashed forth in all the glitter that had
> been one of man's accessories in courtship, but which he
> had dispensed with when the superiority acquired
> through occupational pursuits enabled him to do so.
> Under new stimulation to be attractive, and with the
> addition of ornament to the repertory of her charms,
> woman has assumed an almost aggressive attitude towards
> courtship...
>
> W.I. Thomas, 'Sex and Society', 1907, p. 235

ments are announced in the newspapers with invitations to
place their lists with them. One store in London turns over
two or three million pounds a year in this business, mainly
by manipulating the bride's mother. The more expensive
stores expect a list to fetch about £500 turnover although the
most expensive finds to its chagrin that only half the guests
buy the wedding present from them.[25] The true pattern is
already set in that it is the bride who initiates and controls all
this spectacular consumption, just as the bride's gown and
jewellery and the female guests' attire will establish the
modishness of the whole clan, just as her girl-friend
estimated her success in the marriage stakes by the size of the
rock she sported when her engagement was first announced.
The high consumption factor is maintained throughout by
the imagery of films and plays and books about marriage, in
which every household is warm and light, every wife is slim
and elegant, and every husband successful.

The myth is effortlessly pervasive like the forlorn hope of
winning the pools. Any shabby overworked female reading
of a millionaire's wife in the *Sunday Times* can dream that she

> It is not really surprising to hear of the number of men
> whose wives do not reach a satisfactory climax. As
> vibrators have been mentioned, may I add that it need
> not be the penis-shaped battery model which is difficult to
> 'disguise' if found by your children. We have a standard
> Pifco and this is really fantastic. I would defy anyone to
> claim that his wife would not reach a magnificent climax
> if her clitoris were teased with one of these.
>
> R.W. (Cheshire) Forum, Vol. 2, No. 8

had 'three children, one cook/housekeeper, one nanny, two
cleaners, two gardeners, one Rolls-Royce, one Fiat, one staff
car, one helicopter, country home in Cheshire, London flat
in Belgravia' and 'my husband bought me a lovely little
crocodile bag on chains from Gucci which goes with most
things. Of course, I don't know how much it cost. He also
gave me a mink, dark brown, by Maxwell Croft, which one
can practically live in.... I buy my negligées and
nightgowns from Fortnum's of course. I've no idea how
much they cost. Sometimes my husband gives me them,
which pleases me greatly.... My husband's awfully good at
presents of jewellery.'[26] It would all be spoilt if the envious
little woman reading her *Sunday Times* has a vision of the
industrialist's secretary reminding him that it was his
anniversary, and slipping out at lunchtime with a cheque to
pick up a piece selected by the jeweller's sales manager. Love
seems to perish in hardship or to go underground, so that the
valiant wife says 'I know he loves me. He doesn't say much
and we're past all that petting and stuff. But he'd never do
anything to hurt me or the kids.' It is easy to imagine that
love survives in a cottage with roses round the door, or in a
house in Cheshire with a cook/housekeeper, a nanny, two
gardeners and two cleaners, where the lady of the house is
always scented and beautiful, draped in fine stuffs from

We all know that the male instinctively looks to the woman for chastizement. It is a natural emotion born of the mother and child relationship. I am a willing partner in my husband's recurring urge to be disciplined, not simply for the eroticism of the event but also because my endeavours in this field are amply rewarded in other ways.

I have found that my husband has an almost insatiable desire to please me, not only in sexual affairs but also in general household matters. He has assumed responsibility for the housework, shopping, washing and ironing. I have only to mention that I need a new shelf, that the oven needs cleaning or a room decorating to find it done in no time at all. I am now encouraging him to take an interest in the culinary arts.

I am convinced not only by my own experience but also from other marriages that my husband is not abnormal. I'm sure that nine husbands out of 10, if asked by their wives if they would like to be caned, would answer yes. (Mrs) L.B., Essex.

Forum, Vol. 2, No. 3

Fortnum's, rested and happy in her triumphant husband's loving arms.

But it isn't true and it never was, and now for sure it never will be.

Family

Mother duck, father duck and all the little baby ducks. The family, ruled over and provided for by father, suckled and nurtured by mother seems to us inherent in the natural order. While momma gorilla is breeding and nursing, poppa gorilla mounts guard over her, defending her from the perils of the wild. Even when the wild held no perils, Adam delved and Eve span and God the father was their daddy and walked with them in the twilight if they were good. When they were bad they were flung out of the garden and began a family of their own. Their sons fought as siblings will and murder came upon the world. Somewhere in the Apocrypha lurked Lilith, the destructive woman, who offered love and licentiousness and threatened the family structure. The grandsons of Adam consorted with the daughters of the flesh. The myth of the origin of the patriarchal family in the Old Testament is ambiguous: the father is vindictive, the mother has his vassal, the brothers enact the primal crime, murder for the love of the father, while the harlot beckons from outside the prison of domesticity. But from this source modern Christianity developed its own paradigm of the nuclear family and considered it reflected in the natural law. The structure of the state, naïvely considered as no more than a collection of families, reflects the natural principle: the king/president is a benign but just father of a huge family. The Church also acknowledged one head, a *locum tenens* for God Himself. The man was the soul, and the woman the body: the man was the mind and the woman the heart; the man was the will and the woman the passions. Boys learnt their male role from father and girls their female role from their mother. It seems clear, simple and immutable. Father was responsible for his dependants; he owned the property, transferred it to his first-born son together with his name. The chain of command from the elders to the poorest vassals was complete.

And yet what seems so essential and inevitable is utterly contingent. The patrilineal family depends upon the free gift by women of the right of paternity to men. Paternity is not an intrinsic relationship: it cannot be proved, except

---

> The modern individual family is founded on the open or concealed slavery of the wife.... Within the family he is the bourgeois and his wife represents the proletariat.
>
> Friedrich Engels,
> 'The Origin of the Family' (1943) p. 79

---

negatively. The most intense vigilance will not ensure absolutely that any man is the father of his son.

> Is there no way for men to be but
> Women must be half-workers? We are bastards all...[1]

When there was property to pass on and legitimacy to be upheld, it was imperative to surround women with guards, to keep them in one place, keeping their natural curiosity and urge for movement and expression as undeveloped as possible. The chastity belt which warrior barons clapped around their wives when they went to war was the outward emblem of the fruitlessness of the struggle, the attempt to provide a barricado for a belly. Nowadays women demand trust and offer their free assurance about paternity, honouring the contract that they have made, to be protected, fed and housed in return for ensuring immortality in legitimate issue.

The family which is set up when a young man installs his

bride in a self-contained dwelling is not really well-designed to perform the functions of ensuring paternity. The wife is left alone most of the day without chaperone: the degree of trust demanded is correspondingly greater. The modern household has neither servants nor relatives to safeguard the husband's interest and yet it seems natural and proper, as the logical outcome of all the other patriarchal forms which have preceded it. In fact the single marriage family, which is called by anthropologists and sociologists the *nuclear* family, is possibly the shortest-lived familial system ever developed. In feudal times the family was of the type called a *stem* family: the head was the oldest male parent, who ruled a number of sons and their wives and children. The work of the household was divided according to the status of the female in question: the unmarried daughters did the washing and spinning and weaving, the breeding wives bred, the elder wives nursed and disciplined the children, and managed the cooking, the oldest wife supervised the smooth running of the whole. The isolation which makes the red-brick-villa household so neurotic did not exist. There was friction but it had no chance to build itself into the intense introverted anguish of the single eye-to-eye confrontation of the isolated spouses. Family problems could be challenged openly in the family forum and the decisions of the elders were honoured. Romantic love as a motive for cohabitation was hardly important. A man only needed to desire to breed by a woman who would fit in with his household. Disappointment, resentment and boredom had less scope. The children benefited by the arrangement and in parts of Greece and Spain and Southern Italy still do. Someone, if only grandfather or an unmarried uncle or aunt, always had time to answer questions, tell stories, teach new skills, or go fishing. As soon as children could walk well by themselves they had a little responsibility – the hens, or the dovecote, a lamb or a kid to bring up. They were not sent to bed in a dark room while their elders talked in the kitchen, but allowed to stay and listen and learn until they fell asleep in someone's arms. Then they were quietly undressed and put to bed without waking. There could be no generation gap because the household represented all age groups. When I lived in a tiny hamlet in Southern Italy I saw such a family bravely holding together in spite of the grimmest poverty and the absence of most of the men who were working in Germany, and their children were the happiest, the least coy and irritable of any that I have ever observed. As all the neighbouring families were kin, the community was strongly cohesive. The exigencies of such group living had created strong decorums which were always respected. We would have starved if it had not been for the exchange of whatever goods the kin-families had in excess for our own super-abundances, for we could not have afforded food at the exorbitant prices which the *latifondiste* charged on the open market.

The stem family can provide a source of cohesion which is inimical to state control for it is immovable, and its strongest loyalty is to itself. When the principle is exerted in defiance of instituted authority it can become the infamous *famiglia* of the Mafia. The rituals of family honour have involved the anti-social manifestations of *vendetta* and *omertà* but these are not significant until the familial, regional community is threatened by political authority. The American liberators were quick to see the organizational importance of the Mafia in Sicily; what they did not see was that the kind of cohesion they sought to exploit was already anachronistic and economically non-viable.

The effects of industralization and urbanization in changing the pattern of settlement and requiring the mobility of labour have hastened the decay of the stem family, which declined in Western Europe some time before the sixteenth century. The changes in tenure of land, the decay of regional authority, the centralization of government, enclosures and developement of money rents and absentee landlordism all played a part in the development of the nuclear family, and yet it is only recently that the nuclear family has dwindled to the stump of community living that it now is. When the largest proportion of the working community was in service in large households, when spinsters and unmarried sons lived in the household, when sons and daughters were most often sent away to work in other households, the family remained organic and open to external influences. Husbands and wives could not indulge in excessive introversion about their relationship which was buttressed firmly by the laws against divorce, public opinion, and the uncontrolled size of families. Aging parents were kept and cared for in the household. But there was no longer a family business, no longer a heritage to be developed and served. The denseness of the urban community entailed estrangement from immediate neighbours, and the necessity of finding work led sons outside the immediate purview of the family. The effect of education estranged families even more especially when compulsory education created a generation more literate than their parents. The gradual expansion of education generation by generation is prolonging this effect. By the time Ibsen and Strindberg were writing their domestic tragedies the family had become a prison where the young struggled to escape the dead hand of the old, where the outside community was only represented by the policeman, the doctor and the parson, where the servants were strangers and class enemies. Puritan morality had resulted in hypocrisy, frustration and pornography. Husband and wife danced a dance of diurnal murder. The father–protector, unable to assume any other field of superiority or prowess, was princially moral arbiter although unfitted for the role: the wife was a designing doll, disillusioned about her husband, confused and embittered by her own idleness and insignificance. The syndrome of vicarious leisure, which Veblen describes, had come full circle. Female occupations were more conspicuously meaningless than ever. The embitterment of marriage partners had become so evidently destructive that laws to facilitate divorce began to be promulgated in most western countries. Women began to clamour for the right to work outside domestic service, and expanding industry came to need them, especially with the depredations of the First World War upon manpower. The number of unmarried women became greater, aggravating a problem which had existed since the turn of the century. Gradually the big Victorian-built houses were subdivided into smaller units. In response to requirements for higher density housing the flat proliferated. More and more of the functions of the large household devolved upon the state: the care of the old, of the sick, of the mentally infirm and backward.

The family of the sixties is small, self-contained, self-centred and short-lived. The young man moves away from his parents as soon as he can, following opportunities for

---

If strict monogamy is the height of all virtue then the palm goes to the tapeworm, which has a complete set of male and female sexual organs in each of its 50–200 proglottides or sections and spends its whole life copulating in all its sections with itself.

Friedrich Engels,
'The Origin of the Family' (1943) p. 31

---

training and employment. Children live their lives most fully at school, fathers at work. Mother is the dead heart of the family, spending father's earnings on consumer goods to enhance the environment in which he eats, sleeps and watches television. Children tend more and more since the war to create more vital groups of their own, assuming tribal characteristics of dress and ritual behaviour. Even the girls tend to go to work and set up house with other girls in the enormous bed-sitter belts of major cities. The wife is only significant *qua* wife when she is bearing and raising the small children, but the conditions under which she carries out this important work and the confusion which exists about the proper way to perform it increase her isolation from her community and intensify the parental relationship in these earliest years.

The working girl who marries, works for a period after her marriage and retires to breed, is hardly equipped for the isolation of the nuclear household. Regardless of whether she enjoyed the menial work of typing or selling or waitressing or clerking, she at least had freedom of movement to a degree. Her horizon shrinks to the house, the shopping centre and the telly. Her child is too much cared for, too diligently regarded during the day and, when her husband returns from work, soon banished from the adult world to his bed, so that Daddy can relax. The Oedipal situation which is always duplicated in marriage is now intensified to a degree which Freud would have found appalling. Father is very really a rival and a stranger. During the day the child may be bullied

The complex known to the Freudian school, and assumed by them to be universal, I mean, the Oedipus complex, corresponds essentially to our patrilineal Aryan family with the developed 'patria potestas', buttressed by Roman law and Christian morals, and accentuated by the modern economic conditions of the well-to-do bourgeoisie.

Bronislaw Malinowski
'Sex and Repression in Savage Society', 1927, p. 5

as often as petted: what is certain is that he has too much attention from the one person who is entirely at his disposal. The intimacy between mother and child is not sustaining and healthy. The child learns to exploit his mother's accessibility, badgering her with questions and demands which are not of any real consequence to him, embarrassing her in public, blackmailing her into buying sweets and carrying him. Dependence does not mean love. The child's attitude towards school, which takes him away from his mother after five years of enforced intimacy, is as ambivalent as his feelings about his mother. As long as it is an escape it is welcome but when it becomes demanding the child finds that he can play mother and school off against each other. The jealousy which mothers have of school and the attempt of the school to establish a source of control over the child in opposition to the mother can result in highly fraught situations. The anti-social nature of this mother-child relationship is very evident to schoolteachers especially when it is a question of discipline or treatment of emotional disturbance.[2]

The unfortunate wife-mother finds herself anti-social in other ways as well. The home is her province, and she is lonely there. She wants her family to spend time with her for her only significance is in relation to that almost fictitious group. She struggles to hold her children to her, imposing restrictions, waiting up for them, prying into their affairs. They withdraw more and more into non-communication and thinly veiled contempt. She begs her husband not to go out with the boys, marvels that he can stand in the pouring rain at the football and then be too tired to mend the roof or cut the grass on the finest day. She moans more and more that he doesn't care what the children are up to, that discipline is all left to her, that nobody talks to her, that she's ignorant, that she had given the best years of her life to a bunch of ungrateful hooligans. Politics is a mystery and a boring one; sport is evidence of the failure of men to grow up. The best thing that can happen is that she take up again where she left off and go back to work at a job which was only a stop gap when she began it, in which she can expect no promotion, no significant remuneration, and no widening of her horizons, for the demands of the household must still be met. Work of all kinds becomes a hypnotic. She cleans, she knits, she embroiders. And so forth.

Women trying to counteract the tendency of the nuclear household to isolate them from social contacts have peculiar difficulties. Anne Allen reported this conversation with a young married woman in the *Sunday Mirror*:

'Look,' she said. 'We have about a dozen really good friends. People I am closer to than anyone in my family. People I like better and know better.

'But what happens? *We have to organize ourselves in order to meet.* Someone has to find a baby-sitter. The other couple feel bound to make a nice supper for us.

'Then either the baby is ill, or someone feels tired, and you wish you had not arranged it. Or we all enjoy ourselves so much that it is really sad that it all has to break up so early.

'But just think what it would be like if a close group of friends lived in one building, or one street. It could happen.

'There are architects working on one or two specially planned buildings where everyone has his own bit and a huge communal living area.

'Personally I could not bear to share sexually, and I would be as bad as my mother about sharing a kitchen. I value my privacy too much.

'But there are dozens of times when I long for someone to talk to in the daytime. Or when I am lonely if my husband works overnight. Or when he and I are arguing and I want to get away for an hour.

'I just can't think of any way I would rather live than with my husband and with most of my closest friends around us. After all, thousands of people become close friends with their neighbours. We would just be reversing the procedure.'[3]

Once upon a time everyone lived in a house full of friends with large communal areas, where the streets were full of friends because the immobility of the community meant that all its members knew one another and their family history. The system has its disadvantages: non-conformism often proved intolerable, and the constant attention of the whole community to the actions of individuals had disadvantages more striking than the advantages. In such a community an old lady could not lie for four days at the foot of her staircase with a broken hip but a woman could not conduct a forbidden love affair either. Nowadays people live closer together than ever before but it is overcrowded isolation. Tower blocks contain dozens and dozens of little families who have a great deal in common, but they are strangers to each other. Their front doors shut in a private world which cannot communicate past the blank corridors and lifts except to complain about each other's noise. The women watching their children play in the communal play areas only know the parents of the other children when some outrage demands parental interference. Competitiveness frequently means that each family clings to a fantasy of superiority, racial, moral, religious, economic or class. Town planners lament that tower dwellers will not undertake to keep their communal areas clean and pleasant, and the victims of this rehousing complain that the towers cause special anxieties connected with height and encapsulation. Passing up and down in the lifts they never see each other, they cannot see in each other's windows, or natter in their doorways while cleaning the stoop. Unspontaneous attempts to stimulate intimacy don't work. Women jealously maintain the separateness of their households, fearing all kinds of imaginary corruption of their children and their way of life by the inroads of strangers. Anne Allen's housewife rejects the possibility of sexual sharing, but at least she openly considers it. The kin-community safeguards its own sexual

relationships by incest restrictions which do not have their
initial justification in fears of the results of inbreeding, which
were not known by the first promulgators of anti-incest laws.
Women dwelling in tower blocks may not consciously fear
the effects of intimacy with stranger women, but the tension
is there. Perhaps the failure of such community living could
be avoided by including a pub and a laundrette in each block
but economically it would appear that the jobs being
tirelessly duplicated in each living capsule ought to be shared
if genuine organic interaction is to result.

The architectural results of the nuclear family are
universally deemed disastrous: the ungainly spread of ribbon
developments, of acres of little boxes, has ruined the
appearance of all of our cities. Upkeep of such areas is
prohibitively expensive, access to services is difficult to
arrange. The defendants of high density housing have
practicality and comfort on their side. What they do not
realize is that the nuclear family is pulling against them; no
amount of anthropometric investigation, no clever
orientation of clean and efficient housing units towards light
and warmth and open views can break down the suspicion
that the Oedipal unit feels towards others of its kind. The
stresses and strains of conjugal introspection cannot tolerate
a wider horizon. One alternative is the takeover by the
employer as father, as happens in specially constructed
villages in America where the firms' employees are housed
according to income and position and encouraged to get
together. Wives become faculty wives and corporation
wives. Togetherness is rampant. The long-term results are,
to me at least, unimaginable. Every aspect of family life
comes to be dominated by the firm; just as the unfortunate
man gets his job on a personality assessment relating to his
whole family, he must carry out the firm's role in every
aspect of his personal life. Even his sexual performance may
become a business matter: Masters and Johnson have

delineated the hedonistic norm. No serf, writhing under the law of *jus primae noctis,* handing over his sons to the service of his liege lord, ever had it worse. As securely as any gold-rush miner or freed slave, he owes his soul to the company store. The logical outcome of the control of employment over the movement of labour has come about. His continued security is dependent upon the behaviour of his whole family; the desired result is complete immobility and predictability. This is why faculty husbands have a lower libido rating than others because they have become fat white mice in a hygienic laboratory, not because of the proximity of their women, as Lionel Tiger claimed.[4] Big Daddy the employer, the spectre that looms over *Who's Afraid of Virginia Woolf,* has castrated his sons. The human soul is indestructible however, and if the group is to form the special conscience, then the sin which can incapacitate it must be a group sin, so that no one can split to Big Daddy. The pattern of American decadence is communal drunkenness, first of all, which is the only way into uncensored behaviour, and, ultimately, wife-swapping, the twentieth-century form of incest:

The autumn of 1962, the two couples were ecstatically, scandalously close. Frank and Marcia were delighted to be thrown together so often without seeking it. Janet and Harold in private joked about the now transparent stratagems of the other two lovers. These jokes began to leak out into their four-sided conversations...

The other couples began to call them the Applesmiths.... 'Don't you feel it? It's so *wrong.* Now we're really corrupt. All of us.'[5]

Wife-swapping is seriously advocated by writers in 'journals of human relations', like *Forum,* as a method of revitalizing marriages which have gone stale. Shared but secret behaviour will cement any group into a conspiracy, but the results can be hard to live with. Changing partners is such a thoroughly unspontaneous activity, so divorced from the vagaries of genuine sexual desire – no more than a variant on the square dance. In such a transaction sex is the sufferer: passion becomes lechery. Ringing the changes on modes of *getting pleasure* disguises boredom, but it does not restore life. Sex in such circumstances is less and less a form of communication and more and more a diversion. Like bingo, slot-machines, hula-hoops, and yo-yos, it is fun. Manageable, homely amusement. Not innocent, but calculated; not dynamic, but contained. When Big Daddy countenances such naughtiness, even sex will have come under his benign aegis. The overfed, undersexed white mouse is allowed a brief spell in another's cage to perk him up. Sexual uniformity could be enforced this way: Mr Jones can apply to Mrs Jones what he learnt from Mrs Smith and so on. Universal domesticity buries all.

Anne Allen is a sensible, middling-liberal English housewife. With a matronizing glance at her young interlocutor she continues:.

I find it a rather attractive idea in theory. But in practice I can't think of a dozen, or even half a dozen couples I would like to be that close to. Or who would like to live that way with us....

I don't like the way they bring up their children. I give my children less, or more pocket money, which could lead to fights.

I hate the way they fill their kitchen with strange cooking smells or squalor. Or I feel their beady eyes on my rather wobbly house-keeping.

But most of all, I am helplessly, hopelessly, possessive, and if my husband went off with some nearby dishy wife whenever I shouted at him, there could be murder done.[6]

Anne Allen is more like the average British housewife than the young woman she spoke to, and much more 'normal' than faculty wives or corporation wives or swapped wives. She is not ashamed about the anti-social nature of her family although she might as well have said that there was not *one* couple that she could tolerate at such close quarters, and not

> As a social unit the family means the individual actuated by his most aggressively individualistic instincts; it is not the foundation, but the negation of society. Out of an aggregate of conflicting individualistic interests, human society emphatically has not and could never have arisen. It owed its rise to instincts that obliterated individualistic instincts, that moulded by binding sentiments of interdependency, loyalty, solidarity, devotion, a group larger than the patriarchal family and from its nature capable of indefinite expansion.
>
> Robert Briffault, 'The Mothers', 1931, p. 509

many couples with whom she was in any sense intimate at all. The term *couples* itself implies the locked-off unit of male–female: she did not speak of families. This is virtually what the nuclear family has become. Women's magazines sadly remark that children can have a disruptive effect on the conjugal relationship, that the young wife's involvement with her children and her exhaustion can interfere with her husband's claims on her. What a notion – a family that is threatened by its children! Contraception has increased the egotism of the couple: planned children have a pattern to fit into; at least unplanned children had some of the advantages of contingency. First and foremost they *were* whether their parents liked it or not. In the limited nuclear family the parents are the principals and children are theirs to manipulate in a newly purposive way. The generation gap is being intensified in these families where children must not inconvenience their parents, where they are disposed of in special living quarters at special times of day, their own rooms and so forth. Anything less than this is squalor. Mother must not have more children than she can control: control means full attention for much of the day, and then isolation. So the baby-sitter must be introduced into the house sneakily, for if junior finds out that his parents are going out, he'll scream. I think of the filthy two-roomed house in Calabria where people came and went freely, where I never heard a child scream except in pain, where the twelve-year-old aunt sang at her washing by the well, and the old father walked in the olive grove with his grandson on his arm. English children have lost their innocence, for their first lessons have been in the exploitation of their adult slave. A sterilized parent is a eunuch in his children's harem. To be sure, I recognize that efficient contraception is necessary for sexual pleasure and that sexual pleasure is necessary, but contraception for economic reasons is another matter. 'We can only afford two children' is a squalid argument, but more acceptable in our society than 'we don't like children.' A sterilized parent is forever bound to those children whom he has, more than ever immobile and predictable, and those children are more securely bound to him. 'We can only afford 'two children' really means, 'We only like clean, well-disciplined middle-class children who go to good schools and grow up to be professionals', for children manage to use up all the capital that is made available for the purpose, whatever proportion it may be of the family's whole income, just as housework expands to fill the time available. The sterilized parent is the ulimate domestic animal. Masculine culture contains a strong vein of anti-domesticity, although men can hardly have the experience of it that women have had trained into them. The fantasy of the perfect partner exists alongside the consciousness of what family meant to a growing boy.

Marriage is the only thing that really scares me. With the right girl I suppose it's okay but I couldn't imagine myself having a house and a wife. I like to feel free, to go anywhere and not have to worry. That's one nice thing about not having a girlfriend, you're free to go out and enjoy yourself with the lads. Having a girl ties you down.

The more you go out with a girl, the more involved you get. I'm frightened of becoming engaged. That would finish me – because I'd never break off the engagement, it isn't fair on the girl. Too many teenagers rush into marriage...

The next time I have a steady girl I'm going to make it clear from the start that I want a free night off with the lads every week. Once you lose all your friends, you're stuck to the girl, and you've had it.[7]

You've had it, you're hooked, done for! Involved means tangled up, tied down.

Most people get the best job they can, work for promotion and when they're earning enough money meet a girl and marry her. Then you have to buy a house and a car, and there you are – chained down for the rest of your life. When you get to thirty-five you're frightened to try anything new in case you lose your security. Then it means living with all the regrets about things you wanted to do.[8]

The disenchanted vision of these children has revealed the function of the patriarchal family unit in capitalist society. It immobilizes the worker, keeps him vulnerable, so that he can be tantalized with the vision of security. It gives him a controllable pattern of consumption to which he is thoroughly committed. His commitment is to his small family and his employer not to his community. The effect of wifely pressure on strikers has not to my knowledge been analysed. Often it is responsibility to a family which causes a striker to take drastic action: if the employers can hold out long enough it is this same pressure which will bring him back to work. Wives distrust their husbands' leisure; too often a wife would rather her husband earned less than hung about in the streets with his cronies getting into trouble. One of the saddest comments upon the family in industrial society was offered by the spectacle of the wives of miners thrown out of work by pit closures angrily refusing the solution of pay without work because their husbands would either be around the house all day doing nothing, or getting into mischief with the boys. Many girls undertake their anti-social functions very early, restricting their boyfriends' association with their 'mates' severely in return for sexual favours. This is not altogether the fault of women's selfishness for the male groups that threaten her do not admit her except under special circumstances and in a special capacity. She cannot play darts, drink beer, or kick a football about. Her distrust of these activities is not that her man will consort with other women in the company of his mates, but the knowledge that he enjoys these other activities and is dependent upon them in a way that he does not enjoy or depend upon her. She is jealous not of his sexual favours, but upon the partiality of his sexual passion, and the greater togetherness he might enjoy with men. Every wife must live with the knowledge that she has nothing else but home and family, while her house is ideally a base which her tired warrior-hunter can withdraw to and express his worst manners, his least amusing conversation, while he licks his wounds and is prepared by laundry and toilet and lunch-box for another sortie.

Obviously any woman who thinks in the simplest terms of liberating herself to enjoy life and create expression for her own potential cannot accept such a role. And yet marriage is based upon this filial relationship of a wife who takes her husband's name, has her tax declared on his return, lives in a house owned by him and goes about in public as his companion wearing his ring on her finger at all times. Alteration in detail is not alteration in anything else. A husband who agrees that he too will wear a ring, that they will have a joint bank account, that the house will be in both their names, is not making any serious concession to a wife's personal needs. The essential character of the institution asserts itself eventually. The very fact that such concessions

> ... the signing of a marriage contract is the most important business transaction in which you will ever become involved... One or other of the principals should function as the managing director of the household —preferably the husband; although at times his only qualification for the position is brute strength.... The children as they come along are the new investments undertaken by the firm; and the directors should see to it that there is a good return for the assets invested.
>
> Cyrus Fullerton,
> 'Happiness and Health in Womanhood', 1937, pp. 40–41

are privileges which a wife cannot claim contains its own special consequence of gratitude and more willing servitude. And yet if a woman is to have children, if humanity is to survive, what alternative can there be?

To begin with, the problem of the survival of humanity is not a matter of ensuring the birth of future generations but of limiting it. The immediate danger to humanity is that of total annihilation within a generation or two, not the failure of mankind to breed. A woman seeking alternative modes of life is no longer morally bound to pay her debt to nature. Those families in which the parents replace themselves in two children are not the most desirable ones for children to grow up in, for the neuroses resultant from the intensified Oedipal situation are worse in cases where the relationship with the parents is more dominant than the problems of adjusting to a peer group of brothers and sisters. There is no reason, except the moral prejudice that women who do not have children are shirking a responsibility, why all women should consider themselves bound to breed. A woman who has a child is not then automatically committed to bringing it up. Most societies countenance the deputizing of nurses to bring up the children of women with state duties. The practice of putting children out to nurse did not result in a race of psychopaths. A child must have care and attention, but that care and attention need not emanate from a single, permanently present individual. Children are more disturbed by changes of place than by changes in personnel around them, and more distressed by friction and ill-feeling between the adults in their environment than by unfamiliarity. A group of children can be more successfully civilized by one or two women who have voluntarily undertaken the work than they can be when divided and tyrannized over by a single woman who finds herself bored and imposed upon. The alternative is not the institutionalization of parental functions in some bureaucratic form, nothing so cold and haphazard as a baby farm, but an organic family where the child society can merge with an adult society in conditions of love and personal interest. The family understood not as a necessary condition of existence in a system but as a chosen way of life can become a goal, an achievement of a creative kind.

If women could regard childbearing not as a duty or an inescapable destiny but as a privilege to be worked for, the way a man might work for the right to have a family, children might grow up without the burden of gratitude for the gift of life which they never asked for. Brilliant women are not reproducing themselves because childbearing has been regarded as a fulltime job; genetically they might be thought to be being bred out. In a situation where a woman might contribute a child to a household which engages her attention for part of the time while leaving her free to frequent other spheres of influence, brilliant women might be more inclined to reproduce. For some time now I have pondered the problem of having a child which would not suffer from my neuroses and the difficulties I would have in adjusting to a husband and the demands of domesticity. A plan, by no means a blueprint, evolved which has become a sort of dream. No child ought, I opine, to grow up in the claustrophobic atmosphere of a city flat, where he has little chance of exercising his limbs or his lungs; I must work in a city where the materials for my work and its market are available. No child ought to grow up alone with a single resentful girl who is struggling to work hard enough to provide for herself and him. I thought again of the children I knew in Calabria and hit upon the plan to buy, with the help of some friends with similar 'problems, a farmhouse in Italy where we could stay when circumstances permitted,' and where our children would be born. Their fathers and other people would also visit the house as often as they could, to rest and enjoy the children and even to work a bit. Perhaps some of us might live there for quite long periods, as long as we wanted to. The house and garden would be worked by a local family who lived in the house. The children would have a region to explore and dominate, and different skills to learn from all of us. It would not be paradise, but it would be a little community with a chance of survival, with parents of both sexes and a multitude of roles to choose from. The worst aspect of kibbutz living could be avoided, especially as the children would not have to be strictly persuaded out of sexual experimentation with their peers, an unnatural restriction which has had serious consequences for the children of kibbutzim. Being able to be with my child and his friends would be a privilege and a delight that I could work for. If necessary the child need not even know that I was his womb-mother and I could have relationships with the other children as well. If my child expressed a wish to try London and New York or go to formal school somehwere, that could also be tried without committal.

Any new arrangement which a woman might devise will have the disadvantage of being peculiar: the children would not have been brought up like other children in an age of uniformity. There are the problems of legitimacy and nationality to be faced. Our society has created the myth of the *broken home* which is the source of so many ills, and yet the unbroken home which ought to have broken is an even greater source of tension as I can attest from bitter experience. The rambling organic structure of my ersatz household would have the advantage of being an unbreakable home in that it did not rest on the frail shoulders of two bewildered individuals trying to apply a contradictory blue-print. This little society would confer its own normality, and other contacts with civilization would be encouraged, but it may well be that such children would find it impossible to integrate with society and become drop-outs or schizophrenics. As such they would not be very different from other children I have known.

> For a male and female to live continuously together is...biologically speaking, an extremely unnatural condition.
>
> **Robert Briffault, 'Sin and Sex', 1931, p. 140**

The notion of integrating with society as if society were in some way homogenous is itself a false one. There are enough eccentrics carving out various lifestyles for my children to feel that they are no more isolated than any other minority group within the fictitious majority. In the computer age dis-integration may well appear to be a higher value than integration. Cynics might argue that the children of my household would be anxious to set up 'normal' families as part of the natural counterreaction. Perhaps. When faced with such dubious possibilities, there is only empiricism to fall back on. I could not, physically, have a child any other way, except by accident and under protest in a hand-to-mouth sort of way in which case I could not accept any responsibility for the consequences. I should like to be able to think that I had done my best.

The point of an organic family is to release the children from the disadvantages of being the extensions of their parents so that they can belong primarily to themselves. They may accept the services that adults perform for them naturally without establishing dependencies. There could be scope for them to initiate their own activities and define the mode and extent of their own learning. They might come to resent their own strangeness but in other circumstances they might resent normality; faced with difficulties of adjustment children seize upon their parents and their upbringing to serve as scapegoats. Parents have no option but to enjoy their children if they want to avoid the cycle of exploitation and recrimination. If they want to enjoy them they must construct a situation in which such enjoyment is possible.

The institution of self-regulating organic families may appear to be a return to chaos. Genuine chaos is more fruitful than the chaos of conflicting systems which are mutually destructive. When heredity has decayed and bureaucracy is the rule, so that the only riches are earning power and mobility, it is absurd that the family should persist in the pattern of patriliny. It is absurd that people should live more densely than ever before while pretending that they are still in a cottage with a garden. It is absurd that people should pledge themselves for life when divorce is always possible. It is absurd that families should claim normality when confusion about the meaning and function of parenthood means that children born within a decade of each other and a mile of each other can be brought up entirely differently. To breast feed or not breast feed? To toilet train when and how? To punish, if ever? To reward? It is absurd that so many children should grow up in environments where their existence is frowned upon. It is absurd that children should fear adults outside the immediate family. Generation X, the generation gap, the

Mods, the Rockers, the Hippies, the Yippies, the Skinheads, the Maoists, the young Fascists of Europe, rebels without a cause, whatever patronizing names their parent generation can find for them, the young are accusing their elders of spurious assumption of authority to conceal their own confusion. Vandalism, steel-capped boots, drugs, football rioting, these are chaos and the attempts of instituted authority to deal with them are more chaotic still. The juvenile offender dares the system or one of the systems to cope with him and it invariably fails. The status quo is chaos masquerading as order: our children congregate to express an organic community in ritual and uniform, which can make nonsense of state authority. The Californian police do not dare to interfere with the Hell's Angels who make a mockery of their punitive law by refusing to do the things that their parents might have done if they had had that power. The same sort of mockery is uttered by the Black Panthers. The family is already broken down: technology has outstripped conservatism. The only way the state–father can deal with its uncontrollable children is to bash and shoot them in the streets or send them to a war, the ultimate chaos.

Reich described the authoritarian compulsive family as 'part and parcel, and, at the same time, prerequisite, of the authoritarian state and of authoritarian society'.[9] Like the family, the state belies itself by its own confusion and permissiveness although ultimately it intervenes to exercise its authority chaotically. In England the 'excesses' of youth are contained and allowed to spend themselves until they can be controlled or punished discreetly, so that they do not inflame the dormant young population unduly. The result is political and social chaos, the 'sexual wilderness'. The formlessness, the legal non-existence of my dream household is a safeguard against the chaos of conflicting loyalties, of conflicting educational apparata, of conflicting judgements. My child will not be guided at all because the guidance offered him by this society seeks to lead him backwards and forwards and sideways all at once. If we are to recover serenity and joy in living, we will have to listen to what our children tell us in their own way, and not impose our own distorted image upon them in our crazy families.

Security

There is no such thing as security. There never has been. And yet we speak of security as something which people are entitled to; we explain neurosis and psychosis as springing from the lack of it. Although security is not in the nature of things, we invent strategies for outwitting fortune, and call them after their guiding deity insurance, assurance, social security. We employ security services, pay security guards. And yet we know that the universe retains powers of unforeseen disaster that cannot be indemnified. We know that superannuation and pensions schemes are not proof against the fluctuations of modern currency. We know that money cannot repay a lost leg or a lifetime of headaches or scarred beauty, but we arrange it just the same. In a dim way we realize that our vulnerability to fortune increases the more we rig up defences against the unforeseeable. Money in the bank, our own home, investments, are extensions of the areas in which we can be damaged. The more superannuation one amasses the more one can be threatened by the loss of it. The more the state undertakes to protect a man from illness and indigence, the more it has the right to sacrifice him to the common good, to demolish his house and kill his animals, to hospitalize his children or take them into approved homes; the more government forms upon which his name appears, the more numerous the opportunities for him to be calumniated in high places. John Greenaway fell for the mythology of the welfare state, and allowed the chimera to tantalize him before he was eighteen years old.

I don't feel very secure, and I'd like to marry one day. I suppose it's for security.

You have to feel secure first and foremost. If you have no money in the bank to fall back on you can never be free from worry...

It's not that I have much insecurity at home, I have a good home. I just can't feel secure because of the state of the world...

I daresay if I'm lucky enough to find a secure job bringing in really good money I'll get like the rest of them. It's amazing what a little money in the bank and a nice home will do for you. You start thinking about running a car and keeping your garden tidy and life insurance, and two telly sets and you don't have time to worry about the larger issues of how many people are starving in Africa.

Security can be a killer, and corrode your mind and soul. But I wish I had it.[1]

Probably the only place where a man can feel really secure is in a maximum security prison, except for the imminent threat of release. The problem of recidivism ought to have shown young men like John Greenaway just what sort of a notion security is, but there is no indication that he would understand it. Security is when everything is settled, when nothing can happen to you; security is the denial of life. Human beings are better equipped to cope with disaster and hardship than they are with unvarying security, but as long as security is the highest value in a community they can have little opportunity to decide this for themselves. It is agreed that Englishmen coped magnificently with a war, and were more cheerful, enterprising and friendly under the daily threat of bombardment than they are now under benevolent peacetime, when we are so far from worrying about how many people starve in Africa that we can tolerate British policy in Nigeria. John Greenaway did not realize that his bastions of security would provide new opportunities for threat. The Elizabethans called the phenomenon *mutability*, and mourned the passing of all that was fair and durable with a kind of melancholy elation, seeing in the Heraclitean dance of the elements a divine purpose and a progress to a platonic immutability in an unearthly region of ideas.[2] Greenaway cannot have access to this kind of philosophic detachment; neither can he adopt the fatalism of the peasant who is always mocked by the unreliability of the seasons. He believes that there is such a thing as security: that an employer might pay him less but guarantee him secure tenure, that he might be allowed to live and die in the same house if he pays for it, that he can bind himself to a wife and family as assurance against abandonment and loneliness.

The oddest thing about the twentieth-century chimera of security is that it was forged in the age of greatest threat. No disaster so imminent and so uncontrollable as total war was ever dreamt of before the atomic age. It seems as if men have only to defuse one kind of threat before another takes its place. Disease grows more complicated; the possibilities of aggression and destruction exceed Pope Gregory's wildest dreams. An international agreement proscribes the use of gas and so germ warfare must be developed. And so forth. Insecurity in human life is a constant factor, and I suppose efforts to eliminate it are just about as constant.

Greenaway mixes up security of life and possessions with emotional security, and it is difficult to see how he could do otherwise. Part of the mystery in our use of the idea is the suggestion of blame in the epithet *insecure* when applied to a personality. Moreover, it is assumed that women especially need to feel secure, reassured of love and buttressed by the comforts of home. Women who refuse to marry are seen to be daring insecurity, facing a desolate old age, courting poverty and degradation. But husbands die, pensions are inadequate, children grow up and go away and mothers become mothers-in-law. Women's work, married or unmarried, is menial and low-paid. Women's right to possess property is curtailed, more if they are married. How can marriage provide security? In any case a husband is a possession which can be lost or stolen and the abandoned wife of thirty odd with a couple of children is far more desolate and insecure in her responsibility than an unmarried woman with or without children ever could be. The laws which make divorce easier increase the insecurity of a wife. The jibe of emotional insecurity is a criticism of a woman's refusal to delude herself that she cannot be abandoned; it is hard indeed to rely upon an uncertain relationship which will become even more fragile if it is tested by demands for reassurance. The marriage service promises security: for the religious it is a sacramental sign and the security is security in heaven where husband and wife can be one flesh; for women who understand it as a kind of life-long contract for personal management by one man it is a patently unsatisfactory document. The safeguards and indemnities ought to be written into it at the outset as they are in management contracts and then it would have at least the value of a business document. A sacramental sign in an atheistic age has no value at all. It would be better for all concerned if its contractual nature were a little clearer.[3]

If marriage were a contract with safeguards and indemnities indicated in it it would still not provide emotional security. Its value would be in that it *did not appear to* provide it, so that women would not be encouraged to rely absolutely upon a situation which had no intrinsic permanence. The housewife is an unpaid worker in her husband's house in return for the security of being a permanent employee: hers is the *reductio ad absurdum* of the case of the employee who accepts a lower wage in return for permanence in his employment. But the lowest paid employees can be and are laid off, and so are wives. They have no savings, no skills which they can bargain with eslsewhere, and they must bear the stigma of having been sacked. The only alternative for the worker and the wife is to refuse to consider the bait of security and bargain openly. To do this a woman must have a different kind of security, the kind of personal security which enables her to consider insecurity as freedom.

Women are asked to exercise the virtue of personal security even if they do not have it, for they are supposed not to feel threatened within their marriages and not to take measures to safeguard their interests, although they do do all these things. Self-reliance is theoretically necessary within marriage so logically there is no reason to accept a chimeric security which must not be relied upon if it is to eventuate. The search for security is undertaken by the weakest part of the personality, by fear, inadequacy, fatigue and anxiety. Women are not gamblers even to the small extent that men are. Wives tend to limit their husband's enterprise, especially if it involves risks, and consequently the opportunities for achievement, delight and surprise are limited.

Marriage – having a home and a wife and children – has a very important place in life. A man wouldn't be complete without them –but I don't believe in tying yourself down until you've done something on your own first.

Most people get the best job they can, work for promotion and when they're earning enough money meet a girl and marry her. Then you have to buy a house and a car, and there you are – chained down for the rest of your life. When you get to thirty-five you're frightened to try anything new in case you lose your security. Then it means living with all the regrets about things you wanted to do.[4]

This is how Mike Russell, the twenty-one-year-old reporter on the *Edinburgh Evening News* saw marriage and security in 1964. What he identified was the function of the wife in screwing her husband into his place in the commercial machine. The welfare state justifies its existence by the promise of security and forces the worker to insure against his own restlessness and any accident that may befall him by taking contributions for his old age and illness out of his wages, at the same time as it uses some of his earnings to carry on developing the greatest threats to his continuing existence in the name of defence. A wife is the ally in such repression. The demands of home, mortgages, and hire-purchase payments support the immobilizing tendencies of his employment, militating against his desires for job control and any interest in direct action. If the correct level of remuneration is maintained, and the anomalies of the situation are not too apparent, the married man is a docile and reliable worker. By playing upon insecurity fears about immigrants and discontent with wage freezes and productivity deals, an adroit Tory can convert the working class to the most arrant conservatism.

If women would reject their roles in this pattern, recognizing insecurity as freedom, they would not be perceptibly worse off for it. Cynics notice that economically unmarried couples are often better off on taxation deals and

---

Love from its very nature must be transitory. To seek for a secret that would render it constant would be as wild a search as for the philosopher's stone or the grand panacea: and the discovery would be equally useless, or rather pernicious to mankind. The most holy band of society is friendship.

Mary Wollstonecraft,
'A Vindication of the Rights of Women', 1792, pp. 56–7

---

so forth than married ones. Spiritually a woman is better off if she cannot be taken for granted. Obviously informal relationships can be more binding than formal ones if patterns of mutual exploitation develop, and they usually do, but if women were to keep spontaneous association as an

ideal, the stultifying effects of symbiosis could be lessened.
The situation could remain open, capable of development
into richer fields. Adultery would hold no threat if women
were sure that the relationships they enjoyed were truly
rewarding and not merely preserved by censorship of other
possibilities. Loneliness is never more cruel than when it is
felt in close propinquity with someone who has ceased to
communicate. Many a housewife staring at the back of her
husband's newspaper, or listening to his breathing in bed is
lonelier than any spinster in a rented room. Much of the
loneliness of lonely people springs from distrust and egotism,
not from their having failed to set themselves up in a
conjugal arrangement. The marriage bargain offers what
cannot be delivered if it is thought to offer emotional
security, for such security is the achievement of the
individual. Possessive love, for all its seductiveness, breaks
down that personal poise and leaves its victims newly
vulnerable. Those miserable women who blame the men
who *let them down* for their misery and isolation enact every
day the initial mistake of sacrificing their personal
responsibility for themselves. They would not have been any
happier if they had remained married. When a man woos a
woman he strives to make himself as indispensable as any
woman is to any man: he may even determine to impregnate
her to break down her self-sufficiency. In the struggle to
remain a complete person and to love from her fullness
instead of her inadequacy a woman may appear hard. She
may feel her early conditioning tugging her in the direction
of surrender, but she ought to remember that she was
originally loved for herself; she ought to hang on to herself
and not find herself nagging, helpless, irritable and trapped.
Perhaps I am not old enough yet to promise that the self-
reliant woman is always loved, that she cannot be lonely as
long as there are people in the world who need her joy and
her strength, but certainly in my experience it has always

been so. Lovers who are free to go when they are restless always come back; lovers who are free to change remain interesting. The bitter animosity and obscenity of divorce is unknown where individuals have not become Siamese twins. A lover who comes to your bed of his own accord is more likely to sleep with his arms around you all night than a lover who has nowhere else to sleep.

Hate

Loathing and Disgust

Women have very little idea of how much men hate them. Any boy who has grown up in an English industrial town can describe how the boys used to go to the local dance halls and stand around all night until the pressure of the simplest kind of sexual urge prompted them to *score a chick*. The easier this was the more they loathed the girls and identified them with the guilt that their squalid sexual release left them. 'A walk to the bus-stop was usually good for a wank,' they say bitterly. The girls are detached, acquiescent and helpless, probably hoping that out of the relief they imagine they are giving some affection and protective sentiment might be born. The more reckless get fucked, standing up against a wall, or lying on a leather coat thrown on the ground in the Woolworth's bike sheds. No greater satisfaction ensues from this chilly expedient. 'A wank was as good as a jump in those days.' Afterwards the boys are brusque, hurrying the girls to the bus-stop, relishing only the prospect of telling the other boys about their conquest. In the moments immediately after ejaculation they felt murderously disgusted. 'For when I'm finished I'm finished. I wanted to strangle her right there in my bed and then go to sleep.'[1] They are all permanently broke, living at home with their parents; even if they strike up a steady relationship with one girl, it is a querulous business based on deadly routine and constant whining and bickering. In a rapt and haphazard way they find release in fighting any other bunch of boys who look good for a scrap. They fight bitchily, leaping at unprepared enemies, biting them savagely on the face of the neck, and running away before they can retaliate, dumb with outrage.

To such bitter children the only interesting women are the available ones; they do not think more highly of the unavailable girls, for they find in such exclusivity only the desire to strike a harder bargain: these are the bitches, the others are the slags. A man is bound to end up with one or the other. Marriage is viewed with fatalism; sooner or later you are sure to find yourself screwed permanently into the system, working in a dead-end job to keep a fading woman and her noisy children in inadequate accommodation in a dull town for the term of your natural life. Soon even the energy to fight will ebb away, and the only escape will be momentary, an hour or two in the pub as often as the missus will let you go there. So they see sex as their undoing, a vile servitude with women as its unwitting enforcers.

> One has the right to doubt whether the wars between the baboons are as cruel and deleterious for males and females when they are free.
>
> Paul Schilder,
> 'Goals and Desires of Man', 1942, p. 41

The man who described all this to me assumed that all men felt disgusted by sex afterwards. He was sure that coldness evinced by men after intercourse was actually repulsion. He could not remember ever having disgust-free sex, except with one woman. It is too easy to decide that this is a unique case of a special kind of fastidiousness. It has grown out of the felt loss of human dignity which is the product of boredom and restriction. Where a reasonable degree of affluence entails fewer unaesthetic elements in sexual encounters disgust may be lessened, but as long as sex is furtive and dirty some deep ambivalence to the object of sexual attentions must remain. In extreme cases it may even cause impotence in marriage, because a wife is not to be degraded.

When Freewheelin' Frank told Michael McClure in 1967 that he no longer thought 'dirty or filthy' of women since taking LSD, he was not telling the whole truth. The rebellion of the Hell's Angels reversed traditional aesthetic values so that they imposed the most repugnant sexual rituals upon themselves as a celebration of disgust:

When we talk about eating pussy we make it sound as dirty and vulgar as possible – to make someone barf. Angel mamas are nymphomaniacs who will do anything related to sex. The Angel mama at the time is menstruating, on her period, and real bloody. It is considered the nastier she is, the more class is showed by the member who goes down on her in front of everyone – at least six members – and how he goes about it, while everyone witnesses. . . . Sometimes a member has been known to barf when bein' hassled to do this.[2]

Eldridge Cleaver became a rapist when he came out of San Quentin, 'consciously, deliberately, wilfully, methodically'.

Many whites flatter themselves with the idea that the negro male's lust and desire for the white dream girl is purely an aesthetic attraction, but nothing could be farther from the truth. His motivation is often of such a bloody, hateful, bitter and malignant nature that whites would really be hard pressed to find it flattering.[3]

It is a vain delusion that rape is the expression of uncontrollable desire or some kind of compulsive response to overwhelming attraction. Any girl who has been bashed and raped can tell how ludicrous it is when she pleads for a reason and her assailant replies 'Because I love you' or 'Because you're so beautiful' or some such rubbish. The act is one of

murderous aggression, spawned in self-loathing and enacted
upon the hated other. Men do not themselves know the
depth of their hatred. It is played upon by inflammatory
articles in the magazines designed for morons with virility
problems which sell for high prices in transport cafés: 'Eager
Females: How they reveal themselves', writes Alex Austin in
Male and proceeds to describe a number of harmless
mannerisms, like slipping a shoe off, and showing a hearty

> When she had sucked the marrow from my bones
> And languorously I turned to her with a kiss,
> Beside me suddenly I saw nothing more
> Than a gluey-sided leather bag of pus!
>
> Baudelaire

> If we but seriously consider the nature and qualities of the
> generality of the sex, even in all ages from the fall of man
> to this present, we may well perceive that they have not
> only been extremely evil in themselves; but have also
> been the main instruments and immediate causes of
> Murder, Idolatry, and a multitude of other hainous sins,
> in many high and eminent men...
>
> 'A Briefe Anatomie of Women', 1653, p. 1

appetite (for food) which indicate concealed goatishness in
women.[4] Barry Jamieson describes the underhand tactics of
'The Willing Cheater: Your Wife's Best Friend' in *Stag*.[5]
The object of such articles is to imply that the world is full of
liquorish sluts in flimsy disguises, who will welcome the most
unceremonious advances despite their prissy denials. Such
women are *available, easy, pushovers*. Whatever they get, they

have deserved. Acting upon this kind of imagined discrimination, a certain kind of man whispers obscenities to women passing on the street and laughs at their humiliation and confusion which he construes as evidence that they are guilty of the secret bestial desires that he has touched upon. More often women do not catch the muttered message but the tone of voice and the leer are unmistakable. Men who appraise women with insolent stares in buses and subways and chink the change in their pockets are communicating the same hate-filled innuendo. Whatever delusion it is that persuades men to follow oblivious women up and down crowded city streets derives from this same assumption of animal heat and appetite for degradation hidden under a demure exterior. The lust of loose women is undifferentiated, a remorseless itch, which after the initial susceptibility of male response to female demand is deeply inconvenient and disgusting. The articles I have named also contain descriptions of escape routes from entanglement with such hot bitches. However much women might want to reject this vision of their sex and sexuality it is nevertheless true that the Hell's Angels report no lack of Angel mamas, who actually turn out to take on the whole of a Chapter, despite the fact that the status angel women are the 'old ladies'. There are women who seek degradation as diligently as men seek to deal it to them, although their motivation is vastly different from the fantasy of *Male* and *Stag*, and their number very much less than is implied by the fantasy. Freewheelin' Frank's public image worked so well that he encountered more than his fair share, and the result was what we might expect.

. . . Then I crossed my chin around her neck, squeezing her tight. She went into such fear she became happy. Then from the radio the song 'Everyone has gone to the Moon' began playing. I said 'Do you know where we're at?'

She said 'Make love to me.'

In a rage I said, 'YOU bitch,' and I turned cold and rolled over and listened to the music.... Sometimes during the night, as I would roll over face up, I would see her to my left, laying with her eyes wide open as if she were dead. This helped me to go back to sleep. She wanted to go back to sleep. She wanted to go for a walk one time. I said, 'Go. Lock the door behind you.'

I don't like women, I despise them. I no longer try to please women. I'm mad if they're around for very long. I feel as though I could call them in and dismiss them.[6]

We are conceived somewhere between pissing and shitting, and as long as these excretory functions are regarded as intrinsically disgusting, the other one, ejaculation, will also be so regarded. The involuntary emission of semen during sleep is called a nocturnal *pollution*: the substance itself is viscous and stringy, whitish and acrid, like a more disgusting form of snot, if you regard snot as disgusting. Human beings have extraordinary ways of escaping their conditioning, so that one may see a bowler-hatted gentleman on the train absently picking his nose and eating what he finds there, but if we recall him to full consciousness, deep embarrassment, shame, humiliation, disgust and even loating may result. It is easy when picking a path through the wilderness of sexual *mores* to fall foul of the slough of disgust, for a shameful and compulsive activity can be pushed away by attributing all the shame and all the compulsion to the partner.

The woman tempted me, and I did eat.

When a man is ashamed to masturbate, and instead waylays women for the sake of finding sexual release, the shame that should attach to the masturbatory activity, not significantly different in such a case except that the friction was provided by a female organ and the ejaculation may occur in the vagina, is referred to the woman. The man regards her as a receptacle into which he has emptied his sperm, a kind of human spittoon, and turns from her in disgust. As long as man is at odds with his own sexuality and as long as he keeps woman as a solely sexual creature, he will hate her, at least some of the time. The more hysterical the hatred of sex, the more extravagant the expression of loathing. It is not necessary to quote medieval restrictions on the admission of women to church and the sacraments to demonstrate this, although the examples have the value of being striking and incredible. In the Renaissance, some attempt was made to understand the emotion and the effects of lust.

> The expense of spirit in a waste of shame
> Is lust in action; and till in action, lust
> Is perjured, murderous, bloody, full of blame,
> Savage, extreme, rude, cruel, not to trust;
> Enjoy'd no sooner but despised straight;
> Past reason hunted; and no sooner had,
> Past reason hated, as a swallow'd bait,
> On purpose laid to make the taker mad:
> Mad in pursuit, and in possession so,
> Had, having, and in quest to have, extreme;
> A bliss in proof – and prov'd, a very woe;
> Before, a joy propos'd; behind a dream.
>   All this the world well knows; yet none knows well
>   To shun the heaven that leads men to this Hell.[7]

Shakespeare was right in equating the strength of the lust drive and the intensity of the disgust that followed it. The first manifestations of syphilis in Europe were much more spectatular than the present operations of the disease: the ignorance about the nature of the contagion also helped to colour attitudes towards sex. It is not rare to find in medieval poets a picture of healthy animal enjoyment like the naïve pride of the Wife of Bath in the way that she made her husbands swink. For many humanists the pleasure itself became dubious, and the chase after the sexual object was seen as delusive, even when the lady proved complaisant, for the pleasure was not equal to the fantasms of the lust-stirred brain. But the more the neo-platonists sought to devalue sex, sense and sensory information, the more empiricism flourished, and the more sexual desire, distorted, sublimated, or perverted, burst out in odd manifestations. The end of Shakespeare's poem is still troubled by desire, the very fury of the syntax is evidence of lust's continuing power. Disease, idealism, disgust could not ultimately conceal the libidinous energy of the Elizabethans, who were after all still forced to excrete semi-publicly, to go mostly unbathed, to eat food that our senses would find of the rankest, so that they could not have managed to exist if they had been afflicted with anything like the degree of fastidiousness which characterizes twentieth-century man.

Post coitum omne animal triste est. The Romantics developed the suggestion which had always been present in erotic writing, that actual sexual pleasure was necessarily inferior to the heated imaginings of lust, into a complete statement of the superiority of unheard melodies to heard ones. The great love affairs were those truncated by death, or those never enjoyed because of some other embargo. The mind–body dichotomy, which they might have imagined they derived from Plato, was actually established in the sensibility of Europeans, then justified by Descartes. The Romantic taste for the moribund heroine is itself a manifestation of sexual disgust and woman-hatred. Imagining a female dying is tantamount to killing her: immolated on the altar of morality, she can be enjoyed with a fearful exaltation. The Byronic great lover wasting away with the awful fires of a forbidden love which racked his brain, curled his lip and fed the dull flame in his eye, vitiated the pleasures of all actual events in a dream of what could never be. The act of undying adoration to the unenjoyed was effectively only the rejection of the enjoyed. Even a poet as *now* as Dylan has two kinds of female character in his imagery – the sad-eyed lady of the lowlands, the girl from the north country, who is inviolate and inviolable, *to kalos,* and the others who are human, confused and contemptible. This crude version of romanticism underlies the distinction between two kinds of girls which prevails almost universally in our community, especially in those quarters where avant-garde sexual morality has not succeeded in disguising or banishing disgust as an improper and neurotic feeling. Any woman who goes to bed with a man for the first time knows that she runs the risk of being treated with contempt. Her chosen lover may leave or may turn his back on her immediately after his orgasm and fall, or pretend to, asleep; he may be laconic or brusque in the morning: he may not call again. She hopes that he will not discuss her disparagingly with his friends. The words used to describe women who are not unwilling to have intercourse with men who are eager to have intercourse with them are the transferred epithets of loathing for sex un-dignified by aesthetic prophylaxis and romantic fantasy. For many in this space, falling out of love means the fading of the aura, and the assertion of the bald facts of sexual relationship.

Oh! *Caelia, Caelia,* Caelia *sh(its)*![8]

Sophisticated men realize that this disgust is a projection of shame and therefore will not give it any play, but because they have been toilet-trained and civilized by the same process as the total victims of disgust and contempt, they still feel the twinges. They still say 'Fuck you' as a venomous insult; they still find *cunt* the most degrading epithet outside the dictionary *Cunt-lapping, mother-fucking,* and *cock sucking* are words to provoke a sense of outrage. Being forced to play the role of a woman in sexual intercourse is the deepest imaginable humiliation, which is only worsened if the victim finds to his horror that he enjoys it. There is no way of assessing the extent of this feeling in a civilized community like our own: people tend to minimize it for their self-esteem's sake but nobody feels embarrassed about admit-

> I am inclined to believe that this admission of moral superiority which ordinary men are so ready to yield (to women), is a bribe of compliment and gallantry to quiet the sex under the deprivation of substantial privileges which would really place them on an equality with men: especially as I find that those men who are personally most polite to women, who call them angels and all that, cherish in secret the greatest contempt for them.
>
> J. McGrigor Allen,
> 'The Intellectual Severance of Men and Women',
> 1860, p. 23

ting disgust attendant on promiscuity, although it might be argued that if sex is a good thing it ought not to become disgusting if done often, or with different people. The sophisticated argument is that promiscuity devalues sex, makes it commonplace, impersonal and so forth, but the kind of depression felt by men forced by circumstances to be more or less promiscuous, like travelling musicians, is really still the same old disgust. Very few men who have slept around causually are able to converse humanely with the women who have extended their favours. Many a woman sorrowfully reflects that her more recherché sexual techniques, her more delicate apprehensions of her polymorphous partner's needs, her very sexual generosity has directly entailed her lover's eventual revulsion and estrangement. We may find a key to sexual outrage and murder in the inability of men to shed their inhibitions with the fine woman who is good enough to marry, and their terror and disgust at what the repressed desire eventually forces them to do. The worst aspect of prostitution is that many a prostitute must undergo the bestial rituals which civilized men find necessary for sexual release. Many prostitutes claim this as their social function. The unfortunate girls found strangled with their own stockings and raped with bottles are the victims of male fetishism and loathing, and yet no woman has ever cried out after such an outrage on her sex, 'Why do you hate us so?', although hate it clearly is.

Some of the shock and alarm caused by *Last Exit to Brooklyn* was occasioned by the guilt of readers who recognized the phenomenon of the brutalization of Tralala in the hideous plausibility of her end: if morgue doctors revealed what horrors end up on their slabs we might have worse evidence of the survival of cunt-hatred in our society.

. . . more came 40 maybe 50 and they screwed her and went back on line and had a beer and yelled and laughed and someone yelled that the car stunk of cunt so Tralala and the seat were taken out of the car and laid in the lot and she lay there naked on the seat and their shadows hid her pimples and scabs and she drank flipping her tits with the other hand and somebody shoved the beer can against her mouth and they all laughed and Tralala cursed and spit out a piece of tooth and someone shoved it again . . . and the next one mounted her and her lips were split this time and the blood trickled to her chin and someone mopped her brow with a beersoaked handkerchief and another can of beer was handed to her and she drank and yelled about her tits and another tooth was chipped and the split in her lips were widened and everyone laughed and she laughed and she drank more and more and soon she passed out and they slapped her a few times and she mumbled and turned her head but they couldn't revive her so they continued to fuck her as she lay unconscious on the seat in the lot and soon they tired of the dead piece and the daisychain broke up and they went back to Willies the Greeks and the base and the kids who were watching and waiting to

take a turn took out their disappointment on Tralala and tore her
clothes to small scraps put out a few cigarettes on her nipples pissed
on her jerked off on her jammed a broomstick up her snatch then
bored they left her lying among the broken bottles, rusty cans and
rubble of the lot and Jack and Fred and Ruthy and Annie stumbled
into a cab still laughing and they leaned towards the window as they
passed the lot and got a good look at Tralala lying naked covered
with blood urine and semen and a small blot forming on the seat
between her legs as blood seeped from her crotch. . .[9]

Punished, punished, punished for being the object of
hatred and fear and disgust, through her magic orifices, her
cunt and her mouth, poor Tralala. Women are never
instrumental in crimes of sexual loathing, even when they
are enacted upon the bodies of men. The implications of this
state of affairs have got to be understood by any movement
for female liberation.

Cunt-hatred has survived in our civilization in myriad
small manifestations, most of which would be steadily denied
by the manifesters. The deep aversion for *beaver* in pin-
ups evinced by the selection of poses which minimize the
genital area is partly motivated by a disgust for the organ
itself. Women of considerable experience, like the authoress
of *Groupie,* who delight and glory in their skill at *fellatio* feel,
in Miss Fabian's words, that cunnilingus must be *less groovy*
and would not require it of any man who was making love to
them.[10] Other women are embarrassed by cunnilingus, and
feel sure that men must find it disgusting. Despite my own
intentions, I often feel this way myself, and I cannot pretend
that this is altogether because it is too intimate a proceeding,
or too impersonal. Vaginal secretions are the subject of a
vast folklore; the huge advertising campaigns for deodorants
and sweeteners of the vulvar area deliberately play upon
female misgivings about the acceptability of natural tastes
and odours. One vaginal deodorant is even flavoured with
peppermint to provide an illusion of freshness and inhum-

anity. Others are mentholated. The vagina is described as *a problem* preventing some of the niceness of being close. The excessive use of douches with chemical additives is actually harmful to the natural balance of organisms existing in the vagina, and yet no doctor has dared to denounce it openly. Women desirous of coming to terms with themselves, and of understanding how far they are from actually doing so, might consider their own reactions to the suggestion that they taste their own vaginal secretions on their fingers, or that they taste themselves fresh on the mouth of a lover. Despite my own proselytizing attitude, I must confess to a thrill of shock when one of the ladies to whom this book is dedicated told me that she had tasted her own menstrual blood on the penis of her lover. There are no horrors present in that blood, no poisons; I would such a bleeding finger, I would not scruple to kiss a bleeding lip, and yet. . . The only cure for such superstitions is base empiricism, innocently undertaken.

Repressed disgust for female genitalia is why the many causes of vulvar itches and inflammations are seldom properly investigated, and many women treat themselves ineptly for conditions which they regard as chronic and nervous or moral in origin, until they become incapable of treatment. Cases of incurable trichomonal infection are all due to a combination of fear, superstition and doctors' sloppiness. Penile disorders can be as trivial and risible as athlete's foot, and so can vaginal ones. In each case, examination ought to be performed. The fictitious association of *prurigine vulvae* with excessive sexual desire is an additional reason why female itching is not taken seriously. Along with the fantasy of the flaming itch of the voracious vagina go other notions of the proper coloration and conformation of the nymphae which influence even doctors' conceptions. The cunt of a fresh and virtuous woman is thought to be pink and soft, the clitoris hardly protuberant, the membrane of the labia to be smooth and thin. The purplish tinge of dark-skinned women is suspect, and the ruvidity of the labial tissue is taken to indicate excessive excitation, self-abuse or indulgence.

On the basis of arbitrary assumptions about the coloration and conformation of the nymphae, doctors in America at the turn of the century discovered hundreds of cases of habitual self-abuse and treated them in the most barbarous fashion imaginable – by clitorectomy.[11] Such a remedy for male masturbation has never been suggested, and yet in many cases castration of women was actually practised. In terms of the crudest physiology the practice was inexcusable, for the nerves which supply the clitoris also supply the rest of the ano-vaginal area and masturbation, if it was occurring at all or as much as the doctors said, and if it was having the deleterious effects on the whole organism which they fantasized, such as neurasthenia, anorexa, aberrations in blood pressure, debility and so forth, could quite naturally have been transferred to other areas. The only persuasive motivation for such therapy (for *reason* it cannot have) is cunt-hatred. The infibulation of girls in some primitive tribes also has this punitive and defensive function.

The universal lack of esteem for the female organ becomes a deficiency in women's self-esteem. They are furtive and secretive about their own organs and their functions, but more appallingly there is the phenomenon of the woman who seeks degradation by consorting with her 'inferiors' and inviting her lover to abuse her. A very amusing Italian film was built around the story of a rich woman who made love to her chauffeur when drunk, begging him, 'Chiamami tua serva!' Many of the vile and cruel things which men do to women are done at women's instigation. The most appalling evidence of cunt-hatred can be found in the cases of introduction into the vagina and the urethra of dangerous objects, by women themselves.[12] The earliest gynaecological case-histories contain examples of women who introduced needles and bodkins into the bladder and managed thereby to kill themselves. Even the pioneers of gynaecology were not deluded by their protestations that freakish accidents had occurred. When surgery was in its infancy such abuse was usually fatal. Even now cases of such violence performed upon the self are not altogether rare. Many menstrual disorders derive from inability to accept womanhood and its attendant processes. Many a silly girl swallowing Epsom salts and gin and parboiling herself in a hot bath is not so much endeavouring to procure abortion as punish herself for her female sexuality. Self-loathing is an important factor in nymphomania which is usually compulsive self-abasement. Pop psychology refers to it in jargon as having a low self-image.[13]

Woman are so brainwashed about the physical image that they should have that, despite popular fiction on the point, they rarely undress with éclat. They are often apologetic about their bodies, considered in relation to that plastic object of desire whose image is radiated throughout the media. Their breasts and buttocks are always too large or too small, the wrong shape, or too soft, their arms too hairy or too muscular or too thin, their legs too short, too hefty, and so forth. Not all the apology is fishing for compliments. They are actually apologizing. The compliment is actually necessary reassurance that inadequacies do not exist, not merely reassurance that these inadequacies do not matter. The woman who complains that her behind is droopy does not want to be told, 'I don't care, because I love you,' but 'Silly girl, it's a perfect shape, you can't see it like I can.' It is a commonplace observation that women are forever trying to straighten their hair if it is curly and curl it if it is straight, bind their breasts if they are large and pad them if they are small, darken their hair if it is light and lighten it if it is dark. Not all these measures are dictated by the fantom of fashion.

They all reflect dissatisfaction with the body as it is, and an insistent desire that it be otherwise, not natural but controlled, fabricated. Many of the devices adopted by women are not cosmetic or ornamental, but disguise of the actual, arising from fear and distaste. Soft lighting, frilly underwear, drinks and music, might help to get away with palming off an inferior bill of goods, which under harsh light and quite naked could too easily be disgusting. The universal sway of the feminine stereotype is the single most important factor in male and female woman-hatred. Until woman as she is can drive this plastic spectre out of her own and her man's imagination she will continue to apologize and disguise herself, while accepting her male's pot-belly, wattles, bad breath, farting, stubble, baldness and other ugliness without complaint. Man demands in his arrogance to be loved as he is, and refuses even to prevent the development of the sadder distortions of the human body which might offend the aesthetic sensibilities of his woman. Woman, on the other hand, cannot be content with health and agility: she must make exorbitant efforts to appear something that never could exist without a diligent perversion of nature. Is it too much to ask that women be spared the daily struggle for superhuman beauty in order to offer it to the caresses of a subhumanly ugly mate? Women are reputed never to be disgusted. The sad fact is that they often are, but not with men; following the lead of men, they are most often disgusted with themselves.

Abuse

On 18 December 1969, in the case of Regina versus Humphreys, Mr Frisby Q.C. accused the defence of attempting to show that Miss Pamela Morrow, whom the defendant was charged with having raped, was a 'flippertigibbit'.[1] It seems incredible that twentieth-century lawyers should accuse a girl of being a foul fiend from hell, the same that rode upon Poor Tom's back in *King Lear* and bit him so cruelly.[2] The meaning of the word has declined into a pale shadow of its former force, perhaps because of its indiscriminate use in witch-hunts, but its derivation remains a fact. The element of witch-hunt is never far from trials in which not quite virginal girls are required to give evidence against members of Parliament and there may have been more to Mr Frisby's use of the term than he was aware, but we may follow this pattern of the debilitation by indiscriminate use of terms of the greatest reprobation. The word *hag* used also to apply to a direct satanical manifestation of peculiar grisliness; now it simply means a woman who isn't looking her best. *Hag-ridden* meant the condition of a soul who had been tormented by diabolical spirits in his sleep, and not a husband who had been nagged at. The ineffectualness of the victims of such abuse eventually defused the terms of abuse themselves: *termagant* began its history in the *chansons de geste* as a word meaning a mahometan deity, now it too means a nagging woman. Indiscriminate application has weakened the force of *broad*, originally derived from *bawd*, and *hoyden*, *wanton*, *baggage*, and *fright* (originally a horrifying mask) as well as *tart*, which began as a cant term of affection, became insulting, and is now only mildly offensive.[3]

Unfortunately the enfeeblement of abuse by hysterical overstatement is not the commonest phenomenon in the language of woman-hatred. Many more terms which originally applied to both men and women gained virulence by sexual discrimination. The word *harlot* did not become exclusively feminine until the seventeenth century. There is no male analogue for it in the era of the double standard. The word *bawd* applied to both sexes until after 1700, and the word *hoyden* is no longer applicable to men. Originally a *scold* was a Scots invective – now it means, predictably, a nagging woman. *Witches* may be of either sex, but as a term of abuse *witch* is solely directed at women. A *chit* was originally the young of a beast, came to mean a child, and nowadays means a silly girl.

Class antagonism has had its effect on the vocabulary of female status. Lower-class distrust of airs and graces has resulted in the ironic applications of terms like *madam, lady, dame* and *duchess,* which is fair exchange for the loading of dialect names for women with contemptuous associations, as in *wench, quean, donah, dell, moll, biddy* and *bunter* (once a rag-picker, but now invariably a prostitute). The most recent case in which contempt for menial labour has devised a new term of abuse for women is the usage of *scrubber* for a girl of easy virtue. If such linguistic movements were to be charted comprehensively and in detail, we would have before us a map of the development of the double standard and the degradation of women. As long as the vocabulary of the cottage and the castle are separate, words like *wench* and *madonna* do not clash; when they do both concepts suffer and woman is the loser. The more body-hatred grows, so that the sexual function is hated and feared by those unable to renounce it, the more abusive terms we find in the language.

When most lower-class girls were making a living as

domestics, struggling to keep clear of the sexual exploitation of the males in the household, the language of reprobation became more and more concerned with lapses in neatness, which were taken to be the equivalent of moral lapses. The concept of sluttishness or slatterriness with its compound implication of dirt and dishonour gave rise to a great family of nasty words, like *drab, slut, slommack, slammerkin, traipse, malkin, trollop, draggletail.* The word *slattern* itself withdrew the male portion of its meaning and became exclusively feminine.

The most offensive group of words applied to the female population are those which bear the weight of neurotic male disgust for illicit or casual sex. The Restoration, which reaped the harvest of puritan abuse of gay women, invented a completely new word of unknown derivation to describe complaisant ladies, the ubiquitous *punk.* The imagery of venereal disease added a new dimension to the language: diseased women were *fireships, brimstone, laced mutton, blowens, bawdy baskets, bobtails,* although the vestiges of sensual innocence hung around long enough to endow us with obsolete terms like *bed-fagot, pretty horsebreaker,* as well as loving-ironic use of words like *whore* and *trull,* which were not always wholly bitter in their application. More familiar terms in current usage refer to women as receptacles for refuse, reflecting the evaluation that men put upon their own semen, as *tramp, scow, scupper,* or, most contemporary, the hideous transferred epithet *slag.* Even these words fade from vividness: women themselves use a term like *bag* indiscriminately, although they would recoil from the unequivocal original *douche-bag,* or rhyming slang *toe-rag.*

Perhaps words like *pig, pig-meat* or *dog* are inspired by the sadness which follows unsatisfactory sex: they too lose their efficacy from wide usage as the word *beast* did, and must constantly be replaced. The vocabulary of impersonal sex is peculiarly desolating. Who wants to 'tear off a piece of ass?'

'get his greens?' 'stretch a bit of leather?' 'knock off a bit? of belly? of crumpet?' 'have it away?'

It would be unbearable, but less so, if it were only the vagina that was belittled by terms like *meat, pussy, snatch, slit, crack* and *tail,* but in some hardboiled patois the woman herself is referred to as a *gash,* a *slot.* The poetical figure which indicates the whole by the part is sadly employed when indicating women as *skirts, frills, a bit of fluff* or *a juicy little piece.*

These terms are all dead, fleshy and inhuman, and as such easy to resent, but the terms of endearment addressed to women are equally soullness and degrading. The basic imagery behind terms like *honey, sugar, dish, sweety-pie, cherry, cookie, chicken* and *pigeon* is the imagery of food. If a woman is food, her sex organ is for consumption also, in the form of *honey-pot, hair-pie* and *cake-* or *jelly-roll.* There are the pretty toy words, like *doll* and *baby* or even *baby-doll.* There are the cute animal terms like *chick, bird, kitten* and *lamb,* only a shade of meaning away from *cow, bitch, hen, shrew, goose, filly, bat, crow, heifer,* and *vixen,* as well as the splendidly ambiguous expression *fox,* which emanates from the Chicago ghetto. The food terms lose their charm when we reflect how close they are to coarse terms like *fish, mutton, skate, crumpet,* a *bit on a fork, cabbage, greens, meat* and *bread,* and terms more specifically applied to the female genitalia but often extended to the female herself. Who likes to be called *dry-goods,* a *potato,* a *tomato* or a *rutabaga*?

There used to be a fine family of words which described without reprobation or disgust women who lived outside the accepted sexual laws, but they have faded from current usage. Flatly contemptuous words like *kept-woman* and *call-girl* have taken over the field from *adventuress, woman of the world, woman of pleasure, mistress, inamorata, paramour, courtesan, mondaine.* When Frank Zappa launched the mythology of the *groupie* as high priestess of free love and the group grope, he meant the term to remain free from pejorative colouring,[4] but despite the enormous build-up less than six months later most of the women who hung around musicians treated the appellation as an insult. It is the fate of euphemisms to lose their function rapidly by association with the actuality of what they designate, so that they must be regularly replaced with euphemisms for themselves. It is not too farfetched to imagine that *fiancée* which commonly is the permissive society means *mistress* will itself become a tabu word unless ideology should miraculously catch up with behaviour.

The most scathing vilification of immoral women does not come from men. The feminine establishment which sees its techniques of sexual bargaining jeopardized by the disregard of women who make themselves *cheap* is more vociferous in its condemnation. Too often the errant women abuse themselves with excessive shame and recrimination, degrading themselves more in their own estimation than they do by their behaviour. The compulsiveness of this behaviour is the direct result of repressiveness in education: women are drawn to sexual licence because it seems forbidden and exciting, but the price they pay for such delinquency is too heavy. The result is functional nymphomania, described in Nathan Shiff's *Diary of a Nymph*. A woman in this situation refuses to take responsibility for her own behaviour and instead attributes her deeds to a paraself which takes over. She cannot choose between one sexual partner or another because her will is in abeyance, so that her course is set for self-destruction. Shiff's heroine Christine describes sex as filthy and low, and yearns to feel free from it, to 'be clean again'.[5] The same self-denigrating syndrome appears in a type of letter which appears regularly in the corespondence columns of women's magazines. 'I feel so low and ashamed...'; 'I was so disgusted with myself I found I couldn't respond to my husband's love. Now it is worse. I have read about V.D. and am terrified I could have been infected...' 'I have always loved my husband but three years ago I had a sordid affair which he forgave. . . . I have again been strongly tempted by another man . . .'; 'I know it is impossible to change my past, but I have learned my lesson and regretted ever since what happened . . .'[6] None of the replying matriarchs inquires why the affair was so sordid, why it must be regretted, what lesson it was that was learnt, why shame is so disproportionate or what the woman is really describing when she speaks of temptation. Instead, all sagely counsel that the woman continue to accept her guilt and find expiation in renewed self-abnegation. In 'true romance' stories women mercilessly vilify themselves for quite minor infractions of the sexual code – 'It was so horrible I feel I shall never be clean again. Never. I'm too awful to live. I felt utterly ashamed. I hardly knew this man. How could I be so cheap?'[7]

For educated girls the most telling gibe is that of *promiscuity*, a notion so ill-defined that for practical purposes we must decide that a girl is promiscuous when she thinks herself to be so. Gael Green's conversations with college girls revealed that while they tolerate sex between people who are 'in love', any other kind was promiscuity, an imagined disease so powerful in its effects that accoring to Dr Graham B. Blaine it is the commonest reason for their seeking psychiatric help.[8] Girls who pride themselves on their monogamous instincts have no hesitation in using the whole battery of sex-loathing terms for women who are not. They speak of the 'campus punchboard' or 'an old beat-up pair of shoes', revealing their unconscious fidelity to the notion that for women sex is *despoiling* and *using*.[9] The last word on the pernicious power of the notion of promiscuity was uttered by Jim Moran, battling the double standard in *Why Men Shouldn't Marry*: 'Use of this word [promiscuity] has but one redeeming feature. It identifies the user as a pro-virginity, problem-ridden, puritanical prunt.'[10]

Moran addressed his words chiefly to men: they ought to

be more urgently heeded by women. If women are to be better valued by men they must value themselves more highly. They must not allow themselves to be seduced while in a state of self-induced moral paralysis, trusting to the good-will of the seducer so grudgingly served. They must not scurry about from bed to bed in a self-deluding and pitiable search for love, but must do what they do deliberately, without false modesty, shame or emotional blackmail. As long as women consider themselves sexual objects they will continue to writhe under the voiced contempt of men and, worse, to think of themselves with shame and scorn.

Low regard for the sexual object extends even into the words which denote the simple fact of femaleness. Female and *woman* are not polite terms: I was told as a little girl always to employ the word *lady* or *young lady*. Squeamishness results in ludicrous formulae like *the opposite sex*. Contempt for women can be discerned in a purer form in the use of female terms as abuse for pusillanimous or incompetent men. 'You girl,' say the Londoners, in a tone of the deepest contempt. Feminists might like to consider the gratuitous attribution of the female sex to unspecified objects and creatures, as in this headline which identified the Loch Ness Monster as female, 'If Nessy's there *she's* got a sonar shock coming.' Perhaps we can deduce the latent motive for the attribution from the sadism of the context.

Young and pretty women may delude themselves about the amount of abuse meted out to women, for as long as they remain so they escape most of it. It is easy to pretend that wolf-whistles are gestures of genuine appreciation and that compliments are genuine praise, which they are not. Pretty women sometimes chafe under the effects of the universal supposition that they are morons, but in general it seems easier to exploit male illusions. A woman has only to depart from the stereotype to find herself subjected to all kinds of discrimination and insult, although she may minimize it still for her own mental health. A woman who is not pretty is a *bag*. There are few half measures in popular imagery. A woman who is unacceptably fat is gross, undesirable, ridiculous. A woman who is undesirably thin is scraggy, scrawny and so on. If her legs are not lovely they are awful. If her body suggests too much strength and agility she is hard, tough, unfeminine. If she is efficient and capable or ambitious, it is assumed that she has failed to find satisfaction as a normal woman, even to the extent of implying a glandular abnormality or sexual perversion.

The stereotype of the sex object is only one of the stereotypes used to mask the realities of female humanity. Even this type is not free from abuse. A certain kind of male imagines that women are all the time flaunting themselves to inflame his senses and deny him, in order to build up their deficient egos. He imagines that women get away with outrageous exploitation of male susceptibility. The following extracts appeared in a book of sex instruction republished recently in England, called *Sane and Sensual Sex*.

Man does not (as woman may well think) always like to see her stark naked. He is not necessarily mad keen to see her in scanties or panties or bra. He does not lose his head when her skirt blows up in a high wind, showing all she's got on. He does not enjoy the generous breasts spilling from the top of her dress or forcing their way through her tight sweater. He does not revel in the sight of her bottom swaying, hinged to her hips or inside her skirt that flares all around her, revealing a multitude of frothy petticoats.

Yet – the average girl and young woman thinks this is mass hypnosis to the average man. She runs away with the idea she is sex personified, lusted after by every male in sight. Indispensable to his peace of mind and body. The law of most lands pets and pampers the female from the age of thirteen to the point she is protected from every leer and lascivious look, every bottom-pinch or thigh-tweak that is undesired or unasked for.

Consequently, the female grows up with a Virgin-Mary-

Complex, convinced she is untouchable – until she gives the word 'go'.[11]

One is not surprised to find the author of this extraordinary mixture of yearning and loating spending a disproportionate amount of time praising frilly underwear, and chafing against the imagined dominance of women in sexual matters.

Women will always have the upper hand because she *gives* whereas the man takes,
So she will always spurn the exhibitionist, pretend no interest in the man's sexual charms, disclaim his right to dress well and attractively, on top *and* underneath.
For she thinks that sex-appeal and charm, mysticism and glamour are the prerogative of her sex alone.

His parting shot is meant to be a killer. 'But a man's body wears better than a woman's if he takes care of it. And he is virile and effective long after she has given up the sexual ghost.'[12]

> Most men fall in love with a pretty face but find themselves bound for life to a hateful stranger, alternating endlessly between a workshop and a witch's kitchen.
> Schopenhauer

Pretty women are never unaware that they are aging, even if the process has hardly begun: a decayed beauty is possibly more tormented than any other female stereotype, but even for women who never made any claims on male admiration there are abusive stereotypes which take over her claim to individuality. The studious, plain girl is characterized as a characterless, sexless swot: the housewife is depicted by a head full of curlers and nothing else, aproned, fussing, nagging, unreliable in the kitchen, with the budget, in her choice of clothes and with the family car. As she gets older the imagery becomes more repellent; she becomes obese, her breasts grow huge and sagging, the curlers are never out of her hair, her voice is louder and more insistent; finally she is transmuted into that most hated female image of all, the wife's mother, the ubiquitous mother-in-law. Eventually even a child–wife must grow up, and stop murmuring and snivelling about, and male mockery dates from the moment in which she abandons her filial, adoring station and begins to run her household. 'The pretty girl then blindfolded her man so he would not see that she was turning from a butterly into a caterpillar.'[13]

Philip Wylie lashed himself into a rhetorical frenzy which so accurately caught the frequency of woman-hatred in America that the absurdity of his actual argument did not prevent a spurious phenomenon, 'Momism', from coming into being. Many an intelligent man abandoned his understanding in order to join, like Jimmy Porter, in the luxury of unbridled vilification of women. For example, Wylie actually states that female suffrage is responsible for political corruption in America.

Mom's first gracious presence at the ballot-box was roughly concomitant with the start towards a new all-time low in political scurviness, hoodlumism, gangsterism, labour strife, monopolistic thuggery, moral degeneration, civic corruption, smuggling, bribery, theft, murder, homosexuality, drunkenness, financial depression, chaos and war. Note that.[14]

Of course, he can't be serious. True enough. Such things can only be said in jest, but they are serious none the less. The most telling playground for feelings of rejection about women is the joke department:

A strange sight greeted the young wife as she came home. There was her mother standing on a chair with her feet in a bucket of water. She had one finger plugged into the light socket, and two wires connected to each side of her head. Hubby was poised by the electricity meter with his hand on the switch.

'Ah, you're just in time to see Henry cure my rheumatism!' cried the happy mother.[15]

The fact that there are no such storehouses of jokes against father is not because women have no sense of humour, although it might most commonly be explained that way. How they could survive the endless gibing at their expense without a sense of humour is difficult to explain. Another kind of humorous insult that women take in good part is the drag artists' grotesque guying of female foibles. Some of the transvestite acts are loving celebrations of the sexless trappings of femininity, and should be chiefly of value in pointing out how little femininity has to do with actual sex and how much with fakery and glamour-binding. Many more of them are maliciously conceived caricatures of female types ogling and apeing women's blandishments and hypocrisy while vying with feminine charms. Women are spectators at both kinds of entertainment, laughing and applauding whenever required.

Any woman can continue this investigation of the abuse of womenfolk for herself, but there would not be much point in exciting female paranoia if there were no alternatives. As an essential condition of the diminution of the common practice of belittling women, women themselves must stop pan-handling. In their clothes and mannerisms women caricature themselves, putting themselves across with silly names and deliberate flightiness, exaggerating their indecisiveness and helplessness, faking all kinds of pretty tricks that they will one day have to give up. They ought to take advantage of the genuine praise of women which is appearing, though fitfully, in contemporary culture. When the Troggs sang their praises of their *Wild Thing,* or Family celebrated their *Second Generation Woman*:

> Last thing you gotta do
> Is talk her into loving you
> No need to
>
> She knows when the time is right
> Comes to you without a fight
> She wants to[16]

they opened up new possibilities in the imagery of womanhood, not now circumscribed by hearts and flowers or jewels. *Long Tall Sally* and *Motorcycle Irene* are individuals, not stereotypes, although they are still outnumbered by Girls from the North Country and other impersonal female deities at least they have arrived. It is time we went to meet them.

Misery

Anguish is easier to bear than misery. The woman who is married to a brute, a drunk or a pervert has the world's sympathy as well as masochistic satisfaction. The self-publicizing misery of the abandoned woman justifying her dependence on drugs, drink or sex with strangers by the crime which society has committed against her is not so deeply pitiable as the day-to-day blank misery borne by women who have nothing to complain about. The evidence of this dreary suffering can be found on any aging female face: the wrinkles which disfigure women are lines of strain and repression, lines of worry, not concern. Relaxed, their drawn features are easy to read, but as soon as they realize that they are being observed they guiltily clear their eyes, raise their chins and affect a serenity they do not feel. The prejudice against revolt or complaint by married women is very strong: public airing of boredom or discontent is deep disloyalty, ingratitude and immorality. It is admitted that marriage is a hard job requiring constant adjustment, 'give and take', but it is not so often admitted that the husband-provider is the constant and the woman the variable.

'Daytimes are all right: I'm busy. But the evenings from eight till midnight, along with my knitting or TV, make me feel like a prisoner.

'Because my husband works at the local, if I go out it's with my sister or to evening classes. Surely one hour of a man's company at night is not enough? I feel like a modern Cinderella, and can't stand another twelve years of it. There's a shortage of baby sitters and it's hard to organize a service here because there are very few mothers in my situation close by.'

Let's face one fact: your husband isn't going to change after twelve years. He can't see any harm in his behaviour, and the more you complain, the more ready will he be to run away from your reproaches to the peace of his bar.

You can, though, *change yourself*. First consider your man's many virtues: then make sure the time spent with him is so delightful he's loath to leave.

Finally, reorganize your social life. If you had friends in to cards or a simple meal twice weekly, they wouldn't be your husband, but they'd take your mind off him. And remember –if he were, say, a sailor, he'd be away for years. Come to terms with an absentee husband: and if he begins to realize you are not noticing his absence so much he may be more ready to stay at home.[1]

A wife's only worthwhile achievement is to make her husband happy – it is understood that he may have other more important things to do than make her happy. When her discontent begins to incommode him, he realizes that perhaps he ought to talk to her more, take her out more often, buy her roses and chocolates, or pay her the occasional compliment. It doesn't take much after all. If she has already lapsed into the apathy and irritability of the housewive's syndrome she is not really capable of a conversation, too tired to go out, feels bribed and mocked by flowers.

> **I am admired because I do things well. I cook, sew, knit, talk, work and make love very well. So I am a valuable item. Without me he would suffer. With him I am alone. I am as solitary as eternity and sometimes as stupid as clotted cream. Ha ha ha! Don't think! Act as if all the bills are paid.**
> **Christine Billson 'You Can Touch Me', 1961, p.9**

Nagging, overweight and premature aging are the outward signs of misery, and they are so diffuse among women in our society that they do not excite remark. Women feel guilty about all of them: they are the capital sins of 'letting yourself go'. They invent excuses for them explaining irritability and tiredness by illnesses, claiming pains that do not exist until they make them exist; the insidious headache, backache, loss of appetite, rheumatism. The housewives who suffer from the actual housewives' blight, the 'great, bleeding blisters that break out on their hands and arms' which Betty Friedan noticed are fewer in number than the women who have no such welcome outward sign of their malaise.[2] The statistics about the numbers of women who have surgery for abdominal complaints without organic causes are horrifying. We could guess at some real statistics if we had the market research findings for firms who market 'zest', 'zip', 'energy', 'vitality', 'fitness', 'happiness', 'inner glow', which will 'help you to enjoy life', 'buck you up no end', make you 'relaxed, confident – eager to get on with things', 'help you to become your real self again'. The products that can advertise in this way are free from habit-forming drugs for the most part, although the subtle way in which pain-killers are presented to women as a form of psychotherapy, combating depression and irritability as well as pain, is full of hazards. There are no statistics for aspirin and codeine addiction in this country because they are both sold over the counter. There is no public campaign to warn women of the danger of salicylates.[3] Occasionally a typical housewives' syndrome appears in the professional advice sections of women's papers: Evelyn Home was called upon to deal with this:

Maybe mine's more a problem for you, Dr Meredith, but I'm always bone-tired and therefore bone-idle. And with five children (three at school) you'll guess there's plenty for me to do.

I feel so tired when I wake, I can't think how to cope, let alone start work. I do the minimum of housework, sometimes I don't even get the youngest dressed until just before my husband gets home in the evenings, and only then because he blows his top.

He calls me tired-itis.

How I envy the women who can get up at six and do everything and feel on top of the world. I wish I could do half that they do; now I'm really down and don't feel like trying at all. Recently my thoughts have frightened me; all that stopped me from carrying them out was the thought of the children, whom, though I don't show it, I do love.

It's all there; the guilt, because women's literature is full of the trumpeting of female Stakhanovists crying 'Look how well I do the impossible: everybody love me!', the feeling of incompetence which is turning into illness and debility as she formulates it, the odd relationship with her husband who is her critic, and her uncertain feelings about the children, which are not dispelled by a policy statement which ought to read 'I do love them (but I don't feel it).'

Evelyn Home's response is typical, and no G.P. would thank her for making it, even though it is difficult to think of any workable alternative.

You're quite right: it's a doctor's case, I'm sure of it. Get down to your doctor, explain everything, the weariness, depression, lassitude; he can help.

And cheer up. Many women with far less to cope with than five children and a quick tongued husband feel worse than you and do less. You're all right, except that you're ill (!) Tackle your health first and the other troubles will all fall into place.[4]

Well, it all rather depends on the doctor. Suppose she is as strong as an ox, no iron deficiency? Suppose he does treat her with tonics and vitamins? Suppose he tells her to stop moaning and get on with it, a feat of which G.P.s are not altogether incapable? Suppose he suggests a holiday which they cannot afford, or which turns into a fiasco with even harder and more unwilling work than before? No miracles

will happen. Perhaps she can try a glass or two of tonic wine?
More likely her G.P. will, if badgered sufficiently, prescribe
a happiness pill, an amphetamine, an anti-depressant, a
stimulant. English papers periodically boom with vague
reports of increasing addiction to stimulants and barbiturates
among housewives.

A recent T.V. programme estimated that over a million women in
Britain today are addicted to tranquillizers. To those who have
never taken them it sounds alarming, but those of us who are
actually hooked on them know just how awful it really is. For over a
year, I have been on a brand of pill, described as an anti-depressant
and relaxant.

I started with tranquillizers at the time I went to my family doctor
to ask his advice about a problem concerning my marriage.

This letter appeared in *Forum* as a caution to other women
who might follow the primrose path of symptomatic treatment for an intolerable situation: Mrs J. S. used up two
supplies of pills in all innocence, and then discovered that she
had withdrawal symptoms:

When the new supply ran out I thought I'd try to do without them
On the first day I felt a bit jumpy, but after a couple of drinks in the
evening my nerves quietened down. The following day it was
worse. I was terribly irritable with my husband and the children. I
had palpitations and the palms of my hands were sweaty. As the
days passed, there was no question but that I have become addicted
to tranquillizers. I just had to have more pills.

She went to another doctor to be cured of the addiction,
but he gave her more pills. At least the addiction supplied a
more pressing and uncomplicated problem than her intolerable situation. Her story has no end:

I had to continue taking my tranquillizers to stop worrying about my new worries. Today, I can't imagine life without my pills any more than an alcoholic can without a drink. I was talking with a friend last week who is attending a psychiatrist. Anyway, she was telling me what a marvellous thing analysis is and how her doctor has helped her. I was with her a few hours and I noticed that during that time she twice went to her handbag and took a little pill. I could have sworn that they are the same as mine. She thinks they are little miracle workers. I didn't even bother to explain to her their futility.[5]

Mr Michael Ryman, a psychiatric worker with the drug-addiction unit at All-Saints Hospital, Birmingham, reported that he had watched for eleven years while increasing numbers of housewives (he did not supply figures) trailed into the clinic to be weaned off high dosages of barbiturates,

---

Then Miss Simmons, who is married to the Hollywood producer-director, Richard Brooks, explained: 'I was terribly lonely when Richard was away on his movies. It was like you see on the screen. I was hooked on TV and booze.

· 'It's a disastrous combination. I just sat there with the kids in bed, watching TV and drinking. Night after night.

'It's lovely being with the children. Tracy is now thirteen and Kate is eight. But, of course, they have their own chums.

'And it can be very lonely, sitting there alone in a big house at night. That's how drink became my big problem.'
'News of the World', 5 April 1970

---

tranquillizers and stimulants. He admitted that their success rate with these cases was particularly small. His attitude was moralistic, as the professional attitude always is, eventually. He spoke of women using sleeping pills 'because they cannot sleep or face the sexual advances of a too-ardent husband' (the double-think in the latter idea is masterful), who 'live on tranquillizers to counteract the slightest domestic crisis', who 'swallow anti-depressant capsules to help them through their dull and dreary day'. 'Tranquillizer addicts have, for example, been known to rush to the pill bottle after such minor upsets as boiling potatoes dry, finding a light bulb smashed and getting behind with the weekly wash'.

. He does not ponder why it is that women can get themselves into such a state that trivial matters can become unbearable. It is not surprising that he has such a tiny proportion of successes, if this is the level of analysis to which these women are subjected.[6] The Glasgow Committee of the Royal Scottish Society for Prevention of Cruelty to Children reported that an increasing number of Glasgow mothers were taking drugs 'to escape from reality', another morally suspect activity.[7] The housewives' life is not real: it is anachronistic and thwarting: women have been exposed to too many other kinds of life to revert to four walls and people two foot high without strain. The refusal to accept this as a rewarding life is not a refusal to accept reality. All these symptoms of tiredness, lassitude, 'nerves', as women are apt to call them, are neurasthenia, and have the complex psychosomatic origin that the name implies. No amount of direct medication can be effective, unless women can also be brainwashed into deluding themselves that their monotonous and unremitting drugery in the home is for any purpose or doing any good. A housewife's work has no results: it simply has to be done again. Bringing up children is not a real occupation, because children come up just the same, brought or not. The confusion about the degree of bringing necessary, and the multitude of mistakes which the unsuspecting mother is assured on all sides that she will make, and has made, if things aren't working out, show that she is without guidance yet loaded with responsibility.

Women often imagine that they would be less miserable if they were better off. Perhaps it's a baby-sitter they need, or a maid, or long holidays, or fewer financial worries. The

> ...give their existence some object, their time some
> occupation, or the peevishness of disappointment and the
> listlessness of idleness will infallibly degrade their
> nature...
>
> **From a letter of Charlotte Brontë**

evidence is that the fewer masking problems there are the
greater the strain on the central problem of the marital
relationship itself. In western culture the ultimate success-
figure is the astronaut; the wife of an astronaut can bask in
money and reflected glory. The cosmonaut is the American
Aristocrat; presidents fly to him, he prays on behalf of the
nation standing on the moon: his domestic set-up must have
everything money and planning can provide. A NASA
psychiatrist was quoted as saying that Cape Kennedy was
the world's most active spawning ground for divorce.
Certainly divorces occur there at double the national
average. Housewife alcoholism is higher than anywhere else
in America except Washington. 'Space industry seems to rob
men of emotion.' The deliberate desensitizing of astronauts
has its problems; they might contain themselves brilliantly
on the moon, but they contain themselves everywhere else
too, including their wives' beds, for the degree of sexual
activity at the Cape is agreed to be very low.[8] We may take
the computer society of Cape Kennedy to be the logical
development of the tendencies of our increasingly organized
chaos, even in poor and backward England where people
cannot afford to get divorces. A cosmonaut's wife cannot be
fat and frumpish, so she must express her misery in drunkenness and promiscuity which are at least modish and expensive
habits. In England a 'neglected' and 'downtrodden', 'bored',
'lonely' housewife is likely simply to eat too much, too much
rubbish. Advertising of chocolate bars and biscuits in England
has recently recognized the function of escapist eating. What

we are told to expect from such machine made sludge is 'a taste sensation', an 'explosion', excitement, and visions of faraway places. Television advertising of candy promises hallucinations and orgasms. Certainly a Mars Bar costs less than a divorce.

Female revolt takes curious and tortuous forms, and the greatest toll is exacted by the woman upon herself. She finds herself driving her husband away from her by destructive carping, fighting off his attempts to make love to her, because somehow they seem all wrong. Frigidity is still a major problem, but know-how about the female structure and orgasms will not change it. Women are ill-adapted by

> I resent the fact that my husband doesn't want to make love to me very often but on the rare occasions when he does, I resent that even more and freeze up on him because I feel that he's making a wishy-washy attempt at pretending there's still something between us or that he's not going with another woman at the time (I'm sure he has a few girl friends). We often row about this; sometimes he denies it and sometimes he says I drive him to other women because I'm cold with him. But how can a woman warm up to a man who never says or does anything romantic?
>
> (Mrs) C.T., 'Forum', Vol. 2, No.2

their conditioning to accept sexual reality and orgasm. Often husbands report that frigidity has developed in a wife who seemed to enjoy sex in the early days of marriage. Sexual love is not a matter of orgasm or of romanticism: approaching each other from their opposite poles husbands and wives miss each other in the dark and clutch at phantoms. Contraception takes a toll of female sexuality. It is appalling to reflect that the most popular form of contraception in England is still the sheath. One British couple in five still practises premature withdrawal. One and three-quarter million English women use the pill, not even an eighth of the housewife population. Even if they do use the pill, all problems are not solved. Every week the press features another pill horror story, of a bride dead of thrombosis within weeks of her marriage. A story in the *News of the World* is that the Family Planning Association warns that the 400,000 women supplied by the Association with the pill are suffering an assortment of fifty side effects.[9]

Professor Victor Wynn of St Mary's Hospital, Paddington, says taking the pill can lead to thrombosis, liver disorders, obesity and depression.[10] When he says it, we may begin to believe it, although as a woman who complained of oedema and apathy when taking the pill, I can testify that my G.P. poohpoohed the idea. A number of letters in the *Lancet* in the summer of 1969 discussed the matter of pill-depression and admitted that the pill hormone did interfere with the secretion of tryptophan, 'a dietary chemical essential to good health and which may also be associated with mood control.'[11] The withdrawal of sixteen brands from the market has not done much for the women who are now using the others. The coil has a painful failure rate in about twenty per cent of cases and can be an oddly disquieting resident in the body. Mrs Monica Foot wrote a horrifying account of spontaneous abortion with a bow-type coil in the *Sunday Times* and was reviled for her candour.[12] The diaphragm is a nuisance, is perceptible to the woman, and the spermicides interfere with her secretions and the tactile sensations of the surrounding membrane. Moreover, husbands can drag it out, if they insist upon impregnation. As long as women have to think about contraception every day, and worry about pills, sheaths, and devices of all kinds, and then worry every time a period is due, more irrationality will appear in their behaviour. The almost universal problem of menstrual tension is certainly aggravated for today's woman, and added neurasthenia makes it more acute. Misery, misery, misery.

There are more women who attempt suicide than men, more women in mental hospitals than men[13]; there are hundreds of children injured by desperate parents every year, and even cases of infants bloodily put to death by deranged mothers.[14] Post-natal weeps are a recognized syndrome; some women have suffered them for as long as a year after the birth of the child. The tiny scandalous minority of baby-bashers and husband-murderers get into the press. The majority of women drag along from day to day in an apathetic twilight, hoping that they are doing the right thing, vaguely expecting a reward some day. The working wife waits for the children to grow up and do well to vindicate her drudgery, and sees them do as they please, move away, get into strange habits, and reject their parents. The idle wife girds her middle-aged loins and goes to school, fools with academic disciplines, too often absorbing knowledge the wrong way for the wrong reasons. My own mother, after nagging and badgering her eldest child into running away from home (a fact which she concealed for years by talking of her as if she were present, when she knew absolutely nothing of what she was doing), took up ballet dancing, despite the obvious futility of such an undertaking, studied accountancy, and failed obdurately year after year, sampled religion, took up skiing, and finally learnt Italian. In fact she had long before lost the power of concentration required to read a novel or a newspaper. Every activity was an obsession for as long as it lasted – some lasted barely a month and those are too numerous to list. She resisted television, resisted homemaking and knitting, the usual opiates. She did not play Bingo or housie-housie, partly because of middle-class snobbery. She did not fall in love with a dog, or a budgerigar. Others do.

Of course, single women do not escape female misery, because of the terrific pressure to marry as a measure of feminine success. They dawdle and dream in their dead-end jobs, overtly miserable, because they are publicly considered to be. The phenomenon of single women devoting their lives to aged parents, which has no counterpart in the male sex, is incompletely understood if we do not consider the element of self-cloistering which inspires these women. The mockery of spinsters and acid-faced women is not altogether the expression of prejudice, for these women do exude discontent and intolerance and self-pity. As usual it is a vicious circle.

Given the difficulty of marriage as a way of life, and the greater difficulties of spinsterhood, happiness must be seen by women to be a positive achievement. Ultimately, the greatest service a woman can do her community is to be happy; the degree of revolt and irresponsibility which she must manifest to acquire happiness is the only sure indication of the way things must change if there is to be any point in continuing to be a woman at all.

Resentment

Misery is not borne without resentment. It is commonly admitted that there is a battle waging between the sexes but like most other facts which we dare not directly contemplate it is most commonly referred to facetiously. The battle is universal and deadly serious unlike the isolated skirmishes of the women's liberation movements with the male establishment. Whether it is waged at home or abroad it is always in-fighting without rules or conventions and its conclusion is death. We observe it all the time but we seldom recognize it

> Although he doesn't know it, I have attended his funeral several times. Each time I looked **ADORABLE** in my black tight-fitting suit and Spanish lace veil. And, each time, after a decent period has elapsed, I have remarried a very rich man and become famous for the ethereal look on my beautiful pale face.
>
> Christine Billson, 'You Can Touch Me', 1961, p. 20

for what it is, even when we are in there battling tooth and nail ourselves. Because they have the upper hand, men usually conduct themselves with more grace than women do upon the battleground. Men do not realize that they are involved in a struggle to the death until they have lost it and are facing the ruinous capitulations of the divorce court, when in chagrin at their foolishness in neglecting their defences they give vociferous vent to their conviction that the world is run for the benefit of predatory and merciless women. The winning woman knows that her victory is Pyrrhic.

Female resentment has an astonishing range of public expression. The most catalytic situation is a party. Parties in our society are very rarely occasions of spontaneous festivity. They are usually arranged for a purpose: to introduce a new arrival to a group, to emphasize the importance of an event, to get to know each other. It is a time to stand up and be counted. Men take women to parties and therefore women are at a disadvantage from the outset. The group's cohesion derives from the relationships of the men; order is preserved by acknowledging nuances of rank. The women are expected to pick up on these nuances and subtly strengthen their men's representation in the group. Every woman arriving on her escort's arm knows what her role is, and yet she habitually subverts and destroys the social situation with an astonishing variety of ambiguous tactics. The most obvious, usually practised by women who are not seriously attached, is the stimulation of male rivalry by more or less subtle flirtation. A woman may appear to operate this technique unconciously; she is very rarely entirely in control of it, nonetheless it is extremely effective. In playing this game she may take advantage of tensions already existing in the masculine group and aggravate them. Her best bet is to exploit the male chauvinism which prompts her escort to display his catch for the evaluation of his peers. She may subtly indicate that he is a boor (for her glass has been empty for *hours*), that he is a lovable sweetie (that is to say a schmock), she may welcome anecdotes which tell against him; or if she really doesn't give a damn, she may reject him outright preferably for a friend of his, best of all for his best friend or his most successful rival. More irrevocably attached women only use such techniques in moderation, because they have constructed a whole battery of minor artillery, a sort of lingering death of a thousand cuts to be constantly dealt out to their chosen victim. Joke-telling by the husband is a hazardous endeavour, for his wife will sigh or tell everybody that they have heard it or that Max Bygraves told it so much better; she won't laugh whatever happens. If her husband is the life of the party she will languish and demand querulously to be taken home, or become overcome by liquor curiously fast even to the extent of making an exhibition of herself. If he is having fun she will hiss in his car that he is drunk and making a fool of himself, or remind him that he has to drive home, or, if he remains proof against her, accuse him of gaping after every attractive woman in the room. All this destructiveness derives from her dulled apprehension that she is only there as her husband's appendage: she is not at ease in the social situation. All she was ever prepared to do when she was unattached was to engineer an attachment: now that that is done her little stump of wit and conversation is quite withered away. She feels stupid and probably dowdy: she has never really enjoyed herself, except when she was the object to rivalry and flattery, and she doesn't know how. The sight of her mate playing around evokes her contempt. She bets that he would enjoy himself much better if she wasn't there, a speculation all too often thoroughly grounded in fact. If she doesn't hit back in some snide way her energy has absolutely no outlet. She is wiped out, obliterated, and her older friends murmur among themselves how suppressed she is since she got married, shacked up or whatever. If she should reverse the traditional party situation and coruscate to her husband's disadvantage (and most likely at his expense) bitter revenge will be exacted later, as bitter as anything she could devise herself. It's best to sit it through or try a last blackmailing technique, to sneak off home leaving him wondering what has become of her. Most women adopt the expedient of segregation, so that they can wage war from covered territory.

I have seen more spectacular tactics, which depended upon the publicness of the situation for their effect. One female casualty of my acquaintance used to retire to the lavatory when she could make no headway in the situation, smash her glass and roll in the splinters screaming until some strong man broke the door down and carried her out in picturesque disorder. Another girl provoked a sharp belt in the face, by the simple expedient of screaming unbearably until she got it and then spent all her energy trying to fling herself down three flights of stairs, so that every man there had to lend a hand to restrain her. Another girl used to react suspiciously fast to a modicum of liquor, and tear her clothes off while her mate besought her to cool it, and the rest of the party pretended that they were observing liberated behaviour. This is part of the larger strategy of insinuating that the old man's virility is not equal to his lady's demands, an extreme and bohemian form of flirtation.

The ignorance and isolation of most women mean that they are incapable of making conversation: most of their communication with their spouses is a continuation of the power struggle. The result is that when wives come along to dinner parties they pervert civilized conversation about real issues into personal quarrels. The number of hostesses who wish that they did not have to ask wives is legion. The number who seize the excuse of a wife's absence to invite a man for dinner because the poor fellow cannot do for himself (ostensibly) has its own significance. This must not be taken to indicate that men have not their part to play in the battle. Their tactics are condescension and patronizing of a woman's attempts to contribute to a discussion, simple setting aside of her remarks or ignoring them, exaggerated courtliness to other women, extravagant praise of the cooking (for all the world as if they were constantly starved or poisoned at home), loving mockery of the little woman and so on. Because of their winning position, their techniques do not have to be strident or obscene or anti-social, and this fact itself can drive a woman to madness and direct aggression. I am reminded of one of my girl students who got so tired of being patronized at a Union meeting at the university that she threw a full pint of bitter over the chairman. Her fleeting satisfaction was qualified by the eventual realization that she had lost on all counts.

The real theatre of the sex war despite the atrocities committed in social situations is the domestic hearth; there it is conducted unremittingly. Because of the inequity of the situation and the impossibility of any telling action, the woman must unpack her heart with words and fall acursing like a very drab, a scullion, because, as Hamlet construed from his own example, she lacks gall to make oppression bitter. Verbal aggression is not the reflection of penis envy but the inevitable result of induced impotence. However, the fruitlessness of the reproaches and the endless reiteration of the same spurious complaints (spurious because she is ignorant of what her genuine grievance is) bring about an increasing stridency and a terrible disregard for the real meaning of what she is saying. Her attacks grow more destructive and more unforgivable until she realizes in some helpless way that she is tearing down her house with her own hands, but she is by now powerless to stop brutalizing her own environment. She hears the squalid succession of 'You never's' and 'You always's' and realizes that most of what she is saying is unjust and irrelevant, but something is badly wrong, how else can she say what it is? Her guilt increases; her power to break from a situation which is aging and altering her beyond recognition diminishes every day. Occasionally she breaks down and confesses that she doesn't know what is wrong with her. Her husband suggests that she take a pill and the bitter battle recommences with her upbraiding of his stupidity and heartlessness, his refusal to see that he is partly responsible for her pitiable condition, and so on.

The housewife accepts vicarious life as her portion, and imagines that she will be a prop and mainstay to her husband in his noble endeavours, but insidiously her unadmitted jealousy undermines her ability to appreciate what he tells her about his ambitions and his difficulties. She belittles him, half-knowingly disputes his difficult decisions, taunts him with his own fears of failure, until he stops telling her any-thing. Her questions about his 'day at the office' become a formality. She does not listen to his answers any more than he heeds her description of her dreary day. Eventually the discussion stops altogether. It just isn't worth it. He has no way of understanding her frustration – her life seems so easy. She likewise feels that he cannot know how awful her days can be. Conversation becomes a mere power struggle. She opposes through force of habit. Why should he be always right? Ever right? Men are deluded in the situation because they cannot believe that an issue is merely a pretext for another kind of confrontation. I remember a controversy which raged between my parents about the merits and de-merits of a large tree which was struggling to grow just outside our house. My father painstakingly weighed pros and cons and decided it was best to let it struggle on a little longer for it had been traumatized by the construction of the house and could make a better showing in another season. My mother foxed about, refusing to confront the issue until father decided definitely that he was opposed to its felling. Mother went out the next day and ringbarked it, so it definitely died, and had to be felled after all. My father had decided fairly early on that life at home was pretty unbear-able; and he lived more and more of it at his club, only com-ing home to sleep. My mother did not protest about this, as it gave her an opportunity to tyrannize the children and enlist their aid to disenfranchise my father completely, but many wives impose heavy restrictions on their husband's recreation out of simple jealousy. The objection is made on many counts, of expense, of loneliness (often genuine), of fear of intruders, or need of help with some aspects of running the house. Working-class wives manage to ration their husband's recreation severely, apportioning the money for it after they have taken the pay packet out of the old man's pocket when he has finally arrived home on pay-night. One of the few acts of defiance against the welfare state is the refusal of security which gambling represents and this form of release is most severely opposed by wives, who are acting out their parts in anchoring their men in the system. The release of drunkenness is likewise blocked as much as possible by women, sometimes with good reason, but more often not. The degree of inebriation which is bitterly upbraided by women is so slight that it may be all but imperceptible. Much of the violence which drinking men wreak upon their women is provoked by their voiced or unvoiced reproaches. The wives refuse to recognize their husbands' need of various forms of release because they feel, however bad his situation is, it is not as bad as a woman's lot and women do not seek release, not overtly.

The most sinister aspect of domestic infighting is the use of the children as weaponry and battlefield. Not all women are as desperate as my mother was when she used to mutter to me that my father was a 'senile old goat'. Usually the use of the children both as weapons and causes of contention is more subtle. It is in a woman's interest to keep the children babies as long as she can, because then they cannot disown her even if they are sons, because they need her ministrations. She mocks their father because he cannot know what they need, screams when he takes them out to a football match in the rain, insists on waiting up for them when they go out, both because she is jealous of their freedom, which always seems more than she had, and because she wants to prove that they need her solicitations and surveillance. The most extreme feats of child-exploitation by women are rarer but more striking. The obvious case is the enlistment of the son to depose the father, which is very common in poorer families where dad's inadequacies can be ruthlessly underlined. The son accepts mother's account of her suffering at the hands of his brutal father, and endeavours like Saturn to displace him in his own house. Given a less intense Oedipal situation a son may find himself attacked by his mother in order to get at his father. Once my mother knelt on my small brother's chest and beat his face with her fists in front of my father and was threatened with violent retaliation, the only instance of my father's rising to her bait that I can recall. My brother was three years old at the time.

Much wifely frigidity is the withdrawal of a pleasure as punishment, although this is never admitted. Likewise the exaggeration of illnesses, to the point of valetudinarianism and hypochondria, is often motivated by continual reproach and not organic at all. The subtler form is that which keeps the little woman on her feet through all the vicissitudes of illness, so that everybody feels guilty and never more so than when they feel most irritated by the not so subtle martyrdom she compels them to witness. The withdrawal of rationing of sexual favours is an important weapon in the expression of resentment of the male. It is true that even in reasonably elevated strata of English society (for example, among the wives of some of my colleagues) sex is granted to the husband as a reward for something accomplished or as a consolation for some setback. The blackmail is that there is nothing in it for her, so that her husband feels both bestial and grateful when she allows him the use of his conjugal hole. Nowadays this kind of parleying is frequently conducted in the guise of a birth-control drama, where the wife finds herself unable to bear any form of contraception, even claiming that she finds no pleasure in intercourse unless there is the possibility of issue, or forcing the husband to suffer *coitus interruptus*. When it eventually fails, she can claim that he betrayed her because he is a selfish beast. The variations on this theme are legion. In every case the woman herself is also the loser, but as she has no conception of how she could gain by a different attitude that is not significant in her motivation. She is out to get him.

While a wife may be fondly understood to spur her husband on to greater efforts by her observation of what the Joneses have that they have not, the main reason for pointing out what the Joneses have in the first place is to contrast that with what they have got, thereby stressing the husband's inadequacy. Such a wife goads her husband on to the foreseeable finale of a coronary and a long widowhood, which is somehow not what she wanted at all, because she has never been given an opportunity to understand her own motives for hastening her spouse to his death. This is another aspect of that jealousy of a man's life outside the home, which in extreme cases provokes a wife to badger her husband into giving up a work he loves and which he does very well, for something tedious but lucrative which will keep the family abreast of the Joneses. The Rosamund syndrome, for George Eliot has produced the paradigm in the case of Lydgate's disastrous marriage so that spoiled darling,[1] is the most extreme form of female jealousy of the problem-centred male life, which gives rise to such unforgettable dialogue as 'You love that silly Stradivarius better than you love me' and so forth. The complementary figure is that equally common one of the wife who gave up her Stradivarius to make a good wife to her husband, to whom everybody is too polite to point out that she would have made a lousy violinist anyway. The cheaper form is the listing of the enormously successful men she might have married, or the blanket reproach, 'I've given you the best years of my life!' Men are often led to believe that women's motives for this kind of provoking behaviour are merely acquisitive: in fact the motivation is more often the simpler one, resentment, which inspires a need to prove the husband inadequate, or morally inferior, or both. Any allies can be and are used in the fight. Doctors, analysts, girl friends, even the secretary or the boss, as well as the children, can all be enlisted in the hounding of the husband. The efficacy of the process cannot be construed as a female victory, but simply as the sour fruits of unrecognized revenge.

A far better acount of the miserable destructiveness of womankind is made by Charles M. Schultz in his character-ization of Lucy van Pelt in the brilliant sage of *Peanuts*. Lucy's constant nagging anxiety, her imperviousness to all suffering but her own, her ruthless aggravation of Charlie Brown's inadequacy fears, her self-righteousness, her jealousy of Linus's blanket, her utter incomprehension of Schroeder's music together with her grotesque attempts to vamp him, her crabbiness, her fuss-budgetry, the diabolical intensity of her housekeeping, her inability to smile except maliciously, her effect upon Charlie Brown's ill-fated baseball team, it's all there and any woman who cannot recognize, however dimly, her own image is that unhappy little face, has not yet under-stood the gravity of her situation. Nevertheless, Schultz's portrait of the embattled female is incomplete. To comple-ment Lucy's destructiveness we need the fuller statement of Strindberg's about the mortal combat of the sexes, in *The Dance of Death*, as well as Ibsen's more oblique statements in plays like *Hedda Gabler* and *A Doll's House*. A battle which is fought through inauthenticity and hypocrisy by concealed blows and mutual treachery looks very much like a game, and Eric Berne described some of the most superficial of the tactics that women adopt in his justly celebrated *Games People Play*, but any woman who reads his Section 7, 'Marital Games' could very swiftly add a score or more of other infight-ing techniques which he has omitted. The last comment on the whole gigantic mesh of manipulation which characterizes most of our relationships, but most of all those between the sexes, from father and daughter, to dated and dater, and husband and wife, and mother and son, is most fittingly expressed in Berne's words. 'Many games are played most intensely by disturbed people; generally speaking, the more disturbed they are, the harder they play.' The alternative to game-playing, to the defensive process which is the game of war, is what every woman must now seek for herself, autonomy.

For certain fortunate people there is something which transcends all classifications of behaviour, and that is awareness; something which rises above the programming of the past, and that is spontaneity; and something more rewarding than games, and that is intimacy. But all three of these may be frightening and even perilous to the unprepared. Perhaps they are better off as they are, seeking their solution in popular techniques of special action, such as 'togetherness'. This may mean that there is no hope for the human race, but there is hope for individual members of it.[2]

Rebellion

There have always been women who rebelled against their role in society. The most notorious are the witches, the women who withdrew from 'normal' human intercourse to commune with their pets or familiars, making a living somehow by exploiting their own knowledge of herbal medicine and the credulity of the peasantry, and perhaps indulging in the mysticism of other possibilities, magic white or black, perhaps Satanism. Careful reading of the depositions at witch trials reveals that some of the women were persecuted in the horrible fashion reserved for witches because they were troublemakers inciting the villagers to subversion or open rebellion. One of the punishments, the ducking stool, was the most primitive form of punitive psychotherapy, corresponding to shock treatment of today's melancholic or recalcitrant females.

> There was a woman known to be so bold
> That she was noted for a common scold;
> And on a time, it seems, she wrong'd her Betters
> Who sent her unto Prison, bound in Fetters:
> The Day of her Arraignment being come,
> Before grave elders, this then was her Doom:
> She should be ducked over head and ears,
> In a deep Pond, before her Overseers.
> Thrice was she under Water, yet not fainted,
> Nor yet for aught that I could see, was daunted;
> For, when with Water she was covered,
> She clapped her hands together o'er her head,
> To signify that then she could not talk,
> But yet she would be sure her hands should walk;

She had no power, but yet she had a will,
That if she could, she would have scolded still:
For after that, when they did her up-hale
Fiercely against them all then did she rail
This proves some women void of reasonable Wit;
Which if they had, then would they soon submit.[1]

The invalid conclusion to this tale is typical of male arrogance; the refusal to consider the content of her grievance is characteristic still of conservative accounts of the attempts of women to take action themselves in the hope of changing their condition. The charge of penis envy, or frustration, or perversion, is no more respectable than the anonymous author's assumption that his heroine is void of reasonable wit. We will know a good deal more about the history of feminism when we learn to read between the lines in cases of witchburning and other forms of female persecution. Many female heretics, such as the members of the Family of Love, had joined the sect precisely because they offered new scope for female self-determination.[2] The phenomenon of female gossipry, which entailed cooperation to gull husbands and enrich their wives as well as to procure adultery and abortions, certainly had its feminist elements, and there is evidence that educated women throughout the ages were particularly loath to submit to male sovereignty: as now, it was most frequently the education that was found at fault, and not the male sovereignty.

Much lesbianism, especially of the transvestite kind, may be understood as revolt against the limitations of the female role of passivity, hypocrisy and indirect action, as well as rejection of the brutality and mechanicalness of male sexual passion. All forms of lesbianism involve an invention of an alternative way of life, even if the male-female polarity survives in the relationship to the degree that there is butch and bitch within it. Dildoes are not used by butch lesbians however. The prevalance of tribadism as the principal lesbian mode of lovemaking argues the relative unimportance of the masculine fantasy in the relationship. However, such sexual deviations have been treated with so much lecherous curiosity and violent insult that most lesbians are unable to make their choice of an alternative anything like a political gesture. The operations of relentlessly induced guilt and shame cause the lesbian to conceal her condition, and to misstate her own situation as a result of a congenital blight or the mistakes of her parents. It is true that her inability to play the accepted role in society probably results from a failure in conditioning, but that is not itself a disqualification from the ability to choose lesbianism in an honourable, clear-eyed fashion, rejecting shame and inferiority feelings as a matter of principle, whether such feelings exist or not. The lesbian might as well claim that she had no other acceptable course to follow and become the apologist of her own way of life. Unfortunately, too often she is as blinded by spurious notions of normality as her critics are.

The women who are most conscious of the disabilities which afflict women are those who are educated to the point of demanding and deserving the same kind of advancement as men. In the higher educational establishments in which women are segregated there is a curious air of constipated revolt. Most women teachers are not married and do not have any very significant intercourse with the opposite sex. Their students sometimes suspect them of sexual relationships with each other, and certainly there is an intensity in their personal relationships which would argue some degree of thwarted attraction or affection, although I would maintain that the extreme repressions practised by such women on themselves in other respects indicate impotence in this regard. When a group of girl students presented a rather churlishly expressed list of grievances to the principal of a women's college in which I had the misfortune to be immured for a whole year before I could escape, she and her cronies clung together in her Hollywood-interior lodge, refusing to deal with the matters expressed in the petition, except to complain that they had wanted us to be so happy and we had *hurt* them. It is a kind of female rebellion to eschew cosmetics and the business of attraction, and some of these establishment rebels certainly cultivated respectable slatternliness to an impressive degree. Gentility went by the board as well. One such eminent lady, whose bloated form in a red knitted bathing suit had been known to drive every vestige of colour from a male don's cheek, was famous for farting and belching at table, and I once saw her put a meringue which she had shot on to the floor back on her plate and eat it with complete unconcern. Rather than concede some sort of genetic imbalance in these gifted women I should claim that their braying voices and shattering footsteps were deliberate reactions against feminine murmuring and pussy-footing. They were helped by the existence of an acceptable British stereotype of the aristocratic countrywoman, who is a good sport and more capable with a plough or a snaffle bit than many a man. Only a small proportion of the girls in their charge emulated them, for most of them were still coming through the last stages of puberty, and developing along more orthodox feminine lines despite their mistresses' attempts to keep them playing hockey and beating the men's marks at the end of the year.

Such unremarkable and unconscious forms of rebellion against the feminine role are old and ineffectual. If we were to compare the high incidence of positive homosexuality as well as effeteness and epicenity among male inhabitants of the establishments of higher learning we might discern a valid reaction against the male stereotype of brawn and insensitivity, but as long as the situation remains unrationalized it has little significance except as a personal motivation or a partial factor in neurosis. Rationalization has begun however, and it was first practised by women from this class, the most privileged of their sex. The history of suffragettism and its survival until our own day is beyond the scope of this book, although it is remarkable how many of today's militant women can remember some extraordinary old lady who sought (in vain) to plant the seeds of rebellion in their minds. From time to time wonderfully vivid old women appear on T.V., or are written up in obituaries in *The Times*, to remind us not only of the continuity of the movement but of the tactical address and joyful courage of petticoated, corseted the hatted gentlewomen of a liftetime ago. The progress since their times has not been uniform: women's clothes have fluctuated between the loose and unrestricting and the voluminous and pinching, the novelette heroine has been plucky and good-humoured, and then once more sexy and languishing. The beginning of the second feminist wave, of which this book must be considered a part, was Betty Friedan's research into the post-war sexual sell which got American women out of the factories and back into their homes. Mrs Friedan is a *summa cum laude* graduate of Smith College and held a research fellowship in psychology at Berkeley, a professional woman of considerable reputation and attainments. What she discovered during the five years that she worked on her book has led to her forming the most influential of the women's groups in America, the National Organization of Women, which now has a membership of more than three thousand and branches in many cities. Somewhere on the way she shed the husband to whom she dedicated her book. Her movement is the only one to achieve any degree of recognition from the political establishment. When NOW was formed it was read into the Congressional record; it provides most of the motivation and the personnel for the numerous women's groups and committees which now figure in various Congressional bodies. Clearly, what Mrs Friedan suggests cannot be at all radical. Her whole case rests upon the frustration suffered by the educated woman who falls for the Freudian notion that physiology is destiny. For Mrs Friedan sexuality seems to mean motherhood, an argument which other feminist groups also seem to be misled by, so that in rejecting the normative sex role of women they are forced to stress non-sexual aspects of a woman's destiny at the expense of her libido, a mistake which will have serious consequences. She represents the cream of American middle-class womanhood, and what she wants for them is equality of opportunity within the status quo, free admission to the world of the ulcer and the coronary. She has continued the campaign for the passage of the Equal Rights Amendment, which was begun in 1923, and for the repeal of the abortion laws on the most subtle grounds, arguing that they are unconstitutional as breaches of privacy, limitations on free speech and so forth. She feels that the problems of housewives' neuroses will be solved when they are socialized, encouraged to look beyond the kitchen to the community.[3] So far she has succeeded in 'forcing' the *New York Times* to increase its reputation for fairmindedness and freedom from male chauvinism by desegregating the Want Ads. Of course she could not desegregate the jobs: the immediate result of that tactic was the more qualified women wasted more time and energy reading about, applying for, and being rejected from jobs they had no chance of getting in the first place. As long as even female employers continue to prefer male employees, such token reforms will have only negative results. NOW also boycotted Colgate-Palmolive in a protest against job discrimination, although they have never levelled an attack of any significance against the whole ludicrous cosmetic industry, when the same worthless ingredients make up all the preparations from the cheapest to the most fabulously expensive, and female insecurity is cultivated by degrading advertising so that these mucky preparations can be sold more quickly than ever.

NOW also raided a bar in the Plaza Hotel where women were not admitted except at certain times of the day, and then only if accompanied by a male.

It was not long before intelligent members of NOW realized that their aims were too limited and their tactics too genteel. One of the more interesting women to emerge in the movement is Ti-Grace Atkinson, a leader of the most radical and most elite women's group, the Feminists – A Political Organization to Annihilate Sex Roles. This is a closed group of propaganda makers who are trying to develop the notion of a leaderless society in which the convention of Love ('the response of the victim to the rapist'), the proprietary relationship of marriage, and even uterine pregnancy will no longer prevail. Their pronouncements are characteristically gnomic and rigorous; to the average confused female they must seem terrifying. They have characterized men as the enemy, and, as long as men continue to enact their roles as misconceived and perpetuated by themselves and women, they are undoubtedly right. Nevertheless it is not true that to have a revolution you need a revolutionary theory: they might well find that a theory devised by minds diseased by the system will not be able to avail itself of the facts of a changing situation. It is dangerous to eschew sex as a revolutionary tactic because it is inauthentic and enslaving in the terms in which it is now possible, when sex is the principal confrontation in which new values can be worked out. Men are the enemy in much the same way that some crazed boy in uniform was the enemy of another like him in most respects except the uniform. One possible tactic is to try to get the uniforms off.

The forcing house of most of the younger women's liberation groups was the university left wing. In the November-December number of *New Left Review* in 1966, Juliet Mitchell published the most coherent statement of the socialist feminist position, and reprinted in various forms it remains the basis for most socialist theorizing on the subject, even though it is clearly deficient on the tactical side. *Women – The Longest Revolution* is squarely based on the tenets of Marx, Bebel and Engels. Unlike other theorists she does not fall for Engels's dubious anthropology, but keeps herself to stringent examination of demonstrable fact. '...Far from women's physical weakness removing her from productive work, her social weakness has in these cases evidently made her the major slave of it.'[4]

She sees that increasing industrialization does not therefore guarantee women a place in productive work because it was not incapability of muscular effort that kept her out of it, but rather the development of private property and private ownership of the means of production, and the relegation of women to the status of supermenials enacting vicarious leisure. This role in its turn is determined by the assumed structure of the family as necessarily patriarchal, the distortion of reproduction into a parody of production, of sexuality into sadistic exploitation, and the socialization of the child as woman's unique and prolonged responsibility. These four structures, production, reproduction, sexuality and socialization will have to be reconceived if any major change is to result. Foreseeing perhaps the developments that were soon to ensue from female activity in socialist movements, her conclusion labours to integrate the feminist movement with the proletarian revolution, despite her knowledge that there was no indication in the structure of existent groups or existent socialist regimes that such a brief would be respected:

...Socialism should properly mean not the abolition of the family, but the diversification of the socially acknowledged relationships which are today forcibly and rigidly compressed into it. This would mean a plural range of institutions – where the family is only one, and its abolition implies none. Couples living together or not living together, long-term unions with children, single parents bringing up children, children socialized by conventional rather than biological parents, extended kin-groups, etc. – all these could be encompassed in a range of institutions which matched the free invention and variety of men and women.

It would be illusory to try and specify these institutions. Circumstantial accounts of the future are idealistic and, worse, static. Socialism will be a process of change, of becoming. A fixed image of the future is in the worst sense ahistorical; the form that socialism takes will depend on the prior type of capitalism and the nature of its collapse...The liberation of women under Socialism will not be a 'rational' but a human achievement, in the long passage from Nature to culture is the definition of history and society.[5]

A much more naïve attempt to prove that the struggle of women against oppression was a part of the class struggle had been made as early at 1954, by Evelyn Reed, in the October Discussion Bulletin of the Socialist Workers' Party, in which she attempts to prove that sex rivalry and the emergence of women as sexual objects were the results exclusively of bourgeois capitalism. She invoked the notion of a primitive society free from any form of sex exploitation or property or rivalry, where cosmetics were used simply as a means of identification, describing the propaganda machine of feminity as the deliberate sinister ploy of money hungry capitalists in the nineteenth century expanded to gargantuan limits in the twentieth. The basic trend of the argument is probably correct, but she is so patently arguing from her convictions to her evidence, none of which has any source that she quotes, that the most sympathetic reader is alienated, unless, presumably, he has no way of knowing better. In 1969 her contributions to the woman question were all issued in a pamphlet called *Problems of Women's Liberation: A Marxist Approach*. Her arguments are couched in typical Marxist doctrinaire terminology, buttressed by phony anthropology and poor scholarship. The cover features a reproduction of a figure on an Attic vase, misidentified as a 'goddess symbol of the matriarchy' when it is actually a graceful Bacchante with thyrsus and dead wildcat. Evelyn Reed would have been horrified if she had realized that her work was decorated with the symbol of hippiedom and drug culture, flowing hair, snake diadem and all. There is a symbolism in the error: there is certainly more hope for women in Marcuse than in Marx. The booklet[6] is unusually well-distributed and may be influential, which is in some ways a pity, for much time will be wasted debating invalid conclusions. Juliet Mitchell's article is much better argued and much more scrupulous.

Women active within socialist groups were not reassured that the liberation of the working classes would be their own liberation. Stalin's repeal of the early Soviet legislation which permitted automatic divorce and free abortion, and his institution of rewards for motherhood was a patent betrayal.[7] The increase in the number of female doctors in the soviet was a mere refinement on the female role of service.[8] Female construction workers in Russia are taught no skills and given no tools.[9] In China militarization of women, prohibition of cosmetics and frivolous attire did not entail any amelioration of the woman's role as servant of her family although the more obvious evils of concubinage were eradicated. In the summer of 1967 the women's caucus of the National Convention of the S.D.S. went ahead to draw up a manifesto after expressing their feelings more or less forcefully at an S.D.S. session. Susan Surtheim, who described the session in the *National Guardian,* supported the idea of male liberation groups to correlate with female groups and thought that men should be invited to women's meetings, assuming that the problem was limited to flaws in the sexual roles. The manifesto as it was drawn up mirrored the viewpoint of women like her. It concluded:

1. . . . that our brothers in the S. D. S. [must] recognize that they must deal with their own problems of male chauvinism in their

personal, social and political relationships.

2. It is obvious from this meeting of the S.D.S. that full advantage is not being taken of the abilities and potential contributions of women. We call upon the women to demand full participation in all aspects of the movement from licking stamps to assuming leadership positions.

3. People in leadership positions must be aware of the dynamics of creating leadership and are responsible for cultivating all of the female resources available to the movement.

4. All University administrations must realize that campus regulations discriminate against women in particular and must take positive action to protect the rights of women...

We seek the liberation of all human beings. The struggle for the liberation of women must be part of the larger fight for freedom. We recognize the difficulty our brothers will have in dealing with male chauvinism and we assume our full responsibility (as women) in helping to resolve the contradiction.

Freedom now! We love you![10]

Ironically, the very next month *New Left Notes* printed a speech by Fidel Castro to the Women's Federation of Cuba which ought to have illuminated the flaws in this policy. After recognizing the contribution of women in the struggle for revolution and thanking them for having borne arms alongside the men, he besought them to return to their former menial roles:

Who will do the cooking for the child who still comes home for lunch? Who will nurse the babies or take care of the pre-school child? Who will cook for the man when he comes home from work? Who will wash and clean and take care of things?[11]

By the autumn of 1967 it was evident that women were thinking their position through. Four girl members of the Student Union for peace Action, Canada's leading New Left organization, produced a paper called *Sisters, Brothers, Lovers*

...*Listen*...based upon the comment of Marx that 'social progress can be measured by the social position of the female sex.' In the paper there is some uneasiness about the actual difference between the sexes, as they are not sure whether women have a genetic disadvantage or not, but by adopting the Marxist idea that progress is the overcoming of such ingrained distinction and the irrelevance of such distinction to actual social function and significance, they hope to get by it. They restate the four-point argument of Juliet Mitchell and her theorization on the cultural determination of the role of women. Once again we meet the bitter description of the role of women in radical movements, highlighted by a statement for Stokeley Carmichael: 'The only position for women in S.N.C.C. is prone.'

Some movement women are ready for revolution. We are thinking for ouselves. We are doing the necessary reading, writing, and conversing to find the analysis and theory for the task. We have the background of experience to do this. We have the frustration of being excluded to force us into doing this...[12]

The impression that for them radicalization is an academic process is strengthened by the inclusion of a reading list, the first of a series which have become progressively longer and more comprehensive. Insofar as we are dealing with a movement of university women this is not surprising but for the vast majority of women who never gained any aptitude for this kind of assimilation of ideas, for whom argumentation has no value because they cannot understand it or practise it, such methods remain irrelevant. The most dubious aspect of academic liberationists is their assumption of leadership of a vast murmuring female proletariat, and their adoption of male kinds of grouping and organizational structure to which most women have little success in adapting. There is no indication in their theorizing that they have realized the full extent of the male-female polarity, that they have read their *Soviet Weekly* and been told that members of the State Institute of Teaching Sciences were very worried that the female domination of the teaching industry is producing boys who lack a 'due sense of male authority'.[13]

The academicism of these women extends into most of the women's liberation groups in universities. Ti-Grace Atkinson, as well as being a founder member of the elite group The Feminists, works for Human Rights for Women, an organization which will sponsor research projects into the history and condition of womanhood. It is possibly chastening to reflect that dead suffragettes were financing such projects long before Human Rights for Women came into existence, as well as endowing scholarships for female engineers and the like. Most women's colleges have bequests of this kind, and by and large their contribution to female liberation has been negligible.

The first direct attack on the 1967 Manifesto came from an anonymous male who wrote to *New Left Notes* in December. He suggested that there was danger in placing an under-developed woman in a position of leadership because she would surely fail and so her sense of inferiority would be intensified;[14] moreover, he argued women could not separate themselves from men because they needed them, and their role is to be humbler, more accepting and compassionate than men. He thought that women ought first to educate themselves to make valid challenge for leadership of the movement, and that perhaps they ought to keep their maiden names when they married. Docile S.D.S. women began to murmur and by the next S.D.S. National Convention the murmur had grown to a growl. In *New Left Notes* for 10 June 1968 Marilyn Webb wrote a sharp description of the lot of women members of S.D.S., the accuracy of which stung every radical girl into new resentment, although she did not advocate secession from the male-dominated movement, but

as usual extra work in attaining liberation in the spare time
that was not taken up by typing, distributing leaflets, being
beaten by the police and keeping house and bed for a revolutionary male.[15] At the 1968 convention women misbehaved
and drew the wrath of the men upon themselves. They began
to realize that they were not to be liberated fighting other
people's battles. The men used the conventional arguments
against dominating women and the women, realizing the
insidiousness of the polarity, decided that some hard thinking
had to be undertaken and some completely new strategy
devised.

Two older members of the radical university movement
were preparing a first statement towards such a strategy at
this time. Their newsheet, *Voice of the Women's Liberation
Movement*, was begun and their manifesto, *Towards a Women's
Liberation Movement*, heralded its arrival. The arrest of Carol
Thomas for the second time and her incarceration for a long
sentence added poignancy and urgency to the case.

First they attacked the women's manifesto, pointing out
the defects of its wishy-washy liberal reformism by compar-
ing it with the arguments of city councils about the treatment
of the blacks. By analogy with the development of Black
Power as the first significant attack on the pattern of
paternalistic legislation, they argued for a kind of Woman
Power movement in which the first prerogative was to develop
power, self-confidence and an authentic female strategy.
Beverly Jones pointed out that the women students who were
members of the S.D.S. were privileged women who had not
yet formed any clear idea of the disabilities which increasingly
encumber women as they move on their divinely sanctioned
path towards *kinder* and *küche*. She stressed the need to fight
their own battles in order to find out what the problems really
were, on the S.D.S. pattern 'Confrontation is political awareness.' Women who were successful in the male-dominated
movement had become so by manipulating their special

position and pandering to male values, and as such were no more entitled to speak for their sisters than black businessmen are to represent Harlem; nevertheless, even for them, as yet unmarried and relatively energetic, their dependence upon men for any ego or prestige already made their lives a travesty and a nightmare which they had not the wit or pride to reject. As a married woman she drew a horrific picture of what they ought to expect, and drew up a nine point policy which has since become more or less basic in the young women's liberation groups.

1. Women must resist pressure to enter into movement activities other than their own. There cannot be restructuring of this society until the relationships between the sexes are restructured. The inequalitarian relationships in the home are perhaps the basis of all evil. Men can commit any horror, or cowardly suffer any mutilation of their souls and retire to the home to be treated there with awe, respect, and perhaps love. Men will never face their true identity or their real problems under these circumstances, nor will we...

2. Since women in great measure are ruled by the fear of physical force, they must learn to protect themselves.

3. We must force the media to a position of realism...

4. Women must share their experiences with each other until they understand, identify, and explicitly state the many psychological techniques of domination in and out of the home. These should be published and distributed widely until they are common knowledge. No woman should feel befuddled and helpless in an argument with her husband...

5. Somebody has got to start designing communities in which women can be freed from their burdens long enough for them to experience humanity...

6. Women must learn their own history because they have a history to be proud of and a history which will give pride to their daughters...Courageous women brought us out of total bondage to our present improved position. We must not forsake them but learn from them and allow them to join the cause once more.

The market is ripe for feminist literature, historic and otherwise.
We must provide it.

7. Women who have any scientific competency at all ought to begin
investigating the real temperamental and cognitive differences
between the sexes...

8. Equal pay for equal work has been a project poo-pooed by the
radicals but it should not be because it is an instrument of
bondage...

9. In what is hardly an exhaustive list I must mention abortion
laws.[16]

It would be too easy to cavil at the ignorance of point 7
(research into sex differences has been going on for fifty
years) or at point 8 for its syntactic incoherence. Point 2,
learning to protect oneself, is not such a difficult matter, for
weapons are easy enough to acquire and karate lessons are
included in the syllabus of debutantes' finishing schools: the
difficulty is to render physical violence irrelevant, which is
the only hope of any human being, but none of the feminist
groups has so far emerged with a strategy. Part II of *Towards
a Woman's Liberation Movement* was written by Judith Brown,
research Assistant in Psychiatry at the University of Florida.
She too described the position of radical middle-class women
in S.D.S., and developed the idea of marriage being to
women what interation was to the blacks, using the nigger/
female analogy that has become so popular, and so misleading, in discussions of the female question. She suggested all-
female communes for radical women, but did not see that an
all-female commune is in no way different from the medieval
convents where women who revolted against their social and
biological roles could find intellectual and moral fulfilment,
from which they exerted no pressure on the status quo at all.
Her consideration of celibacy as a tactic made the conventual
aspect of her strategy even more apparent. Lesbianism and
masturbation as alternatives to integration do not weaken

the force of the convent parallel significantly. The manifesto ends with an unsigned incoherent lament for the second arrest of Carol Thomas and her incarceration for a considerable period. The point is not made that she was specifically victimized as a woman, indeed the charge on which she was arrested is not named, but as a demonstration of solidarity between revolutionary women perhaps it has some value.

We have not conned ourselves into political paralysis as an excuse for inaction – we are a subjugated caste. We need to develop a female movement, most importantly, because we must fight this social order, with all of the faculties we have got, and those in full gear. And we must be liberated so that we can turn from our separate domestic desperation – our own Apocalypse of the Damned – toward an exercise of social rage against each dying of the light. We must get our stuff together, begin to dismantle this system's deadly social and military toys, and stop the mad dogs who rule us every place we're at.[17]

The female quest for self-knowledge suddenly discovered a whole new arsenal, the work of Masters and Johnson, published in 1966 with the title *Human Sexual Response.* The implications for female liberation were first savagely outlined by Mette Eiljerson and then read in the original Danish by a Feminist, Anne Koedt. The argument of Miss Koedt's *The Myth of Vaginal Orgasm,* that orgasmic potency became through the anatomical ignorance of Freud and Reich an unattainable goal for woman and a cause of greater shame and inauthenticity in sexual behaviour, is undubitably correct, but her corollaries, that the mistake was the deliberate result of male chauvinism, that the vagina is irrelevant to female sexual pleasure, that men insist on penetration because the vagina is the pleasantest place for a penis to be (a touch of female chauvinism here!), are at best doubtful. 'Men fear that they will become sexually expendable if the clitoral organ is substituted for the vaginal as the basic pleasure for women...'[18]

One wonders just whom Miss Koedt has gone to bed with. Most men are aware of the clitoris and are really frightened of being desired simply as a sexual object. The man who is expected to have a rigid penis at all times is not any freer than the woman whose vagina is supposed to explode with the first thrust of such a penis. Men are as brainwashed as women into supposing that their sexual organs are capable of anatomical impossibilities. Miss Koedt's assumptions show that she has seen through her own brainwashing but not through theirs. Her last point is most peculiar.

Lesbianism – Aside from the strictly anatomical reasons why women might seek women lovers, there is a great fear on men's part that women will seek the company of other women on a full, human basis. The establishment of clitoral orgasm as fact would threaten the heterosexual *institution*. The oppressor always fears the unity of the oppressed, and the escape of women from the psychological hold men now maintain. Rather than imagining a future free relationship between individuals, men tend to react with paranoid fears of revenge on the part of women (as witnessed with the V. Solanas events).[19]

One wonders who shot whom according to Miss Koedt's version! In most cases male unity is preserved at the expense of outlawing any sexual contact between male members of the group. Sex is simply not a cohesive force. Homosexual groups within society as we know it are not noted for their cohesiveness or cooperation, although that is not itself a refutation of homosexuality in a different situation where guilt and dishonesty were not inescapable concomitants. The most subtle of the assumptions behind such a paper is that the status quo, which in this case is the vaginal sensitivity of middle-class American lovers in the 1960s, is the only possible situation: in developing her theory Anne Koedt condemns all women to that condition. Until the experiments are carried out in Tahiti and other outlandish places (if they still exist) we will not know what level of insensitivity is anatomically determined. At all events a clitoral orgasm with a full cunt is nicer than a clitoral orgasm with an empty one, as far as I can tell at least. Besides, a man is more than a dildo. Nancy Mann wrote a corrective to Miss Koedt's article, which is now issued with it by the *New England Free Press*. She attempts a new explanation of female failure to achieve orgasm, mostly on the grounds that we are not doing it right, that we are not turned on to the essential nature of the experience. Her conclusion is a hopeful one for women who really don't want to masturbate or learn tribadism.

I'm sure it's no coincidence that so many people in this country have bad sex. It goes along with the general disregard for human pleasures in favour of the logic of making profit. Obviously people have real control over and responsibility for their actions in sex. But for women to blame it all on to men (or men to blame it all on women) is bad politics...Sex, work, love, morality, the sense of community – the things that have the greatest potential for being satisfying to us are undermined and exploited by our social organization. That's what we've got to fight.

If you can't get along with your lover you can get out of bed. But what do you do when your country's fucking you over?[20]

The obvious softening of Anne Koedt's grim satisfaction at ousting the penis does not protect Nancy Mann from the snide bitchery of female columnists; in her sneering article in *New York,* Julie Baumgold managed to imply that Miss Mann's surname, as good a Jewish name as her own, was evidence of female chauvinism and penis envy.[21] In fact, despite the generally derisive attitude of the press, female liberation movements have so far been very much a phenomenon of the media. The gargantuan appetite of the newspapers for novelty has led to the anomaly of women's liberation stories appearing alongside the advertisement for emulsified fats to grease the skin, scented douches to render the vagina more agreeable, and all the rest of the marketing for and by the feminine stereotype. Female liberation movements are good for news stories because of their atmosphere of perversion, female depravity, sensation and solemn absurdity.

The summer of 1968 was not only momentous for the women's movement because women emerged as a coherent group in the New Left but also because Valerie Solanas shot Andy Warhol. Suddenly S.C.U.M., the Society for Cutting Up Men, was big news, battling with Bobby Kennedy's assassination for the front page. There is, apart from Miss Solanas herself, little evidence that S.C.U.M. ever functioned. She was too easily characterized as a neurotic, perverted exhibitionist, and the incident was too much a part of Warhol's three-ring circus of exploited nuts for her message to come across unperverted. But people read her book for thrills, and got more than they bargained for. More than any of the female students she had seized upon the problem of the polarity, of the gulf which divides men and women from humanity and places them in a limbo of opposite sides. She advanced the most shocking strategy for allowing women to move back to humanity – simply, that they exterminate men. It was probably the fierce energy and lyricism of her uncompromising statement of men's fixation on the feminine, and their desperate battle to live up to their own penile fixation, which radicalized Ti-Grace Atkinson out of NOW, and even gingered up those ladies' slogans until they managed to purify their ranks of such brutality, and eventually gave birth to WITCH, Women's International Terrorist Conspiracy from Hell. WITCH is essentially an experiment with the media. Public Bra-burning, hexing the Chase Manhattan Bank, and invading the annual Bride Fair at Madison Square Garden dressed as witches and bearing broomsticks were all bally-hoo operations, and, given the susceptibility of the commercial system to its own methods, they worked, to the point of causing the Wall Street market to drop five points, but nowadays, through fear of the Tactical Police Force and other forms of establishment reprisal, what is essentially a publicity movement has gone anonymous and underground.

After the first rush of derisive publicity women's liberation has adopted a suspicious and uncooperative attitude to the press, a tactic which has in no way improved their public image or even protected it from figuring so large in Sunday supplements and glossy magazines. In fact, no publicity is still bad publicity, especially when women are so tied to a life-long habit of careless reading that most of the sneering was lost on them, and where it was not its obviousness provoked a certain sympathy for the individuals who were being so grossly ill-treated by the media which were exploiting them. Women were glad to know that 'something is happening here', even if 'what it is ain't exactly clear'. Every time a statement by a woman seeking liberation, either from taxation which prevents her from practising her profession as a married woman or from sexual dominion and inauthenticity, reaches the newspapers, the response is enormous, and the controversy spreads over several issues, if we take the article by Vivian Gornick in the *Village Voice* as an example.[22] For every woman who writes a letter to the editor there are hundreds who can't manage it, and every time a male writes in derision and fear the point is underlined a hundredfold. It is to be hoped that more and more women decide to influence the media by writing for them, not being written about. The influence could extend to other media as well, for the enormous belly of daily television must be fed, and if feminist programmes are financed by cosmetic firms so much the better. We might as well let them pay the costs of their own grave-digging. In any case, insulting and excluding reporters is no defence against them; censorship is the weapon of oppression, not ours.

There are many other women's liberation movements now operating in America, from the university chapters, which count twenty-five as a large turnout and remain local manifestations dealing with their own problems, to groups like the Red Stockings, formed when they were jeered by the men at the anti-inaugural demonstration in Washington, who concentrate on consciousness-raising in the Marcusian sense, to the 17 October movement of which Anne Koedt and Shulamith Firestone are members, to Cell 55, to Abby Rockefeller's Boston-based Women's Liberation movement, whose conference last summer was attended by five hundred women who got up at 10 o'clock on a Sunday morning to watch a karate demonstration (Rockefeller and Roxanne Dunbar have green belts), to the Congress to Unite Women (which sadly only marshalled five hundred women). The movement is endlessly divided and dividing but this may be taken as a sign of life, if not power.

In England Women's Liberation workshops are appearing in the suburban haunts of the educated housewife, and in the universities. There is no great coherence in their theory and no particular imagination or efficiency to be observed in their methods. The Tufnell Park Liberation workshop produced a paper called *Shrew* which is badly distributed. After five phone-calls to try and secure back numbers I gave up. When these worthy ladies appeared at the Miss World contest with their banners saying 'We are not sexual objects' (a proposition that no one seemed inclined to deny) they were horrified to find that girls from the Warwick University movement were chanting and dancing around the police. They begged them to desist because it was so unladylike and their image was already so shabby, and when the next issue of *Shrew* appeared it contained an official lamentation about the demeanour of these strange women, assuming in pity for their uncouthness that they were Coventry housewives with four children apiece, the very people the Women liberators were anxious to help! In fact, the Coventry chapter is one of the few which are attended by working-class women who tell the privileged girls how it is, a tendency which could well be followed by other privileged women who have not so far learned to demand anything but the vacuous notion of 'equal opportunity'.[23]

Nevertheless, despite chaos and misconception, the new feminism grows apace. The new Feminist Theatre, sponsored by Red Stockings, fills the Village Gate in New York. Although few women are misled by the red herring of learning male violence as a revolutionary tactic or practising celibacy, wives and mothers did march round the Hudson Street alimony jail with posters announcing that they didn't want alimony. As Gloria Steinem remarked, the growth of the liberation movement has 'happened not so much by organization as contagion'.[24] The actual movement extends farther and deeper than the underground organization whose publications are disseminated by the N.E.F.P. and Agitprop, and even wider than Mrs Friedan's female establishment. An anti-female-liberation motion was overwhelmingly defeated by a predominantly male audience at a university debate that I spoke at lately, when a similar debate five years ago, although argued much better than this, was roundly defeated. When I addressed a very mixed and uneccentric audience at an adult education centre on Teesside the week before, soft-spoken nervous women spoke in front of their husbands about the most subversive ideas. Nurses are misbehaving, the teachers are on strike, skirts are all imaginable levels, bras are not being bought, abortions are being demanded...rebellion is gathering steam and may yet become revolution.

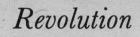

Revolution

Revolution

Reaction is not revolution. It is not a sign of revolution when the oppressed adopt the manners of the oppressors and practise oppression on their own behalf. Neither is it a sign of revolution when women ape men, and men women, or even when laws against homosexuality are relaxed, and the intense sexual connotation of certain kinds of clothes and behaviour are diminished. The attempt to relax the severity of the polarity in law bears no relation to the sway that male-female notions hold in the minds and hearts of real people. More women are inspired to cling to their impotent femininity because of the deep unattractiveness of Barbara Castle's seamed face and her depressing function as chief trouble-shooter of the Wilson regime than are inspired to compete like she did for man's distinction in a man's world. We know that such women do not champion their own sex once they are in positions of power, that when they are employers they do not employ their own sex, even when there is no other basis for discrimination. After all they get on better with men because all their lives they have manipulated the susceptibilities, the guilts and hidden desires of men. Such women are like the white man's black man, the professional nigger; they are the obligatory woman, the exceptional creature who is as good as a man and much more decorative. The men capitulate.

That women should seek a revolution in their circumstances by training themselves as a fighting force is the most obvious case of confusing reaction or rebellion with revolution. Now that warfare, like industry, is no longer a matter of superior physical strength, it is no longer significant in the battle of women for admission to humanity. In our time violence has become inhuman and asexual. It is associated with wealth, in the manufacture of sophisticated armament, in the maintenance of armies of police of all varieties, in the mounting of huge defences which by their very existence precipitate the chaos of war. War is the admission of defeat in the face of conflicting interests: by war the issue is left to chance, and the tacit assumption that the best man will win is not at all justified. It might equally be argued that the worst, the most unscrupulous man will win, although history will continue the absurd game by finding him after all the best man. We have only to think of Hochhuth's attempt to pass judgement on England's role in the overkill of Germany and the judicious blindnesses of Winston Churchill to recognize this inevitable process. Wars cannot be *won*, as any Englishman ruefully contrasting his postwar fortunes with those of guilty Nazi Europe is confusedly aware. Women who adopt the attitudes of war in their search for liberation condemn themselves to acting out the last perversion of dehumanized manhood, which has only one foreseeable outcome, the specifically masculine end of suicide.

The Boston Women's Liberation Movement justify their interest in karate on the grounds that women are terrified of physical aggression in the individual circumstance, and need to be liberated from that fear before they can act with confidence. It is true that men use the threat of physical force, usually histrionically, to silence nagging wives: but it is almost always a sham. It is actually a game of nerves, and can be turned aside fairly easily. At various stages in my life I have lived with men of known violence, two of whom had convictions for Grievous Bodily Harm, and in no case was I ever offered any physical aggression, because it was abundantly clear from my attitude that I was not impressed by it. Violence has a fascination for most women; they act as spectators at fights, and dig the scenes of bloody violence in films. Women are always precipitating scenes of violence in pubs and dance-halls. Much goading of men is actually the female need for the thrill of violence. Most fights are degrading, confused affairs: most men do not hit the thing they aim at, and most end up letting themselves get hurt in their own confused masochism. The genuinely violent man does not play about with karate or the Marquess of Queensberry's rules – he uses a broken bottle, a wheelbrace, a tyre lever or an axe. He does not see the fight through, but seeks to end it quickly by doing as much harm as he can as soon as he can.

It would be genuine revolution if women would suddenly stop loving the victors in violent encounters. Why do they admire the image of the brutal man? If they could only see through the brawn and the bravado to the desolation and the misery of the man who is goaded into using his fists (for battered-looking strong men are always called out by less obviously masculine men who need to prove themselves). Why can they not understand the deification of the strong-man, either as soldier, wrestler, footballer or male model, seeing that his fate so closely approximates their own? If women would only offer a genuine alternative to the treadmill of violence, the world might breathe a little longer with less pain. If women were to withdraw from the spectatorship of wrestling matches, the industry would collapse; if soldiers were certainly faced with the withdrawal of all female favours, as Lysistrata observed so long ago, there would suddenly be less glamour in fighting. We are not houris; we will not be the warrior's reward. And yet we read in men's magazines how the whores of American cities give their favours for free to the boys about to embark for Vietnam.

The male perversion of violence is an essential condition of the degradation of women. The penis is conceived as a weapon, and its action upon women is understood to be somehow destructive and hurtful. It has become a gun, and in English slang women cry when they want their mate to ejaculate, 'Shoot me! Shoot me!' Women cannot be liberated

---

The Woman's Fight
(Tune: 'Juanita')

Soft may she slumber on the breast of mother earth
One who worked nobly for the world's rebirth.
In the heart of woman, dwells a wish to heal all pain,
Let her learn to help man to cast off each chain.

Woman, oh woman, leave your fetters in the past:
Rise and claim your birthright and be free at last.
Mother, wife and maiden, in your hands great power lies:

Give it all the freedom, strength and sacrifice.
Far across the hilltop breaks the light of coming day,
Still the fight is waiting, then be up and away.

           I.W.W. Songs

---

from their impotence by the gift of a gun, although they are as capable of firing them as men are. Every time women have been given a gun for the duration of a specific struggle, it has been withdrawn and they have found themselves more impotent than before. The process to be followed is the opposite: women must humanize the penis, take the steel out of it and make it flesh again. What most 'liberated' women do is taunt the penis for its misrepresentation of itself, mock men for their overestimation of their virility, instead of seeing how the mistake originated and what effects it has had upon themselves. Men are tired of having all the responsibility for sex, it is time they were relieved of it. And I do not mean that large-scale lesbianism should be adopted, but simply that the emphasis should be taken off male genitality and replaced upon human sexuality. The cunt must come into its own. The question of the female attitude to violence is inseparable from this problem. Perhaps to begin with women should labour to be genuinely disgusted by violence, and at least to refuse to reward any victor in a violent confrontation, even to the point of casting their lot on principle with the loser. If they were to withdraw their spectatorship absolutely from male competition, much of its motivation would be gone.

Although many women do not necessarily find themselves attracted to the winners in violent conflicts but prefer to hover over the gallant defeated, in the wider social sense they all prefer winners. An eminent lady professor, addressing an adult education group at a northern university, lamented the fact that male chauvinism prevented educated men from dating the equally qualified and very accessible girls at the same institution. The girls could not be expected to hobnob with less educated, inferior men, and so they went out with no one. But if men are content to spend their leisure time with their intellectual inferiors, why cannot women be so? Women may remark with contempt that men are nine-to-five intellectuals, and can only relax when the heat is off and they can chat with a moron. They play Daddy the all-knowing, and their chosen dates play breathless daughter. By and large the gibe is true. But it is also true that in too many cases female intellectuals are arrogant, aggressive, compulsive and intense. They place too high a value on their dubious educational achievements, losing contact with more innocent recreations. They seek a male whose achievements will give value to their own, an ego to replace their own insufficiency, and most men are quick to sense the urgency of the quest. Many men tire of morons easily, but are more deeply repelled by blue-stockings. Rather than seek to be squired and dated by their rivals why should it not be possible for women to find relaxation and pleasure in the company of their 'inferiors'? They would need to shed their desperate need to *admire* a man, and accept the gentler role of loving him. A learned woman cannot castrate a truck-driver like she can her intellectual rival, because he has no exaggerated respect for her bookish capabilities. The alternative to conventional education is not stupidity, and many a clever girl needs the corrective of a humbler soul's genuine wisdom. In working-class families, the paternal role of the father is not as pronounced as it is in middle-class homes, for often working-class women are quicker with their letters and more adept at manipulating the authorities than their husbands are.[1] A worker husband could well be proud of a 'thinker' mate. Marriage would mean that after taxation her earnings made little difference to the family's financial situation. Professional earnings in this country are so low and hours so long that no man need feel his earning capacity undermined by his wife's, however highly qualified she was. Socialist women, now fulminating in segregated groups after waiting hand, foot and buttock on the middle-class revolutionary males in the movement, might be better off placing their despised expertise and their knowledge of the basic texts at the service of the class they were meant for. Women's achievement is assessed in terms of how far up out of their class they succeed in mating. A revolution in consciousness might reverse that notion. Of course, it must be done genuinely – there is no scope for condescension.

If women are to effect a significant amelioration in their condition it seems obvious that they must refuse to marry. No worker can be required to sign on for life: if he did, his employer could disregard all his attempts to gain better pay and conditions. In those places where an employer has the monopoly of employment this phenomenon can be observed. It should not be up to the employer to grant improvements out of the goodness of his heart: his workers must retain their pride by retaining their bargaining power. It might be argued that women are not signed up for life in the marriage contract because divorce is always possible, but as it stands divorce works in the male interest, not only because it was designed and instituted by men, but because divorce still depends on

money and independent income. Married women seldom
have either. Men argue that alimony laws can cripple them,
and this is obviously true, but they have only themselves to
blame for the fact that alimony is necessary, largely because
of the pattern of granting custody of the children to the
mother. The alimonized wife bringing up the children without father is no more free than she ever was. It makes even
less sense to sign a life-long service contract which can be
broken by the employer only. More bitter still is the reflection
that the working wife has her income assessed as a part of her
husband's, and he on the other hand is not even obliged to tell
her how much he earns. If independence is a necessary concomitant of freedom, women must not marry.

What does the average girl marry for? The answer will
probably be made – love. Love can exist outside marriage –
indeed for a long time it was supposed that it *always* did.
Love can take many forms, why must it be exclusive?
Security? Security is a chimera, especially if it is supposed to
mean the preservation of a state of happy togetherness which
exists at the time of marriage. Should no obvious disasters
like adultery or separation occur, people still change: neither
partner will be, ultimately, the person who got married in
the beginning. If a woman gets married because she is sick of
working, she asks for everything she gets. Opportunities for
work must be improved, not abandoned. If a woman marries
because she wants to have children, she might reflect that the
average family has not proved to be a very good breeding
ground for children, and seeing as the world is in no urgent
need of her increase she might do better, for contraception is
very possible, to wait until some suitable kind of household
presents itself. The scorns and disabilities suffered by the
single girl who cannot have a mortgage and is often considered an undesirable tenant can be experienced and
challenged only by a single girl; cowardly marriage is no way
to change them. Even though there are more problems

attendant upon bringing up an illegitimate child, and even friendly cohabitation can meet with outrage and persecution from more orthodox citizens, marrying to avoid these inconveniences is a meaningless evasion.

It is all very well to state so categorically that a woman who seeks liberation ought not to marry, but if this implies that married women are a lost cause, any large-scale female emancipation would thereby be indefinitely postponed. The married woman without children can still retain a degree of bargaining power, on condition that she resolves not to be afraid of the threat of abandonment. The bargaining between married people generally works unevenly: the wife eventually finds that her life has changed radically, but not her husband's. This state of affairs is by and large considered just: for example, a Home Office decision recently refused a woman the right to live in her country of origin because she had married an Indian and 'it was customary for the woman to adopt her husband's country of origin.'[2] The same goes for his home town, or his workplace, his chosen domicile and his friends. The inequality in the give-and-take of marriage can best be explained by an emotional inequity at the heart

---

The Rebel Girl
Words and Music by Joe Hill, Copyright 1916
CHORUS
That's the Rebel Girl, that's the Rebel Girl!
To the working class she's a precious pearl.
She brings courage, pride and joy
To the fighting Rebel Boy;
We've had girls before but we need some more
In the Industrial Workers of the World,
For it's great to fight for freedom
With a Rebel Girl.

I.W.W. Songs

of it, although in many cases this inequity is a bluff. Many men are almost as afraid of abandonment, of failing as husbands as their wives are, and a woman who is not terrified of managing on her own can manipulate this situation. It is largely a question of nerve. As the stirring of the female population grows, it ought to follow that various kinds of cooperative enterprise spring up to buttress the individual's independence, although there are probably fewer women's clubs and cooperative societies now than there were between the wars, if we consider the picture painted in *Girls of Independent Means*. The principal value in organizing is not the formation of a political front but the development of solidarity and mutual self-help, which can be useful on quite a small scale. Going home to mother is a pretty vapid ploy, because mother is usually difficult to live with, reproachful, conservative and tired of her children's problems. Most women still need a room of their own and the only way to find it may be outside their own homes.

The plight of mothers is more desperate than that of other women, and the more numerous the children the more hopeless the situation seems to be. And yet women with children do break free, with or without their offspring. Tessa Fothergill left her husband, taking her two children, and began the struggle to find a flat and a job on her own. She had so much difficulty that she decided to found an organization for women with her problems and called it Gingerbread. Another similar group already existed, called Mothers-in-Action.[3] However slow the progress past official obstruction may be, it is easier accomplished together. Eventually a woman's newspaper will be founded in which such groups could announce their formation and canvass for collaborators. Most women, because of the assumptions that they have formed about the importance of their role as bearers and socializers of children, would shrink at the notion of leaving husband and children, but this is precisely the case in which brutally clear rethinking must be undertaken. First of all, the children are not *hers*, they are not her property, although most courts strongly favour the mother's claim against the father's in custody cases. It is much worse for children to grow up in the atmosphere of suffering, however repressed, than it is for them to adapt to a change of regime. Their difficulty in adapting is itself evidence of the anti-social strengthening of the umbilical link, and it is probably better for the children in the long run to find out they do not have undisputed hold on mother. In any case, the situation ought to be explained because they always feel unease, and worry more about obscure possibilities than they do about facts. A wife who knows that if she leaves her husband she can only bring up the children in pauperdom, although she could support herself, must make a sensible decision, and reject out of hand the deep prejudice against the runaway wife. In many cases, the husband is consoled by being allowed to retain the children and can afford to treat them better with less anxiety than a woman could. He is more likely to be able to pay a housekeeper or a nanny than a woman is. And so forth. Behind the divorced woman struggling to keep her children there always looms the threat of 'taking the children in to care' which is the worst of alternatives. A woman who leaves her husband and children could offer them alimony, if society would grant her the means.

The essential factor in the liberation of the married woman is understanding of her condition. She must fight the guilt of failure in an impossible set-up, and examine the set-up. She must ignore interested descriptions of her health, her morality and her sexuality, and assess them all for herself. She must know her enemies, the doctors, psychiatrists, social workers, marriage counsellors, priests, health visitors and popular moralists. She must analyse her buying habits, her day-to-day evasions and dishonesties, her sufferings, and her real feelings towards her children, her past and her future.

Her best aides in such an assessment are her sisters. She must not allow herself to be ridiculed and baffled by arguments with her husband, or to be blackmailed by his innocence of his part in her plight and his magnanimity in offering to meet her half-way in any 'reasonable' suggestion. Essentially she must recapture her own will and her own goals, and the energy to use them, and in order to effect this some quite 'unreasonable' suggestions, or demands, may be necessary.

It is not a complete explanation of the development of the subjugation of the female sex to say, as Ti-Grace Atkinson does, that men solved the biological mystery of procreation. In fact they did not and have not solved the mystery of paternity. It is known that a father is necessary, but not known how to identify him, except negatively. Women have

> All that is good and commendable now existing would continue to exist if all marriage laws were repealed tomorrow...I have an inalienable constitutional and natural right to love whom I may, to love as long or as short a period as I can, to change that love every day if I please!
>
> Victoria Claflin Woodhull, 20 November 1871

freely counteracted this disability of paternity by offering, after perhaps initially being forced by incarceration and supervision to offer, guarantees of paternity and its concomitant, fidelity. Now that cloistering of wives is an impossibility, we might as well withdraw the guarantees, and make the patriarchal family an impossibility by insisting on preserving the paternity of the whole group – all men are fathers to all children. The withdrawal of the guarantee of paternity does not necessarily involve 'promiscuity', although in its initial stages it might appear to. The promiscuity of casual secretaries in choosing their employment can work as a

revolutionary measure, forcing recognition of their contributions to the firm and its work; likewise, the unwillingness of
women to commit themselves with pledges of utter monogamy and doglike devotion might have to be buttressed by
actual 'promiscuity' to begin with.

Women must also reject their role as principal consumers in
the capitalist state. Although it would be a retrogressive step to
refuse to buy household appliances in that women's work
would be increased and become more confining than it need
be, it would be a serious blow to the industries involved if
women shared, say, one washing machine between three
families, and did not regard the possession of the latest model
as the necessary index of prestige and success. They could
form household cooperatives, sharing their work about, and
liberating each other for days on end. Their children instead
of being pitted against one another could be encouraged to
share the toys that lie discarded as soon as they are sick of
them. This would not be so repugnant to children as parents
hope. I can recall being beaten for giving away all my toys
when I was about four. I really didn't want them any more.
Children do not need expensive toys, and women could
reject the advertising that seeks to draw millions of pounds
out of them each Christmas. Some of the mark-up on soap
powders and the like could be avoided by buying unbranded
goods in bulk and resisting the appeal of packaging. In the
same way food can be bought in direct from the suppliers,
and if women combine to cheat the middlemen they have an
even better chance of making it work. 'Cheaper by the
dozen' does not have to be limited to one family. Women
ought also to get over the prejudice attaching to second-hand
clothes and goods. The clothes children grow out of can be
shared about and if children weren't always victims of oversell they wouldn't mind. Baby carriages and the like are
already swapped around in most working-class families. Part
of the aim of these cooperative enterprises is to break down

the isolation of the single family and of the single parent, but principally I am considering ways to short-circuit the function of women as chief fall-guys for advertising, chief spenders of the nation's loot.

Most women would find it hard to abandon any interest in clothes and cosmetics, although many women's liberation movements urge them to transcend such servile fripperies. As far as cosmetics are used for adornment in a conscious and creative way, they are not emblems of inauthenticity: it is when they are presented as the real thing, covering unsightly blemishes, disguising a repulsive thing so that it is acceptable to the world that their function is deeply suspect. The women who dare not go out without their false eyelashes are in serious psychic trouble. The most expensive preparations in the cosmetic line are no different in essence from the cheapest; no miraculous unguents can actually repair failing tissue. It is as well to consider diet and rest for the raw material of beauty, and use cosmetics strictly for fun. The cheapest and some of the best fun are the colours used on the stage in greasepaint. Kohl is the best eye make-up, and the cheapest, and can be bought in various forms. Instead of the expensive extracts of coal marketed with French labels, women could make their own perfumes with spirit of camphor, and oil of cloves and frankincense, as well as crumbled lavender, patchouli and attar of roses. Instead of following the yearly changes of hairstyle, women could find the way their hair grows best and keep it that way, working the possible changes according to their own style and mood, instead of coiffing themselves in a shape ordained by fashion but not by their heads.

Some of these trends are already apparent. Most young girls do not inhabit the hairdressers anything like as much as their mothers do. They have vanquished the couturier single-handed and wear whatever they please, from the oldest and most romantic to the most crass adaptations of men's sporting

gear. There are signs that they are abandoning prestige
eating habits as well, especially alcohol and the wine game.
Many of them are finding ways of survival as students that
they will not abandon as grown women. The pattern of rejection of cigarettes and beer for illicit marijuana has far-
reaching effects for the economy if it is taken up on any large
scale. The taste for macrobiotic food and much less of it
reflects both an attitude to eating and to the marketing of
food. So far only a minority is following such trends, but it is
a much larger minority than we find trumpeting behind the
banners of women's liberation. Yet it is liberation that they
are seeking, just the same. The hippie rejection of violence
may be considered to have failed, for policemen were not
ashamed to respond to a flower with a baton, but the
question has been defined and the debate is not over yet.

The chief means of liberating women is replacing of compulsiveness and compulsion by the pleasure principle.
Cooking, clothes, beauty, and housekeeping are all compulsive activities in which the anxiety quotient has long since
replaced the pleasure or achievement quotient. It is possible
to use even cooking, clothes, cosmetics and housekeeping for
fun. The essence of pleasure is spontaneity. In these cases
spontaneity means rejecting the norm, the standard that one
must live up to, and establishing a self-regulating principle.
The analogy is best understood in the case of drugs: women
use drugs as anodynes, compulsively, to lessen tension, pain,
or combat anxiety symptoms, entering almost automatically
into a dependence syndrome so that it becomes impossible to
discern whether the drug caused the symptom for which the
drug was taken, and so it goes on. The person who uses
marijuana has no need to do so: he uses it when he wants to
feel in a certain way, and stops his intake when he is at the
point that he wants to be at. He is not tempted to excuse his
use as a kind of therapy, although regulations about the use
of cannabis are trying to force some such construction of the

situation. In the same way; it ought to be possible to cook a meal that you want to cook, that everybody wants to eat, and to serve it in any way you please, instead of following a time-table, serving Tuesday's meal or the tastefully varied menu of all new and difficult dishes you have set yourself as a new cross, and if you simply cannot feel any interest in it, not to do it. Unfortunately the ideology of routine is strongly established in this country, and even delinquent housewives use their bingo and their stout as a routine, that 'they don't know what they would do without'. Housework is admitted to be a typical vicious circle; work makes more work and it goes on. It is so difficult to break such a circle that it seems almost essential to break right out of it, and insist on doing something else altogether. Regular periods of 'freedom' are still contained within the circle, and this is why they won't work. Most forms of compromise will not do the job, although they may alleviate symptoms of strain temporarily. For the same reason, incorporating some self-chosen work in the circle will not work insofar as incentive and energy are constantly being vitiated. There is no alternative but rupture of the circle.

For some the rupture of the circle has meant that the centre cannot hold and chaos is come upon the world. The fear of liberty is strong in us, but the fear itself must be understood to be one of the factors inbuilt in the endurance of the status

---

For my arguments, Sir, are debated by a disinterested Spirit – I plead for my sex, not for myself. Independence I have long considered the grand blessing of life, the basis of every virtue – and independence I will ever secure by contracting my wants, though I were to live on a barren heath.

Mary Wollstonecraft,
'A Vindication of the Rights of Women', 1792, p. iv

quo. Once women refuse to accept the polarity of masculine-feminine they must accept the existence of risk and the possibility of error. Abandonment of slavery is also the banishment of the chimera of security. The world will not change overnight, and liberation will not happen unless individual women agree to be outcasts, eccentrics, perverts, and whatever the powers-that-be choose to call them. There have been women in the past far more daring than we would need to be now, who ventured all and gained a little, but survived after all. Vociferous women are guyed in the press and sneered at by others who collect a fat pay-packet and pride themselves on femininity as well, but at least they are no longer burnt. It is too much to expect that women who have set out to liberate themselves should become healthy, happy, creative and cooperative as if by magic, although generally the more appalling symptoms of depersonalization do disappear. The old conditioned needs and anxieties linger on, continuing to exact their toll, but now they are understood for what they are and borne for a purpose. The situation will only emerge in all its ramifications when it is challenged, and women might initially be horrified at the swiftness with which police forget their scruples about hitting women, or the vileness of the abuse which is flung at them, but such discoveries can only inspire them more doggedly to continue. The key to the strategy of liberation lies in exposing the situation, and the simplest way to do it is to outrage the pundits and the experts by sheer impudence of speech and gesture, the exploitation of cliché 'feminine logic' to expose masculine pomposity, absurdity and injustice. Women's weapons are traditionally their tongues, and the principal revolutionary tactic has always been the spread of information. Now as before, women must refuse to be meek and guileful, for truth cannot be served by dissimulation. Women who fancy that they manipulate the world by pussy power and gentle cajolery are fools.[4] It is slavery to have to adopt such tactics.

It is difficult at this point to suggest what a new sexual regime would be like. We have but one life to live, and the first object is to find a way of salvaging that life from the disabilities already inflicted on it in the service of our civilization. Only by experimentation can we open up new possibilities which will indicate lines of development in which the status quo is given term. Women's revolution is necessarily situationist: we cannot argue that all will be well when the socialists have succeeded in abolishing private property and restoring public ownership of the means of production. We cannot wait that long. Women's liberation, if it abolishes the patriarchal family, will abolish a necessary substructure of the authoritarian state, and once that withers away Marx will have come true willy-nilly, so let's get on with it. Let the men distribute leaflets in factories where the proletariat have become hire-purchase slaves instead of communists. The existence of hire-purchase slaves is also based upon the function of the wife as a stay-at-home consumer. Statistics show that almost all hire-purchase contracts are entered into by married people. If women revolt, that situation must change too. Women represent the most oppressed class of life-contracted unpaid workers, for whom slaves is not too melodramatic a description. They are the only true proletariat left, and they are by a tiny margin the majority of the population, so what's stopping them? The answer must be made, that their very oppression stands in the way of their combining to form any kind of solid group which can challenge the masters. But man made one grave mistake: in answer to vaguely reformist and humanitarian agitation he admitted women to politics and the professions. The conservatives who saw this as the undermining of our civilization and the end of the state and marriage were right after all; it is time for the demolition to begin. We need not challenge anyone to open battle, for the most effective method is simply to withdraw our cooperation in building up a system which oppresses us, the valid withdrawal of our labour. We may also agitate hither and thither, picket segregated bars and beauty competitions, serve on committees, invade the media, do, in short, what we want, but we must also refuse, not only to do some things, but to want to do them.

Experience is too costly a teacher: we cannot all marry in order to investigate the situation. The older sisters must teach us what they found out. At all times we must learn from each other's experience, and not judge hastily or snobbishly, or according to masculine criteria. We must fight against the tendency to form a feminist elite, or a masculine-type hierarchy of authority in our own political structures, and struggle to maintain cooperation and the matriarchal principle of fraternity. It is not necessary for feminists to prove that matriarchy is a prehistoric form of community, or that patriarchy is a capitalist perversion in order to justify our policies, because the form of life we envisage might as well be completely new as inveterately ancient. We need not buy dubious anthropology to explain ourselves, although women with a studious bent might do well to research the historic role of women in some attempt to delimit our concepts of the natural and the possible in the female sphere. The time has come when some women are ready to listen, and their number is growing; it is time also for those women to speak, however uncertainly, however haltingly, and for the world to listen.

The surest guide to the correctness of the path that women take is *joy in the struggle*. Revolution is the festival of the oppressed. For a long time there may be no perceptible reward for women other than their new sense of purpose and integrity. Joy does not mean riotous glee, but it does mean the purposive employment of energy in a self-chosen enterprise. It does mean pride and confidence. It does mean communication and cooperation with others based on delight

in their company and your own. To be emancipated from
helplessness and need and walk freely upon the earth that is
your birthright. To refuse hobbles and deformity and take
possession of your body and glory in its power, accepting its
own laws of loveliness. To have something to desire, something to make, something to achieve, and at last something
genuine to give. To be freed from guilt and shame and the
tireless self-discipline of women. To stop pretending and
dissembling, cajoling and manipulating, and begin to
control and sympathize. To claim the masculine virtues of
magnanimity and generosity and courage. It goes much
further than equal pay for equal work, for it ought to
revolutionize the conditions of work completely. It does not
understand the phrase 'equality of opportunity', for it seems

> Establishment of Truth depends on destruction of False-
> hood continually,
> On Circumcision, not on Virginity, O Reasoners of
> Albion!
>
> Blake, 'Jerusalem', pl. 55, ll 65–6

that the opportunities will have to be utterly changed and
women's souls changed so that they desire opportunity
instead of shrinking from it. The first significant discovery
we shall make as we racket along our female road to freedom
is that men are not free, and they will seek to make this an

> ..among the disbelievers of revealed religion I have not
> found during a life of half a century, a single opponent to
> the doctrine of equal rights for males and females.
>
> Long, 'Eve', 1875, p. 112

argument why nobody should be free. We can only reply that
slaves enslave their masters, and by securing our own manu-
mission we may show men the way that they could follow

when they jumped off their own treadmill. Privileged women will pluck at your sleeve and seek to enlist you in the 'fight' for reforms, but reforms are retrogressive. The old process must be broken, not made new. Bitter women will call you to rebellion, but you have too much to do. What *will* you do?

Notes

SUMMARY

1. 'Boadicea Rides Again', *Sunday Times Magazine,* 21.9.1969.
2. Ibsen, *A Doll's House,* Act III.

GENDER

1. The embodiment of anthropological and ethnological prejudice is the stupendous three volume study of H.H. Ploss and M. and P. Bartels; the plates of the original German edition were destroyed by Hitler, but not before Dr Eric Dingwall had prepared an English version, *Woman* (London, 1935). Hereinafter it is referred to as Ploss and Bartels.
2. F.A.E. Crew, *Sex Determination* (London, 1954), p. 54.
3. Ashley Montagu, *The Natural Superiority of Women* (London, 1954), pp. 76-81.
4. The Cropwood Conference on Criminological Implications of Chromosomal Abnormalities, held at the University of Cambridge in the summer of 1969, discussed this matter at length. The bibliography on the XYY syndrome now reaches upwards of 500 titles.
5. Gray's *Anatomy* (London, 1958), pp. 219-20.
6. Robert Stoller, *Sex and Gender* (London, 1968), *passim.*

BONES

1. See for example Joan Fraser, *Stay a Girl* (London, 1963), p. 3:

A woman needs a different type of exercise from a man. He needs movements aimed at developing his physical strength and hardening his muscles, but a woman does not want hard muscles. She needs a non-fatiguing form of exercise, movement which refreshes and relaxes her. One which, besides toning up her muscles, joints, glands, respiratory and digestive organs, will give her everyday movements a grace, litheness and poise which enhance her femininity.

2. The pedomorphism of women has always been remarked upon, e.g. by Bichat in his *General Anatomy* (London, 1824), and of course by Ploss and Bartels (*op. cit.*, p. 90), but these commentators did not see that it might prove to be an advantage as did W.I. Thomas in *Sex and Society* (London, 1907), pp. 18, 51, and Ashley Montagu (*op. cit.*, pp. 70-1).
3. See Gray's *Anatomy (op. cit.)*, pp. 402-7.
4. Evidence for the slighter differentiation in pelvic formation among primitive or hardworking women can be derived from Ploss and Bartels, who cite for example Hennig's 'Das Rassenbecken', from *Archaeologie für Anthropologisten* (1885-6), Vol. 16, pp. 161-228.

CURVES

1. R. Broby-Johansen's *Body and Clothes* (London, 1969) is the fullest account to date of the interaction between body, self-image and clothing, including the shifting of the erogenous zones and the siting of fat.
2. Sophie Lazarsfeld, *The Rhythm of Life* (London, 1934), p. 158.
3. Pauline Reage, *The Story of O* (Traveller's Companion, Paris, 1965), p. 18 and *passim*. Thorstein Veblen offers a sociological explanation of curves as signifying luxury and debility in *The Theory of the Leisure Class* (London, 1899) pp. 141-6.

4. Kenneth Tynan, 'The Girl who turned her Back', *Mayfair*, Vol. 4, No. 3, March 1969.

5. This eulogy of fat from Ploss and Bartels (*op cit.*, p. 86) reveals just how inportant it must have been to our grandfathers:

There is something alien and repellent in very angular and flat surfaces in women, such as appear among certain primitive races, owing to overwork and poor living at an age when European women are still in the prime of life.

The adipose layer may be considered a most important secondary sexual character in women. It produces the tapering roundness of the limbs, the curves of the throat, nape and shoulders, the swelling of bosom and curving roundness of buttocks; all the character·stic signs of womanhood. This adipose layer also produces the smooth cushioned shape of the knee which differs so from the masculine form. And the massive roundness (which sometimes appears dispro-portionate) of the upper thigh in women, tapering rapidly towards the smooth dimpled knee, is caused by the same fatty layer.

HAIR

1. The assumption that women grew much more hair on their heads than men was almost universal. Bichat (*op. cit.*, Vol. II, p. 446) even goes so far as to say 'one might think that nature had thus compensated the fair sex for their deficiency in many other parts'. *Cf. The Works of Aristotle the Famous Philosopher* (London, 1779), p. 374. While baldness is a sex-linked characteristic, it is not proper to maintain that women do not go bald. The intensity of the sexual prejudice has resulted in the utter concealment of female baldness, which is much commoner than is generally supposed.

SEX

1. E.g. Samuel Collins, *Systema Anatomicum* (London, 1685),

p. 566, and Palfijn's *Surgical Anatomy* (London, 1726), plates facing pages 226 and 227, also his *Description Anatomique des Parties de la Femme* (Paris, 1708, the plates are not numbered) and Spigelius, *De humani corporis Fabrica* (1627), Tab. XVII, Lib. VIII, and *Les Portraits Anatomiques* of Vesalius (1569), and the *Tabulae Anatomicae* of Eustachius (1714).

2. *A Pleasant new Ballade Being a merry Discourse between a Country Lass and a young Taylor,* c. 1670.

3. *The High-prized Pin-Box. Tune of, Let every Man with Cap in's Hand* etc., c. 1665.

4. Samuel Collins (*op. cit.*), pp. 564-5.

5. Theodore Faithfull answering correspondence in *International Times* No. 48, January 17-30, 1969.

6. A.H. Kegel, 'Letter to the Editor', *Journal of the American Medical Association,* Vol. 153, 1953, pp. 1303-4. His work is discussed by Daniel G. Brown in 'Female Orgasm and Sexual Inadequacy', *An Analysis of Human Sexual Response,* ed. Ruth and Edward Brecher (London, 1968), pp. 163-4.

7. Mette Eiljersen, I Accuse! (London, 1969), p. 45.

8. Herbert Marcuse, *Eros and Civilisation* (London, 1969), pp. 52-3

9. Jackie Collins, *The World is full of Married Men* (London, 1969), pp. 152-3.

THE WICKED WOMB

1. One such book, written by a lady doctor to introduce girls to menstruation, is Erna Wright's *Periods without Pain* (London, 1966); the grim diagrams she employs do not even show the clitoris, nor is it mentioned in the text.

2. The ancient fear of the womb has been discussed at length by H.R. Hays in *The Dangerous Sex: The Myth of Feminine Evil* (London, 1966).

3. *Cf.* the comments by Daniel G. Brown (*loc. cit.,* pp. 148-9)

on the necessity of women's taking over the study of their own sexuality.

4. Bisshof's *Observations and Practices Relating to Women in Travel etc.* (London, 1676), p. 76.

5. Chlorosis has been described as 'an anaemic condition seen in young women and girls and thought to have been due to tight corsets, constipation, frequent pregnancies, poor hygiene and diet'. (*The British Medical Dictionary,* ed. Sir Arthur Salusbury McNalty, London, 1961.) It was as often thought by popular medicine to have been caused by the frustration of the virgin's desire to couple and bear children, *vide The Works of Aristotle in Four Parts* (London, 1822), pp. 21-2. In fact it had been associated with iron deficiency by Baverius in the fourteenth century, but the connection with virginity obscured the issue for theorists like Johan Lange who wrote a treatise on the virgins' illness in 1554. In 1730, Hoffmann further complicated the issue by connecting it with hysteria. Learned studies demonstrated it prevalence in boarding schools and among female students generally, and it was even connected with a heart condition at one stage. (See *An Introduction to the History of Medicine* by Fielding H. Garrison (Philadelphia, 1929, pp. 167, 207, 271, 314, 360, 571, 647). Nowadays it is generally agreed that no definable disease called chlorosis exists.

6. The bibliography of hysteria is enormous, from Hippocrates *Liber Prior de morbis mulierum* of which a version by Cordeus appeared in 1583, and *In Libellum Hippocrates de Virginum Morbis* of Tardeus (1648). The affliction was a popular and lucrative specialization. Many young doctors chose to write about it in Latin dissertations. British Museum T.559 contains thirty odd tracts dating between 1668 and 1796 which may serve as examples of the way in which heterogeneous symptoms were lumped together under the blanket of hysteria.

7. Ploss and Bartels (*op. cit.*), Vol. I, pp. 611-31, 'The Seclusion of Girls at Menstruation'.

8. Sylvia Plath's poetry is a monument to woman strangled in phylogenetic toils. Her imagery builds fantastic structures of female carnality obsessed with the dream of violation and death. Some of the dominant motifs and the basic tensions are illustrated by her short poem, 'Metaphors':

> I am a riddle in nine syllables,
> An elephant, a ponderous house,
> A melon strolling on two tendrils,
> A red fruit, ivory, fine timbers!
> This loaf's big with its yeasty rising.
> Money's new minted in this fat purse.
> I'm a means, a stage, a cow in calf.
> I've eaten a bag of green apples,
> Boarded the train there's no getting off.
>
> (*The Colossus,* London, 1960, p. 41)

STEREOTYPE

1. Thorstein Veblen (*op. cit.*), *passim.*
2. *E.g.*

> I thought my mistress' hairs were gold,
> And in her locks my heart I fold;
> Her amber tresses were the sight
> That wrapped me in vain delight;
> Her ivory front, her pretty chin,
> Were stales that drew me on to sin;
> Her starry looks, her crystal eyes
> Brighter than the sun's arise.
>
> (Robert Greene, *Francesco's Fortunes.*)

3. *E.g.*

> When I admire the rose,
> That Nature makes repose

> In you the best of many,
> And see how curious art
> Hath decked every part,
> I think with doubtful view
> Whether you be the rose or the rose be you.
>
> (Thomas Lodge, *William Longbeard*)

4. *E.g.*

> Her cheeks like apples which the sun hath rudded,
> Her lips like cherries charming men to bite,
> Her breast like to a bowl of cream uncrudded...
>
> (Edmund Spenser, *Epithalamion*)

5. *E.g.*

> The outside of her graments were of lawn,
> The lining purple silk, with gilt stars drawn,
> Her wide sleeves green and bordered with many a grove...
> Buskins of shells all silvered used she
> Branched with blushing coral to the knee,
> Where sparrows perched, of hollow pearl and gold,
> Such as the world would wonder to behold;
> Those with sweet water oft her handmaid fills,
> Which as she went would chirrup through the bills.

It is only proper to point out that in this passage Marlowe is setting Hero up as a foil to the natural beauty of Leander, beloved of the gods, who is presented quite naked. Hero as a stereotype might be considered one of the themes of the poem.

6. Corbett *v* Corbett (otherwise Ashley) before Mr Justice Ormerod (Law Report, February 2, 1970, Probate, Divorce and Admiralty Division). *News of the World,* 8.2.1970, *Sunday Mirror,* 3, 8, 15 February 1970.

ENERGY

1. Carl Vogt, 'La Question de la Femme', *Revue d'Anthro-*

pologie, 1888, Tome III, fasc. lv, pp. 510-2, quoted in Ploss and Bartels (*op. cit.*), Vol. I, p. 126.

2. *Vide* 'Sublimation: its Nature and Conditions' in J.C. Flügel, *Studies in Feeling and Desire* (London, 1955).

3. The traditional view is expounded by McCary in *The Psychology of Personality* (London, 1959), pp. 7-9.

4. S. Freud, *Three Essays on Sexuality,* The Standard Edition of The Complete Works (London 1953), Vol. vii, p. 219.

BABY

1. William Blake, 'Infant Sorrow', *Songs of Experience* (*Poetry and Prose of William Blake,* ed. Geoffrey Keynes, London 1967, henceforward referred to as *Nonesuch,* p. 76).

2. *Sunday Mirror,* 19.10.1969.

3. William Blake, 'Infant Joy', *Songs of Innocence* (*Nonesuch,* p. 62).

4. For an explanation of the principle see Paul Schilder, *The Image and Appearance of the Human Body: Studies in the Constructive Energies of the Psyche* (London, 1935), pp. 120-2 and Norman O. Brown, *Life Against Death* (London, 1968), Part IV, 'The Self and the Other; Narcissus' (pp. 46-57).

5. Maria Montessori, *The Secret of Childhood* (London, 1936), p. 191.

6. Freud notes this phenomenon in *New Introductory Lectures in Psychoanalysis* (Complete Works, Vol. xxii, p. 117). The expounders of feminine wiles boast of it, *e.g.* M. Esther Harding, *The Way of all Women* (London, 1932), p. 7, and Mary Hyde, *How to Manage Men* (London, 1955), p. 6.

7. Philip Roth, *Portnoy's Complaint* (London, 1969), p. 125.

8. J. Dudley Chapman, *The Feminine Mind and Body* (New York, 1967), quotes Oscar Hammerstein II, 'You can have fun with a son, but you gotta be a father to a girl' (*Carousel*), p. 19.

9. *Vide* Anna Anastasi, *Differential Psychology* (London), and

Walter Wood, *Children's Play and its Place in Education* (London, 1913), pp. 83-4.

GIRL

1. *Vide* Karen Horney, *Feminine Psychology* (London, 1967), pp. 40-2, also Cap. II 'The Flight from Womanhood' *passim*. *Cf.* Margaret Mead, *Male and Female* (London, 1949), p. 144.
2. Helene Deutsch, *The Psychology of Women* (London, 1946, 1947), Vol. I, pp. 7, 22. Deutsch even goes so far as to state that the greatest danger to her uncontrollable girl patients was that they should unconsciously provoke the lust of their male companions because 'they have no sexual urge, they desire no sexual gratification and because of the absence of desire they feel secure' (p. 42).

PUBERTY

1. Deutsch (*op. cit.*), pp. 136-7, *cf.* Horney (*op. cit.*), pp. 100-101 and Lewis M. Terman, *Genetic Studies of Genius* (London, 1936), Vol. III, pp. 93-4.
2. J. Dudley Chapman (*op. cit.*), p. 69.
3. James Hemming, *Problems of Adolescent Girls* (London, 1950), pp. 93-4.
4. *Ibid.*, p. 130.
5. A.C. Kinsey, W.B. Pomeroy, C.E. Martin and P.H. Gebhard, *Sexual Behaviour in the Human Female* (Philadelphia, 1953), p. 173.
6. Hemming (*op. cit.*), p. 15.
7. Horney (*op. cit.*), p. 234.
8. *Ibid.*, p. 244.
9. John Aubrey, *Remaines of Gentilisme and Judaisme* (1686-7), edited and annotated by James Britten (London, 1881), p. 153.

THE PSYCHOLOGICAL SELL

1. August Strindberg, *The Father*, Act II, Sc. vii. Although he is patently ill-served by his wife's superstition and incomprehension of his work, the Captain still imagines that there was once a good old time when 'one married a wife' and enjoyed 'sensual love' and not a business partnership.

2. Naomi Weisstein, 'Kinder, Küche, Kirche as Scientific Law: Psychology reconstructs the Female', *Motive*, March-April 1969, pp. 78-85.

3. *Ibid.*, p. 80.

4. Ian Suttie, *The Origins of Love and Hate* (London, 1935), p. 221.

5. Ernest Jones, 'The Early Development of Female Sexuality' in *Papers on Psychoanalysis* (London, 1948), p. 438.

6. S. Freud, *Three Essays on the Theory of Sexuality* (*op. cit.*), p. 219 (my ital.).

7. Norman O. Brown, *Life Against Death* (*op. cit.*), p. 121.

8. S. Freud, *Civilisation and its Discontents: Complete Works, op. cit.*, p. 144.

9. Deutsch (*op. cit.*), Vol. I, p. 101.

10. Horney (*op. cit.*), pp. 232-3.

11. Deutsch (*op. cit.*), p. 151.

12. Bruno Bettelheim, 'Women and the Scientific Professions', *M.I.T. Symposium on American Women in Science and Engineering*, 1965.

13. E. Erikson, 'Inner and Outer Space: Reflections on Womanhood', *Daedalus*, 1964, No. 93, pp. 582-606.

14. Joseph Rheingold, *The Fear of Being a Woman* (New York, 1964).

15. J. Krafft-Ebing, *Psychopathia Sexualis* (London, 1893), p. 13, *cf.* Margaret Mead (*op. cit.*), pp. 209-10:

The human female who has learned through a long childhood education to value a great variety of rewards, and fear a great variety of punishments, finds that her receptivity – although perhaps retaining a slight degree of periodicity – is actually subject to a great deal of modulation. Where receptivity requires so much less of her – merely a softening and relaxing of her whole body, and none of the specific readiness and sustained desire that is required of the male – she can learn to fit a simple compliancy together with a thousand other considerations of winning and keeping a lover or a husband, balancing the mood of the moment against 'the mood of tomorrow, and fitting her receptivity into the whole pattern of a relationship. There seems little doubt that the man who has learned various mechanical ways to stimulate his sexual specificity in order to copulate with a woman whom he does not this moment desire is doing far more violence to his **nature** than the female who needs only to receive a male to whom she gives many other assents, but possibly not active desire.

16. Erich Fromm, *The Art of Loving* (London, 1969), p. 20.

THE RAW MATERIAL

1. Eleanor Maccoby, *The Development of Sex Differences* (London, 1967), *passim,* especially the 'Classified Summary of Research in Sex Differences', (pp. 323-51).
2. Lewis M. Terman, *Genetic Studies of Genius (op. cit.),* p. 294.
3. Maccoby (*op. cit.*), p. 35.
4. *Ibid.,* pp. 36, 37.
5. *Ibid.,* p. 44.

WOMANPOWER

1. See Mary Ellman, *Thinking About Women* (London, 1969), *passim.* Mailer explains his concept of the novel as the Great Bitch and how women cannot be said to get a piece of her in 'Some Children of the Goddess', *Cannibals and Christians* (London, 1969), p. 132.
2. The term is culled from Cynthia Ozick 'The Demise of the Dancing Dog', *Motive,* March-April, 1969.
3. Otto Weininger, *Sex and Character* (London, 1906), p. 236.

4. *Ibid.,* p. 241.

5. *Ibid.,* p. 250.

6. Valerie Solanas, *The S.C.U.M. Manifesto* (New York, 1968), pp. 73.

7. Weininger (*op. cit.*), p. 274. The claim that deceitfulness is a secondary sexual characteristic of the female mind has been made by many observers, including feminists like Mary Wollstonecraft who saw it as an essential consequence of female degradation and B.L. Hutchins, *Conflicting Ideals: Two Sides of the Woman Question* (London, 1913), 'Girls have been brought up on intensely insincere ideals' (p.30).

8. Weininger (*op. cit.*), p. 100. The assumptions that women perceive differently from men, are subjective rather than men and so on, despite the failure of testing to indicate any justification for them, are taken on trust by psychologists who deal with femininity. Deutsch luxuriates in extolling the value of women's subjective, intuitive perception as the desirable complement to male objectivity and mental aggression.

9. T.S. Eliot, 'The Metaphysical Poets', *Selected Essays* (London, 1958), pp. 287-8.

10. Antonin Artaud, 'Letters to Anais Nin' translated by Mary Beach, *International Times,* No. 16. Letter of 14th or 15th June, 1933.

11. This quotation appears in Marshall McLuhan, *The Medium is the Massage* (London, 1967) ascribed to A.N. Whitehead, and a book called *Adventures in Ideas.* I cannot recall seeing it in *Adventures of Ideas* but it does catch the drift of much that Whitehead did say, e.g. 'The Anatomy of Some Scientific Ideas' in *The Organisation of Thought* (London, 1917), pp. 134-90 *passim,* or *Science and the Modern World* (Cambridge, 1927) Cap. v, 'The Romantic Reaction' (pp. 93-118) *passim,* or indeed *Adventures of Ideas* (Cambridge, 1933), pp. 150-1, 173, 184-5.

12. Weininger (*op. cit.*), p. 149.

13. J. Needham, *Science and Civilisation in China* (Cambridge, 1954), Vol. II; p. 58.

14. S. Freud, *Some Psychic Consequences of the Anatomical Distinction Between the Sexes*, Complete Works, Vol. xix, pp. 257-8.

15. Weininger (*op. cit.*), p. 146.

16. *Ibid.* p. 186.

17. Norman O. Brown, *Life Against Death (op. cit.)*, p. 145.

18. *Ibid.*, p. 276.

19. Norman O. Brown, *Love's Body* (New York, 1966), p. 80.

20. Weininger (*op. cit.*), p. 198.

21. Edward de Bono, *The Uses of Lateral Thinking* (London, 1967), p. 31, *cf.* A.N. Whitehead, *An Introduction to Mathematics* (London, 1911), p. 138 and William James, *Some Problems in Philosophy*, Cap. X.

22. Leopold Von Sacher-Masoch, *Venus in Furs* (London, 1969), p. 160.

23. Rainer Maria Rilke, *Letters to a Young Poet* (Edinburgh, 1945), p. 23.

WORK

1. Unless otherwise stated statistics in this section are drawn from the *Annual Abstract of Statistics*, No. 105, 1968.

2. *Higher Education, Evidence – Part One, Volume E: Written and Oral Evidence received by the Committee appointed by the P.M. under the Chairmanship of Lord Robbins* (London, 1963), pp. 1552-3.

3. The Ford strike was largely the result of the efforts of Rose Boland, the women's shop steward. One of its results was the formation of the National Joint Action Campaign Committee, the most committed left-wing women's group.

4. See 'Equal Pay for Equal What' by Hugo Young and 'How Equal is Equal?' by Vincent Hanna, in the *Sunday Times*, 1.2.1970.

5. Shirley Enticknap explained the objections of men trade

unionists to their loss of control of women's working hours in *The News of the World*, 7.9.1969.

6. *The Times*, 19.5.1969.

7. Reported in *Black Dwarf*, 10.1.1969.

8. *The Times*, 21.5.1969.

9. *The Times*, 4.6.1969.

10. See Pauline Pinder, *Working Wonders*, P.E.P. Broadsheet No. 512. Mrs Britain 1969 is a schoolteacher with four children.

11. The results of the Alfred Marks Bureau Inquiry were published on 19.7.1969 (*Sunday Times*, 20.7.1969).

12. *Sunday Times*, 27.7.1969.

13. From the classified advertisements of *The Times*, 4.7.1969.

14. Mary Hyde (*op. cit.*), pp. 91, 96, 102.

15. *The Times*, 22.5.1969.

16. *Petticoat*, 28.6.1969.

17. *The Times*, 22.5.1969.

18. *The People*, 11.5.1969.

19. *The News of the World*, 20 and 27.4.1969.

20. *Daily Mirror*, 7.7.1969.

21. Suzy Menkes, *How to be a Model* (London, 1969).

22. 'The Great Nude Boom', *The People*, 1.6.1969.

23. It seems that strippers do not belong to their union, and dare not join because of the abundance of black-leg labour available. The average earnings are 6/- a strip, at fifty strips a week, in very poor conditions. (*The People*, 22.2.1970.)

24. Witness the case of Valerie Stringer, a qualified electrical engineer who cannot find work (*The People*, 25.1.1970) and Dallas Bradshaw, a wireless operator who has fallen foul of the seamen's prejudice that a woman at sea brings bad luck.

25. The selection of names is arbitrary. Every day the business sections of the newspapers salute the new female arrivals in positions of power.

THE IDEAL

1. In the Renaissance simple statements of the Platonic concept of love were disseminated as commonplace. To the basic arguments drawn from the *Convivium* and other dialogues were added the eulogies of Cicero and Plutarch and the theories of Heraclitus and Aristotle. The essence of this mixture can be found in many places, from the courtesy books like the *Cortigiano* and de la Primaudaye's *Academie* to the commonplace books and moral tracts for the consumption of the newly literate, e.g. Sir Thomas Elyot's *The Boke of the Governour* (1531), Section 31, *The Booke of Friendship of Marcus Tullius Cicero* (1550), John Charlton's *The Casket of Iewels* (1571), Baldwin's *Treatise of Moral Philosiphy* (1550), Bodenham's *Politeuphuia* (1597) and Robert Allott's *Wits Theater of the little World* (1599). Possibly the most accessible and the most elegant formulation, is Bacon's *Essay of Friendship*.

2. Schilder (*op. cit.*), p. 120, *cf.* Norman O. Brown, *Life Against Death (op. cit.)*, pp. 50-1.

3. William Blake, Poems from MSS, *c.* 1810 (*Nonesuch,* p. 124), *cf.* Suttie (*op. cit.*), pp. 30-1.

4. *The People,* 12.10.1969.

5. A.H. Maslow, *Motivation and Personality* (New York, 1954), pp. 208-46; quotation from pp. 245-6.

6. Norman O. Brown, *Life Against Death (op. cit.)*, p. 144.

7. William Shakespeare, 'The Phoenix and the Turtle' (*The Complete Works,* ed. W.J. Craig, Oxford, 1959, p. 1135).

8. S.E. Gray, *Womanhood in its Eternal Aspect* (London, 1879), p. 4.

ALTRUISM

1. William Blake, 'The Clod and the Pebble', *Songs of Experience (Nonesuch,* p. 66).

EGOTISM

1. William Blake, 'The Clod and the Pebble', *Songs of Experience* (*Nonesuch,* p. 66).
2. Erich Fromm (*op. cit.*), p. 38.
3. *Honey,* August 1969, 'She Loves me Not'.
4. *Weekend,* October 8-14, 1969.
5. Mary Hyde (*op. cit.*), p. 70.
6. Compton Mackenzie, *Extraordinary Women* (London, 1967), p. 107.
7. Letter to 'Evelyn Home', *Woman,* May 3, 1969, Vol. 64. No. 1664.
8. Lillian Hellman, *An Unfinished Woman* (London, 1969), p. 278.

OBSESSION

1. Christopher Marlowe, *Hero and Leander,* p. 178.
2. Jean Racine, *Phèdre,* I, iii, pp. 151-2.
3. William Shakespeare, *Romeo and Juliet,* I, i, pp. 196-200 (*Works, op. cit.,* p. 766).
4. Kingsley Amis, 'An Ever-fixed Mark', *Erotic Poetry,* ed. William Cole (New York, 1963), p. 444.
5. *Sweethearts,* Vol. II, No. 57, December, 1960, 'Kisses can be False'.
6. *Ibid.*
7. Quoted in Albert Ellis, *The Folklore of Sex* (New York, 1961), p. 209.
8. *Sweethearts (loc. cit.),* 'When Love Calls'.
9. *Datebook's Complete Guide to Dating,* edited by Art Unger (New Jersey, 1960), p. 89.
10. Mary Astell, *An Essay in Defence of the Female Sex* (London, 1721), p. 55.
11. Ti-Grace Atkinson, *vide infra* 'Rebellion', quoted from an article by Irma Kurtz in the *Sunday Times Magazine,* 14.9.1969.

12. O. Schwarz, *The Psychology of Sex* (London, 1957), p. 20.

ROMANCE

1. The publishers Mills and Boon asked Dr Peter Mann to analyse their readership and have bound up his report as 'The Romantic Novel, a Survey of Reading Habits' (1969).
2. *Woman's Weekly*, 2.7.1969.
3. *Mirabelle*, 8.11.1969, 'Saturday Sit-in'.
4. Georgette Heyer, *The Regency Buck* (London, 1968), p. 15.
5. *Ibid.*, p. 5.
6. *Ibid.*
7. Barbara Cartland, *The Wings of Love* (London, 1968), p. 152.
8. *Ibid.*, p. 47.
9. *Ibid.*, p. 137.
10. *Ibid.*, p. 191.
11. Lucy Walker, *The Loving Heart* (London, 1969), p. 226.
12. *Ibid.*, p. 32.
13. *Ibid.*, p. 171.
14. *Ibid.*, pp. 53, 85-6, 91, 112, 191, 207, 228.
15. *Ibid.*, pp. 253-4.
16. Run as a series by the *Sunday Mirror* 26 October-16 November 1969.
17. Violette Leduc, *La Bâtarde* (London, 1967), pp. 341-2.
18. 'The Sexual Sophisticate' quoted in Phyllis and Eberhard Kronhausen, *Sexual Response in Women* (London, 1965), p. 61.
19. Maxine Davis, *The Sexual Responsibility of Women* (London, 1957), p. 91.
20. Cartland (*op. cit.*), p. 62.
21. D.H. Lawrence, *Women in Love* (London, 1968), p. 354.
22. From the advertising campaigns of Winter, 1969-70.
23. 'Woman to Woman', *Woman*, July 19, 1969, Vol. 65, No. 1675.
24. Jenny Fabian and Johnny Byrne, *Groupie* (London, 1969).

25. Rey Anthony, *The Housewives Handbook on Selective Promiscuity* (Tucson, 1960 and New York, 1962).

THE OBJECT OF MALE FANTASY

1. *Penelope,* No. 194, October 14th, 1969, 'A Girl called Pony'.
2. Norman Mailer, *An American Dream* (London, 1966), p. 16.
3. Kate Millett, 'Sexual Politics: Miller, Mailer and Genet', *New American Review,* No. 7, August 1969.
4. Mailer (*op. cit.*), p. 9.
5. *Ibid.,* p. 23.
6. *Ibid.,* p. 25.
7. *E.g.* Umar in 'Umar Walks the Earth!' *Strange Tales,* Vol. I, No. 156, May, 1967, the villainess Hydra in *Captain America,* the Black Widow in *Captain Marvel,* Karnilla, Queen of the mystic Norns, who menaces *Thor.*
8. *E.g.* La Contessa Teresa di Vicenzo in *On Her Majesty's Secret Service.*
9. Mailer (*op. cit.*), p. 39.
10. Mickey Spillane, *Bloody Sunrise* (London, 1967), p. 74.
11. Mailer (*op. cit.*), p. 36.
12. *Ibid.,* p. 168.
13. *Ibid.,* p. 172.
14. *Ibid.,* p. 102.
15. John Philip Lundin, *Women* (London, 1968), pp. 60-1.
16. *Ibid.,* p. 101.
17. James Jones, *Got to the Widowmaker* (London, 1969), p. 282.
18. The Poems of Emily Dickinson, ed. M.D. Brainchi and A.L. Hampson (London, 1933), p. 131.

THE MIDDLE-CLASS MYTH OF LOVE AND MARRIAGE

1. Denis de Rougemont, *Love in the Western World, cf.* C.S.

Lewis, *The Allegory of Love.*

2. *Hail Maidenhad,* ed. O. Cockayne, Early English Text Society Publications No. 19 (1866), pp. 28-39.

3. C.L. Powell, *English Domestic Relations* 1487-1653 (Columbia, 1927), p. 126.

4. Rabelais, Five Books of the Lives, Heroick Deeds and Sayings of Gargantua and his sonne Pantagruel (London, 1653), Caps LII-LVII.

5. Gordon Rattray Taylor, *Sex in History* (London, 1965), p. 138.

6. Erasmus, *Two dyaloges wrytten in Laten one called Polythemus or the Gospeller, the other dysposing of thynges and names* translated into Englyshe by Edmonde Becke, Sig.M5 verso.

7. The story appeared in the *Decamerone,* not for the first time, and was instantly taken up as a theme, by Petrarch, who wrote a Latin treatment of it, and then several French versions appeared to proliferate in the sixteenth century in a rash of ballads and poems and plays e.g. *The Antient True and admirable History of Patient Grissel* (1619), *The Pleasant and sweet History of Patient Grissell* (1630), *The Pleasant Comodie of Patient Grissill.* By H. Chettle, T. Deloney, and T. Haughton (1603), *The Most Pleasant Ballad of Patient Grissel. . . To the tune of the Brides Goodmorrow* (T. Deloney? 1600 and 1640).

8. E.g., *The Boke of Husbandry. . .Made first by the Author* Fitzherbert, . . .Anno Domini 1568, fol. xxxvi verso. The ten properties of woman:

The .i. is to be mery of chere, ye .ii. to be wel placed, the .iii. to haue a broad forhed, the .iii. to haue brod buttocks, the .v. to be hard of ward, ye .vi. to be easy to leap upon, ye .vii. to be good at long iourney, ye .viii. to be wel sturring under a man, the .ix. to be always busy wt yet mouth, ye .x. euer to be chewing on ye bridle.

9. Peter Laslett, *The World We Have Lost* (London, 1965).

10. John Campion, *Two Books of Airs;*

Jack and Joan they think no ill,
But loving live and merry still...

11. Nicholas Breton, *The Court and Country* (1618), *The Works in Verse and Prose of Nicholas Breton,* ed. A.B. Grosart (London, 1879), Vol. II.

12. *E.g.* Barclay in *The Ship of Fooles,* Ascham in *The Schole-master,* Lodge in *Wits Miserie,* among many others.

13. 4 & 5 Philip and Mary c. 8, and 39 Elizabeth c. 9.

14. E.g. the popular Elizabethan ballad, *The Brides Good-morrow.* (The version in the B.M. dates from 1625.)

15. Antoine de la Sale, *Les Quinze Joies de Marriage* rendered by Thomas Dekker as *The Batchelar's Banquet* (1603).

16. One farce which exists in both French and English and demonstrates the archetypal pattern is *Johan Johan and Tyb his Wife.*

17. When Lady Mary Gray, a tiny woman bred too close to royalty for her own comfort, married Keys, a sergeant porter of no breeding and a huge man, for her own safety, the scandal was very great. (Strype, *Annals of the Reformation* (1735-37), Vol. II, p. 208).

18. Sir Philip Sidney, *Astrophel and Stella,* especially Sonnets XXIX, XXXVI, XLI, LII, LXXII, LXXVI, LXXXI, LXXXII, *cf.* Samuel Daniel, *Delia* and Sir Thomas Wyatt, Poems from the Egerton MS.

19. Edmund Spenser, *Amoretti* and *Epithalamion,* published in 1595.

20. William Habington, *Castara* published anonymously in 1634. The first part deals with courtship and the second, which deals with marriage, has the epigraph *Vatumque lascivos triumphos, calcat Amor, pede coniugali.*

21. *E.g.* Thomas Deloney, *The Gentle Craft, A Discourse Containing many matters of Delight*...London...1637. Chapter 5 relates 'How the Emperours Fair Daughter Ursula, fell in love with young Crispine comming with shooes to the Court;

and how in the end they were secretly married by a blind Frier.'

22. The Fair Maid of Fressingfield is the subject of the sub-plot of *Friar Bacon and Friar Bungay* (1592) by Robert Greene.

23. *The Golden Legend* was a compilation of Saints stories made according to the calendar of feasts by Jacobus de Voragine, Bishop of Genoa in the thirteenth century. It was one of the first books to be printed, and went through edition after edition in all places where there were printing presses, the first international best-seller.

24. Gillian Freeman, *The Undergrowth of Literature* (London, 1969), pp. 50-1.

25. *Sunday Times*, 3.8.1969, 'Making Money out of Marriage'.

26. *Sunday Times*, 15.6.1969, 'First Catch your Millionaire'.

FAMILY

1. William Shakespeare, *Cymbeline*, II, v. 1-2 (*Works op. cit.* p. 1024).

2. Some evidence of this can be gained from the Plowden Report, summarized in the *Sunday Mirror*, 8.3.1970.

3. *Sunday Mirror*, 23.11.1969, 'Let's All Cuddle'.

4. Lionel Tiger, *Men in Groups* (London, 1969), pp. 209-10.

5. John Updike, *Couples* (London, 1968), pp. 138, 141, 150.

6. *Sunday Mirror (loc. cit.)*.

7. Charles Hamblett and Jane Deverson, *Generation X* (London, 1964), p. 43.

8. *Ibid.*, pp. 48-9.

9. Wilhelm Reich, *The Sexual Revolution* (New York, 1969), p. 71.

SECURITY

1. Hamblett and Deverson (*op. cit.*), pp. 41, 111.

2. *E.g.* Edmund Spenser, *Two Cantos of Mutabilitye* published in 1609 'parcell of some following Booke of the Faeire Queene' which was never completed.
3. I suspect that a contract made by a man and a woman respecting the conditions of their cohabitation would be regarded by law as a contract for an immoral purpose, and hence not binding in law (!).
4. Hamblett and Deverson (*op. cit.*), pp. 48-9.

LOATHING AND DISGUST

1. Frank Reynolds as told to Michael McClure, *Free-wheelin' Frank* (London, 1967), p. 86.
2. *Ibid.,* pp. 55, 7, and 12-13.
3. Eldridge Cleaver, *Soul on Ice* (New York, 1968), pp. 16-7.
4. 'Eager Females – How they reveal themselves', *Male,* Vol. 19, No. 6, June 1969.
5. *Stag,* Vol. 20, No. 5, May 1969.
6. Reynolds (*op. cit.*).
7. William Shakespeare, Sonnet CXXIX (*Works, op. cit.*) p. 1124.
8. Dean Swift, 'Cassinus and Peter', *The Poems of Jonathan Swift,* ed. Harold Williams, Oxford, 1937, p. 597.
9. Hubert Selby, *Last Exit to Brooklyn* (London, 1966), pp. 82-3.
10. Jenny Fabian and Johnny Byrne, *Groupie* (London, 1969).
11. R.L. Dickinson and Laura Beam, *The Single Woman* (London, 1934), pp. 18, 252, 258, 262, 264.
12. *Ibid.,* p. 231.
13. *E.g.* Albert Ellis and Edward Sagarin, *Nymphomania* (London, 1968), pp. 45, 54, 59, 103-4, 118-9, 122-3.

ABUSE

1. *Evening News,* 18.12.1969.
2. William Shakespeare, *King Lear,* III, iv. 117-22 and IV. i. 62-3 (*Works op. cit.*) pp. 926, 930.
3. The Sources for this section are mainly the *New English Dictionary* (Oxford), and Wentworth and Flexner's *Dictionary of American Slang* and E. Partridge, *Smaller Slang Dictionary* (London, 1961), and Farmer and Henley, Slang and its Analogues (London, 1890).
4. *Rolling Stone,* No. 27, February 15th, 1969.
5. Nathan Shiff, *Diary of a Nymph* (New York, 1961).
6. Letter to 'Mary Grant', *Woman's Own,* 19.7.1969, and to 'Evelyn Home', *Woman,* 15.3.1969, and to 'Mary Marryat', *Woman's Weekly,* 2.7.1969.
7. 'Love Needs no Words', *New Romance* No. 3, November, 1969 and 'When Someone Needs You', *True Story,* No. 565, December, 1969.
8. Gael Greene, *Sex and the College Girl* (London, 1969), p. 111, quoting a Queen's University Conference on Mental Health, reported in the *New York Times,* May 19th, 1963.
9. *Ibid.,* pp. 45-6, and 111-3.
10. Jim Moran, *Why Men Shouldn't Marry* (London, 1969), p. 43.
11. Gilbert Oakley, *Sane and Sensual Sex* (London, 1963), p. 51.
12. *Ibid.,* pp. 52-3.
13. Philip Wylie, *Generation of Vipers* (New York, 1942), pp. 187-8.
14. *Ibid.,* pp. 188-9.
15. *Best Mother-in-Law Jokes* compiled by J.D. Sheffield (London, 1969), p. 1 and *passim.*
16. From the single 'Second Generation Woman' Reprise RS23315 published by Dukeslodge Enterprises.

MISERY

1. Letter to 'Evelyn Home', *Woman,* 2.8.1969.
2. Betty Friedan, *The Feminine Mystique* (New York, 1963), pp. 20-1.
3. An *Observer* report on the patent medicine industry (4.1.1970) stated that of £50,000,000 a year, £15,000,000 was spent on painkillers, £6,000,000 on tonics and vitamins, and £6,500,000 on advertising.
4. Letter to 'Evelyn Home' in *Woman,* 22.3.1969.
5. *Forum,* Vol. II, No. 8, pp. 69-70.
6. *The People,* 23.11.1969.
7. *The Times,* 9.5.1969.
8. *News of the World,* 6.7.1969.
9. *News of the World* 30.11.1969 reporting the compilation of the Family Planning Association's publication, *The Pill and You.*
10. Professor Victor Wynn is in charge of the Alexander Simpson Laboratory for Metabolic Research at St Mary's Hospital in Paddington (reported in *The People,* 14.12.1969), *cf.* research by Dr Anne Lewis and Mr Masud Noguchi reported in *The Observer,* 15.6.1969.
11. Reported in *The Observer,* 20.7.1969.
12. *Sunday Times,* 1.6.1969.
13. Dr W.J. Stanley, in *The British Journal of Social and Preventive Medicine,* November, 1969.
14. *Vide* '78 Battered Children'. Report of the N.S.P.C.C. (September, 1969), and *Sunday Times,* 30.11.1969.

RESENTMENT

1. George Eliot, *Middlemarch.*
2. Eric Berne, *The Games People Play* (London, 1964), p. 162.

REBELLION

1. *The Anatomy of a Woman's Tongue divided into Five Parts* (London, 1963), Epigram III, p. 173.
2. The Family of Love were an English sect which originated in Holland under the leadership of Hendrick Niclaes; it sought to reunify men in the Mystical Body. See *A brief rehearsal of the belief of the good-willing in England* (1656), *A Description of the sect called The Family of Love; with their Common Place of Residence.* Being discovered by Mrs Susannah Snow of Pinford near Chertsey in the County of Surrey, who was vainly led away for a time through their base allurements (1641), and *The Displaying of an horrible sect of... Heretiques* (1578).
3. Betty Friedan, *The Feminine Mystique* (New York, 1963).
4. Juliet Mitchell, 'Women – The Longest Revolution', *New Left Review,* November-December 1966, p. 18.
5. *Ibid.,* pp. 36-7.
6. Evelyn Reed, *Problems of Women's Liberation: A Marxist Approach* (New York, 1969).
7. Reich (*op. cit.*), pp. 153-269.
8. Tiger (*op. cit.*), pp. 110-1.
9. Kyril Tidmarsh, 'The Right to do the Hardest Work', *The Times,* 16.2.1967. See also *Women in the Soviet Economy* by T. Dodge (Baltimore, 1966).
10. Quoted in *Towards a Female Liberation Movement* by Beverly Jones and Judith Brown (New England Free Press), p. 2.
11. *New Left Notes,* August, 1967.
12. Judi Bernstein, Peggy Morton, Lina Seese, Myrna Wood, *Sisters, Brothers, Lovers... Listen...* (New England Free Press), p. 7.
13. *Soviet Weekly,* May 17th, 1969, p. 5.
14. Anonymous letter in *New Left Notes,* December, 1967.
15. Marilyn Webb, 'We Have a Common Enemy', *New Left Notes,* June 10, 1968.

16. Jones and Brown (*op. cit.*), pp. 20-2.

17. Ibid., p. 37.

18. Anne Koedt, *The Myth of Vaginal Orgasm* (New England Free Press), p. 5.

19. *Ibid.*

20. Nancy Mann, *Fucked-up in America (ibid.)*

21. Julie Baumgold, 'You've come a long way, Baby', *New York*, June 9th, 1969, p. 30.

22. Vivian Gornick, 'The Next Great Moment in History is Theirs', *Village Voice*, November 27th, 1969.

23. Mention ought also to be made to the N.J.A.C.C. (*vide supra* 'Work', and Mide McKenzie's Feminists, who produced the mimeographed *Harpies Bizarre*. Women's Liberation Workshop has now expanded to five groups, while another group in Nottingham puts out a duplicated sheet called *Socialist Woman,* and another at Bristol, *Enough is Enough.* A conference at Oxford, 28th February to 1st March, drew five hundred participants, along with 400 children and fifty menfolk.

24. Gloria Steinem, 'The City Politic', *New York,* March 10th 1969.

REVOLUTION

Anna Martin, *The Married Working Woman,* published by the National Union of Women's Suffrage Societies, July, 1911.

Among the poorer families especially, the mental superiority of the wife to the husband is very marked. The ceaseless fight these women wage in defence of their homes against all the forces of the industrial system, develops in them an alertness and an adaptibility to which the men, deadened by laborious and uninspiring toil, can lay no claim.

2. Mrs Mary Chatterji was told by the Home Office that 'it is considered that a wife should in general be prepared to

make her home in her husband's country' (*The Times,* 3.2.1970).

3. Gingerbread, Flat 45, Porchester Gardens, London, W2, and Mothers-in-Action, 10 Lady Somerset Road, London NW5 (*Sunday Times, 25.2.1970*).

4. Diane Hart sought to launch a Petticoat Party in May 1969, when she inserted an advertisement in *The Times* which read 'Ladies, don't just sit there. If you are sick of castles in the air, sit in the House of Commons. Wanted, 630 ladies willing to gamble £500 each, fighting a constituency'. Needless to say no political party resulted. She stood for election herself and was duly defeated. Three American charmers formed a Pussycat League to express Pussycat Power, which would obtain universal sway by caresses and coddling (*Sunday Mirror,* 2.11.1969). No appreciable political or other results have ensued from this hardly novel technique.